Revelation
Day by Day

Revelation
Day by Day

Edited by
R. Leslie Holmes
&
Richard Allen Bodey

BakerBooks
A Division of Baker Book House Co
Grand Rapids, Michigan 49516

Published by Baker Books
a division of Baker Book House Company
P.O. Box 6287, Grand Rapids, MI 49516-6287

Printed in the United States of America

Library of Congress Cataloging-in-Publication Data

Revelation day by day / edited by Robert Leslie Holmes & Richard Allen Bodey.
    p.   cm.
    ISBN 0-8010-6363-9
    1. Bible. N. T. Revelation—Meditations. I. Holmes, Robert Leslie, 1945– II. Bodey, Richard Allen.
    BS2825.54 .R48 2001
    242'.5—dc21   2001037362

For current information about all releases from Baker Book House, visit our web site:
              http://www.bakerbooks.com

This book is dedicated with love and appreciation
to
Betty Chapman,
a great encourager of this work and
faithful servant of Jesus Christ

Contents

Preface

Back in the dark days of Watergate when people wondered if the U. S. Constitution would hold, Senator Sam Ervin, Chairman of the Special House-Senate Committee on Watergate received a telephone call. From the other end of the line, a man said that the Lord had told him to present the real facts concerning the alleged cover-up. The wise senator listened and replied that he could not allow such testimony because it would risk being regarded as hearsay. He hastened to add, "However, if the good Lord would come and tell the committee himself, you can be sure we would all listen."

No book of the Bible has suffered more from the testimony of hearsay witnesses than the Book of Revelation. And no book has been more misunderstood and abused or suffered more from misinformation. That is why this book had to be written. Revelation is uniquely the testimony of Jesus Christ, the Lord.

In the pages that follow, you will find a daily bite-sized nugget of truth that explains, illustrates, and adds practical application to the Book of Revelation. We have endeavored to bring the scholarship of some of today's leading Christian communicators to bear on what the Book of Revelation has to say to our generation. We intentionally recruited a healthy cross section of contributors across denominational lines and sought out people who have a high regard for Scripture. Each contributor was given absolute freedom to choose the Scripture translation he or she preferred. However, you will soon note that, unless it is otherwise stated, the most often used translation is the New International Version. We did ask the writers to avoid the divisive issues that keep people from reading this Bible book, and we accept full responsibility for any disappointment you, the reader, may sense because of that decision. It is our conviction that Revelation is not primarily a book about millennial issues but a book of pastoral care by the Good Shepherd.

The messages of the various contributors have been divided into 260 easy to understand devotionals so that, in the space of one year, the reader might increase his or her understanding of John's apocalyptic vision by reading a passage five days each week. We hope that the remaining two days each week will be used to reflect upon what has been read.

We express our deep appreciation to the contributors and trust they will be pleased to be a part of the finished product. We are especially indebted to the Baker Book House staff for their investment of time, energy, and encouragement in this project. Bob Hosack and Paul Engle were especially helpful to us in this regard and we thank them. Without their wise counsel and grace this project might have never seen the light of day. Thank you, Bob and Paul.

10

We are grateful too, to our wives, Barbara Holmes and Ruth Bodey, who encouraged and supported us along the way. Their sacrifices to that end are especially valued.

Of special help was Betty Chapman of the First Presbyterian Church of Pittsburgh who invested much energy in typing and retyping many of the pages. We will always remember her patience and her smiling disposition, and we dedicate this volume to her.

We send this volume forth with the prayer that what is written here will not only please the Lord who sits on Revelation's throne but will also encourage you to walk day-by-day more closely to him. To the Lamb be all glory forever.

Robert Leslie Holmes
Richard Allen Bodey

Alphabetical
List of Contributors

Lane Adams

For ten years, Dr. Adams was Associate Evangelist for the Billy Graham Evangelistic Association, conducting forty-three citywide crusades in five nations. He is the author of *Come Fly with Me* and *How Come It's Taking Me So Long?* Born in New Orleans, he was educated at Columbia Theological Seminary and pastored churches in Florida and Tennessee. A Presbyterian minister, he resides in California.

Richard Allen Bodey

A minister in the Presbyterian Church in America, Richard Allen Bodey holds degrees from Princeton Theological Seminary, Westminster Theological Seminary, and Trinity Evangelical Divinity School. Dr. Bodey taught at Trinity Evangelical Divinity School, Deerfield, Illinois, and Reformed Theological Seminary, Jackson, Mississippi. He is contributing editor of *Good News for All Seasons, Inside the Sermon, The Voice from the Cross,* and *If I Had Only One Sermon to Preach.* He was coeditor (with Leslie Holmes) of *Come to the Banquet.*

Robert E. Coleman

Robert E. Coleman is director of the School of World Mission and Evangelism and professor of evangelism at Trinity International University in Deerfield, Illinois. He also serves as ministerial associate of the Billy Graham Evangelistic Association. Dr. Coleman is founding member of the Lausanne Committee for World Evangelization and a past president of the Academy for Evangelism in Theological Education. A graduate of Southwestern University, Asbury Theological Seminary, Princeton Theological Seminary, and the University of Iowa, hundreds of articles and twenty-one books have come from his pen, including *The Master Plan of Evangelism, Singing with the Angels,* and *The Coming World Revival.* Translations of one or more of his books are published in ninety-five languages, with English editions alone approaching five million copies in print.

Emmitte Cornelius

Educated at Jackson State University and Reformed Theological Seminary, Cornelius served pastorates in Jackson and Edwards, Mississippi, and was the founder and president of Macedonian Call Missionary Fellowship. He taught at Mississippi Baptist Seminary. He has contributed to *Lamp unto My Feet.*

Michael Duduit

Michael Duduit is associate professor of communications and Christian studies and executive vice president of Union University in Jackson, Tennessee. He is also the editor in chief of *Preaching: The Professional Journal for Those Who Preach.* A Southern Baptist, Dr. Duduit was educated at Stetson University, Southern Baptist Theological Seminary, and Florida State University. He is the author of *Joy in Ministry: Messages from Second Corinthians,* and editor of several books.

Charles F. Edgar III

Charles F. Edgar III is the rector of St. Mark's Episcopal Church in Glen Ellyn, Illinois. He is a graduate of Wheaton College, Trinity Evangelical Divinity School, and The University of the South. He has written previously for *Sewanee Theological Review*.

William M. Flannagan

A former moderator of the Evangelical Presbyterian Church, Dr. Flannagan is senior minister at First Presbyterian Church in Rome, Georgia. He was educated at King College, Bristol, Tennessee, and Union Theological Seminary. He has had articles published in *Presbyterian Outlook* and *Guideposts*.

Albert H. Freundt

Albert Freundt is a minister in the Presbyterian Church (U.S.A.). He has degrees from King College, Columbia Theological Seminary, and McCormic Theological Seminary, and had a long teaching career at Reformed Theological Seminary in Jackson, Mississippi. Dr. Freundt is a contributor to numerous religious journals and periodicals, and to a dozen dictionaries and encyclopedias.

13

George C. Fuller

George C. Fuller was born in Fort Wayne, Indiana. A minister in the Presbyterian Church in America, he graduated from Haverford College, Princeton Theological Seminary, Babson College, and Westminster Theological Seminary. In addition to serving as a pastor in Alabama, Maryland, and Minnesota, he was formerly executive director of the National Presbyterian and Reformed Fellowship and president of Westminster Theological Seminary. Dr. Fuller is currently a pastoral minister in Cherry Hill, New Jersey. He is the author of *Play It My Way*.

William H. Hinson

The pastor of the First Methodist Church of Houston, Texas, William H. Hinson is the author of several books, including *Solid Living in a Shattered World, Triumphant Living for Turbulent Times,* and *Faith, Lies, and the Opinion Polls.* A son of Georgia, Dr. Hinson was educated at Georgia Southern University, Boston University, and Candler School of Theology at Emory University.

Barbara M. Holmes

A native of Belfast, Northern Ireland, Barbara M. Holmes has lived in Mississippi, Georgia, Florida, and California. She currently resides in Pittsburgh, Pennsylvania. Her educational journey started in Ireland and continued at the University of Southern Mississippi, where she earned bachelor's and master's degrees in education. She has traveled extensively and spoken to women's groups and at national conferences.

14

Robert Leslie Holmes

An Ulster-Scot, Robert Leslie Holmes is the minister of the First Presbyterian Church of Pittsburgh, Pennsylvania. His previous pastorates were in California, Florida, Georgia, and Mississippi. He graduated from the University of Mobile, Alabama, Reformed Theological Seminary, and Columbia Theological Seminary. Through the media ministry of First Presbyterian Church, he is heard across the United States weekly. He has written previously for a variety of journals and magazines. He is the author of several books and numerous magazine articles. He was coeditor of *Come to the Banquet.*

Derl G. Keefer

Derl G. Keefer, a minister in the Church of the Nazarene, pastors a congregation in Three Rivers, Michigan. His previous pastorates were in Indiana and Illinois. He graduated from Southern Nazarene University and Nazarene Theological Seminary. He was a contributor to *Come to the Banquet*, and his sermons have been published in *Preaching, Clergy Journal*, and *Resource Magazine*, as well as *Preachers' Manual* and *Clergy Journal's Annual Manual*.

David L. Larsen

Ordained in the Evangelical Covenant Church, Dr. Larsen is a graduate of Stanford University and Fuller Theological Seminary. He is professor emeritus of preaching at Trinity Evangelical Divinity School. His books include *The Anatomy of Preaching, Caring for the Flock, The Evangelism Mandate, A History of Biblical Preaching from the Old Testament to the Modern Era*, and *Digging Deeper, Going Farther*.

Anne Graham Lotz

Anne Graham Lotz, the second child of Billy and Ruth Graham, was born in North Carolina. After teaching Bible Study Fellowship each week for twelve years without missing a class, Anne responded to God's call to an itinerant ministry of Bible teaching in 1988. At that time she founded AnGeL Ministries. She has ministered on every continent and in over twenty countries. Her contributions in this volume are adapted from her book, *The Vision of His Glory*.

Joel Nederhood

Educated at Calvin College and Calvin Theological Seminary, Dr. Nederhood is a minister in the Christian Reformed Church in North America. He has been director of *The Back to God Hour* of the Christian Reformed Church and pastor of preaching and worship at Cottage Grove Christian Reformed Church in South Holland, Illinois. Twenty-five years of his radio messages were published in *The Radio Pulpit*. He has authored many books, including, *The Church's Mission to the Educated American, God Is Too Much, The Holy Triangle,* and *The Forever People.*

James Rea

Born in Belfast, Northern Ireland, James Rea was educated at Edgehill Theological College, Belfast, and Westminster College, Oxford. He is a minister in the Methodist Church in Ireland, and was honored by Queen Elizabeth II for his work with social programs in his community. He is senior minister of Thomas Street Methodist Church, Portadown, Northern Ireland.

Charles W. Roberts

A son of Pine Bluff, Arkansas, Chuck Roberts graduated from Arkansas State University and Columbia Theological Seminary. He is the pastor of First Presbyterian Church in Pascagoula, Mississippi. He has written a number of articles for denominational publications.

16

Simon Schrock

An Amish Mennonite, Simon Schrock was ordained to the ministry in 1977 and to the office of Bishop in 1981. He presently serves as Bishop of Faith Christian Fellowship, Catlett, Virginia. He is the author of *Getting On with Living, Price of Missing Life, One-Anothering, Vow Keepers-Vow Breakers,* and *A Smoother Journey.* He is president of Choice Books of Northern Virginia.

William L. Self

A native of Winston-Salem, North Carolina, William L. Self is a Southern Baptist pastor. Former president of the Georgia Baptist Convention and the Foreign Mission Board of the Southern Baptist Convention, he is currently pastor of the Johns Creek

Baptist Church in Alpharetta, Georgia. He was educated at Stetson University, Southeastern Baptist Theological Seminary, and Emory University. The author of numerous articles and several books, Dr. Self was appointed Special Ambassador to Liberia by former President Gerald R. Ford.

Roger L. Steiner

Born in Erie, Pennsylvania, Roger Steiner attended Pennsylvania State University and Lutheran Theological Seminary. A minister in the Evangelical Lutheran Church in America, he is currently pastor at Trinity Lutheran Church in Avalon, Pennsylvania.

John H. White

Born in Newburgh, New York, and educated at Geneva College, Reformed Presbyterian Theological Seminary, University of Pittsburgh, and Pittsburgh Theological Seminary, John H. White is president of Geneva College in Beaver Falls, Pennsylvania. A former president of the National Association of Evangelicals and past chairman of the board of World Relief, Dr. White is the editor of *The Book of Books*, author of *From Slavery to Servanthood*, and a contributor to other publications. He is a minister in the Reformed Presbyterian Church in North America.

Luder G. Whitlock

Luder G. Whitlock was born in Jacksonville, Florida. A minister in the Presbyterian Church in America, he graduated from the University of Florida, Westminster Theological Seminary, and Vanderbilt University. Dr. Whitlock has served churches in Florida and Tennessee, and has taught at Reformed Theological Seminary in Jackson, Mississippi, where he currently is serving as president. Dr. Whitlock has contributed to many theological books and offers his services to advisory boards covering a wide range of interests.

17

Not As Scary
As You Think

The revelation of Jesus Christ, which God gave him to show his servants what must soon take place. He made it known by sending his angel to his servant John, who testifies to everything he saw—that is, the word of God and the testimony of Jesus Christ.

Revelation 1:1–2

Our four-year-old grandson, Benjamin, will not watch a TV show or video that he considers scary. When a scene that makes him uneasy appears on the screen, he either leaves the room or turns off the TV. As a result, he has missed some classics.

Some of us have done much the same with the Book of Revelation. Many have misinterpreted it through the centuries, while others have abandoned it altogether. Luther would have denied Revelation a place in the New Testament, along with James, Jude, 2 Peter, and Hebrews. And Zwingli said, "With the Apocalypse we have no concern, for it is not a biblical book."

Revelation *is* biblical. It is the New Testament representative of a very common kind of literature included in both the Old and New Testaments. The Book of Revelation is commonly called the *Apocalypse*, meaning to reveal, or to make known. Apocalyptic literature was the product of an undefeatable, indestructible Jewish hope.

Many readers have difficulty understanding Revelation. But it can and should be understood, for it has had an enormous influence on religion, history, and culture. It also has an urgent message for the contemporary church. It has inspired great minds in the fields of art, architecture, and music. Consider, for example, Albrecht Durer's series of woodcuts of the four horsemen of the Apocalypse. The form of the medieval cathedral down to the smallest detail was patterned after the heavenly city in Revelation 21:1–26. We see the influence of Revelation in great oratorios such as Handel's *Messiah*, and stately hymns such as *Holy, Holy, Holy* ("casting down their golden crowns around the glassy sea"). Revelation's vision of the redeemed social order has provided stimulus for resistance to injustice and oppression, influencing Daniel Berigan's *Beside the Sea of Glass* and Martin Luther King Jr.'s *We Shall Overcome*.[1]

Revelation does not speak *about* our time; it speaks *to* our time. We need to listen.

William L. Self

1:1–2

The God Who Speaks

Blessed is the one who reads the words of this prophecy, and blessed are those who hear it and take to heart what is written in it, because the time is near.

Revelation 1:3

I recently preached through the Book of Revelation. In each service, we listened to several chapters of the book read aloud without commentary. The text was carried by its own strength and the voice of Christ spoke through it. I suggest that in your private devotions or public worship, if possible, read large sections of the Book of Revelation and let it speak without commentary. We must understand that it is not a riddle to be unraveled but a word to be received.

Revelation is dominated by a situation that was intolerable for its readers. Believers were torn between the Roman government's effort to establish one centralized religion that worshiped Caesar and their allegiance to Jesus Christ. They were severely persecuted if they refused to give lip service to Caesar as lord. Their leader John had been exiled to a penal colony on the island of Patmos in the Aegean Sea. "Where is God in the midst of all of this?" they asked. John assures them that the God who spoke in the Old Testament and has been with his people through history is the same God revealed in Jesus Christ, and he will be faithful to them in this situation. We must understand that what the reader is about to receive is the revelation of Jesus, the exalted Lord of the church, who is present with his people in their worship, and addresses them in this prophetic word.

John assumes there will be Christian congregations assembled for worship and that this book will be read as a message from the risen Christ. The document is addressed to these congregations and suggests that the church is important to God. Our culture tends to disregard the church or to see it as a social club, a religious country club, or excess baggage in our lives. This is not a biblical position. When God does anything in the world, he does it through his church. The church is the best thing God has going for him in this world.

William L. Self

A Special
Letter from God

John, To the seven churches in the province of Asia: Grace and peace to you from him who is, and who was, and who is to come, and from the seven spirits before his throne, and from Jesus Christ, who is the faithful witness, the firstborn from the dead, and the ruler of the kings of the earth.

Revelation 1:4–5a

The Book of Revelation is a personal letter from God to his churches. It was written specifically to seven churches in Asia Minor. There were more than seven churches in this region, but God singles out those in Ephesus, Smyrna, Pergamum, Thyatira, Sardis, Philadelphia, and Laodicea.

The number seven appears often in the Revelation. There are seven lampstands (1:12), seven stars (1:16), seven lamps (4:5), seven seals (5:1), seven horns and seven eyes (5:6), seven trumpets (8:2), seven angels and plagues (15:6), and seven bowls (15:7). The number seven is regarded as the perfect number because seven stands for completeness. Here we see that when John wrote to the seven churches, he was writing, in fact, to the whole church.

Why did John choose these seven churches? He chose them because of their special influence and authority. They were his churches, and by speaking to them he sent a message, first to those who knew him and loved him, and then through them to every other church in every generation.

His description of Jesus Christ in this letter is highly significant. Christ is the "faithful witness, the firstborn from the dead, and the ruler of the kings of the earth." John is essentially saying that the identity of Jesus is not a puzzling question. Jesus is always for us. Because many readers of this book will witness to the lordship of Christ by giving their own lives for him, John makes it clear that the death and resurrection of Jesus was the beginning of a long succession of deaths and resurrections among his followers.

He wants his readers to know, in their hardship, that Jesus has been there ahead of them. In their martyrdom, the resurrected Jesus will be there with them. Whatever we face, or whatever we carry, we do not do it alone. The living Christ is with us in every situation.

William L. Self

21

Love That
Will Not Let Us Go

To him who loves us and has freed us from our sins by his blood, and has made us to be a kingdom and priests to serve his God and Father—to him be glory and power for ever and ever! Amen.

Revelation 1:5b–6

The hardest thing for us to realize is that God loves us unconditionally. We talk a lot about it, but we do not live as if we really believe it.

Christ loves us, not with a vague general philanthropy toward the masses but with knowledge of each of us and with concern for us as individuals. This love has given us the privilege of citizenship in the kingdom of heaven. Moreover, Christ has made us to be a kingdom of priests under his God and Father. This is a most unusual gift, because a priest enjoys the privilege of direct access to God. All of us may enter the secret place with confident, happy hearts, knowing that we have personal access to God through our Lord Jesus Christ. With his birth at Bethlehem, all the functions of the priesthood were once and forever committed to him and to all who are united with him. That is to say, all true members of the invisible church at the instant of their conversion become priests (1 Peter 2:5; Rev. 1:6; 20:6). There is no possibility of limiting this privilege to the clergy. To put it another way, we are all ministers. God has appointed every one of us to participate in the work of Christ in this world, because we all share in his royal priesthood.

William L. Self

Hang in There

*Look, he is coming with the clouds, and every eye will see him, even those
who pierced him; and all the peoples of the earth will mourn because of
him. So shall it be! Amen. "I am the Alpha and the Omega," says the Lord
God, "who is, and who was, and who is to come, the Almighty."*

Revelation 1:7–8

Every pastor knows the anxiety people experience as they wait
for the results of medical tests. Every week, it seems, someone
shares with me the anxiety he or she or a loved one is facing while
hanging on tenterhooks waiting for word from the pathologist.
Often, a pep talk cannot smother their anxiety.

The Christians to whom this letter was addressed were also in
the grip of fear. They were being killed. They were losing their
families and friends because of persecution. All seemed dark and
hopeless. John tells them that the best way to be certain God would
not fail them in the present was to remember what he had done
in the past. The Lord had helped them in the past, and John writes
confidently of the triumphant return of Christ, who will rescue
Christians from the cruelty of their enemies.

John writes of the promise of Christ's return to kindle their
hope and ours. This passage of Scripture rings with the assurance,
"So shall it be! Amen." That is to say, "Yes, indeed, it shall be!"

Whatever your long dark night is, whatever the horror you are
living through, do not imagine that God has abandoned you.
Remember John's message that in Christ, God loves each one of
us with a love we do not deserve. Remember that he has promised to triumph over every situation in which we find ourselves.
Although his timetable may not be ours, we know that he will
never abandon us in any dark place. We can rest secure in the love
of God and in the certainty of his faithfulness. The night may be
dark and the passage long, but we know that he comes to us, and
is present with us in every circumstance. As we await his Second
Coming, we are comforted by his presence with us now.

William L. Self

23

Through Tribulation to the Kingdom

I, John, your brother and companion in the suffering and kingdom and patient endurance that are ours in Jesus.

Revelation 1:9a

A member of our congregation who was an ordinary, middle-aged, suburban mother came into my office to talk with me. She had enjoyed a very predictable, normal life. But, in a whirlwind of events over a six-month period, she lost her husband in a fishing accident and her son in a university dormitory accident.

She said sometimes she felt abandoned by God. Then she spoke of some people who tried to minister to her during her trauma. "I could tell from their words whether they had suffered through any hardship. Those who had experienced little grief tried to wipe away mine with glib words—'It'll be all right. . . . Your husband and son are in a better place. . . . Some day you will understand. . . . Just have faith. . . . I know how you feel.'" She felt they implied that this was something to be taken lightly, or she was to snap out of it. Their comfort enraged her.

Others who had experienced great pain and trauma did understand her pain. Offering no advice, they simply gave themselves. She said she found healing through their shared pain.

John declares here that he is a partner in the tribulation of his readers. He knows the trials they are going through. He does not come to them from an exalted position. The person who has gone through affliction is instantly recognized by another who is going through it—they are partners in tribulation.

An interesting word—tribulation. Tribulation acts like the weight of a great boulder on a person's life. It is our response to the pressure of events. The only thing that can resist this pressure is steadfast endurance. This is the gift of God. The kingdom of God is not designed for lovers of ease and comfort. The kingdom journey is a difficult journey and it requires the greatest endurance of all.

William L. Self

24

Where Is God
When We Need Him?

*I, John, . . . was on the island of Patmos because of the word of God and the
testimony of Jesus.*

Revelation 1:9b

During World War II, a man escaped from a prisoner of war camp.
In retaliation, the camp officer hung a twelve-year-old boy from
the camp gallows and made the other prisoners watch. As the boy's
lifeless body swung on the rope, one of the prisoners shouted, in
anger and derision, "Where is God now?" After a silent moment,
another prisoner pointed to the gallows and said, "He is right
there." Indeed he was. The crucified God was with them. Many
times we feel separated from God. But, whenever we hurt, we'll
find Jesus right there with us.

John was on the Isle of Patmos, a barren little slice of land off
the coast of Asia Minor—modern Turkey—when he wrote this
book. Patmos is ten miles long and five miles wide. It is crescent-
shaped, the horns of the crescent pointing to the east, and boasts
a good natural harbor. Banishment to a remote island was a common form of Roman punishment. John was sentenced to it along
with many other political prisoners. They were stripped of their
civil rights and all their property.

The island made a tremendous impact on the writing of John.
He could see nothing but the sea on all sides. The sea is a symbol
of that which separated him from those he loved and for whom
he cared. It was out of the hard labor and weariness of banishment on the Isle of Patmos that John speaks. In our anxiety and
in what seems like banishment at times, we can listen to his
encouragement. John gives us assurance that, though the sea may
separate, there will be a day when there will be no more sea (21:1).

None of us desires pain, nor do we seek it. But we know that,
through our painful experiences, our Lord shapes and refines us
so that he can use us more effectively. We also know that he is
with us in our trials and, through them, is making us more authen-
tically Christlike.

William L. Self

In the Spirit
on the Lord's Day

On the Lord's Day I was in the Spirit, and I heard behind me a loud voice like a trumpet....

Revelation 1:10

One day, I was talking on a cordless telephone that I have in my study when, in the middle of the conversation, the phone went dead. Not only was I inconvenienced, but I was terribly embarrassed by this event. When I investigated why the battery was dead, I remembered that I had left the phone off the hook the night before, disconnected from its power source.

Something like this can happen to Christians living in our fast-paced modern society. God intends us to reconnect ourselves to our source of power every week. He has given us one day in seven for this purpose, but our society has taken the Holy Sabbath and turned it into a Great American Weekend. The first day of the week used to be called the Lord's Day, because it is a gift of God to us so that we can celebrate our Lord's resurrection and spiritually recharge ourselves. God did not give us this day by accident. We need to be with God's people each Lord's Day so that we can find a holy center from which we can draw spiritual strength and energy to face whatever we may encounter in the week to come. Those who neglect the observance of Sunday lose a vital force. Those who habitually refuse to rest and worship are living on reserves. They are literally working themselves to death.

"Sunday is a hollow, scooped out of the windy hill of the week," said the Scottish author George McDonald. On the Isle of Patmos John said, "I was in the Spirit on the Lord's Day."

William L. Self

Do You Know the Trivia, or Do You Know the Lord?

In his right hand he held seven stars.

Revelation 1:16a

The King James Version contains 3,566,480 letters, 733,746 words, 31,163 verses, and 1,189 chapters. The longest chapter in the Bible is Psalm 119, and the shortest is Psalm 117. The middle verse of the Bible is Psalm 118:8. The longest word in the Bible is Maher-Shalal-Hash-Baz (Isa. 8:1). The longest verse is Esther 8:9, and the shortest is John 11:35.

Learning about the Bible is good, but many people spend their time merely amassing facts, and some are on a lifelong expedition to accrue more facts about the Bible. A recent Gallup Poll showed that 82 percent of Americans believe the Bible is either literal or the inspired Word of God, but only 21 percent engage in any kind of significant Bible study. We derive little good from believing that the Bible is trustworthy, if we are not trusting the Lord of the Bible.

In this chapter of Revelation, we have a vision of the risen Lord that we do not find anywhere else in the Bible. He holds seven stars in his hand. Can you imagine that the very same hand that holds the stars rests upon the head and shoulders of a frightened child or a grieving mother? The hand of Christ is strong enough to uphold the heavens and gentle enough to wipe away our tears. The presence of Christ is far more important than facts about Christ, or even the book that tells about him.

Yes, know the Bible. Know the details of the Bible, but move from knowing the details of the Bible to knowing the living presence of the eternal Christ who holds the stars in his hands.

William L. Self

27

Fear Not to Live or Die

When I saw him, I fell at his feet as though dead. Then he placed his right hand on me and said: "Do not be afraid. I am the First and the Last. I am the Living One; I was dead, and behold I am alive for ever and ever! And I hold the keys of death and Hades."

Revelation 1:17–18

Most of us have had experiences in our lives when it seems that everything is falling apart. The Christians to whom John wrote were no exception. Jesus told them not to be afraid, then gave them three great encouragements. He told them not to fear to live, because he is the living one. He told them not to fear to die, because he was dead and now he is alive again. And he told them not to fear anything that would come after death because he has the "keys of death and Hades." There is not a thing that can ever happen to us that we should be afraid of, because Jesus has gone through it all ahead of us. Whatever you face today, you can face it with the comforting assurance that Jesus has been there first.

Most of us live in bondage to the fear of death, to the image of death as a thief. When death steals our beloved, we feel a profound sense of injustice. We need to understand that Jesus Christ has gone on ahead of us to make it very clear that death is neither a thief nor an annihilator but a transition.

Peter Marshall, in a sermon on December 7, 1941, at the U.S. Naval Academy, told about the little boy suffering from leukemia whose mother read to him every afternoon. He enjoyed the stories of King Arthur, but the knights often died in the stories. When the little boy asked, "Does it hurt to die?" his mother said, "Do you remember when you played all day and came in so tired? The next morning you awoke with no idea how you got into your bed. The truth is that your big brother picked you up, carried you upstairs, and put you into your bed. You went to sleep in one room and awakened in another room upstairs." She went on to explain that we die in one room, but when we wake up in another, we find that Jesus (our big brother) has come and taken us up the stairwell.

William L. Self

Don't Fear the Future

I am the Living One; I was dead, and behold I am alive for ever and ever!
And I hold the keys of death and Hades.

Revelation 1:18

Joy Davidman was a gifted American who went to Russia in the late 1930s. Like many intellectuals, she joined the Communist Party. As she began to become disillusioned with it, she started listening to the BBC. She heard C. S. Lewis deliver the lectures later published in his book *Mere Christianity* and was converted. She later moved to England and studied with C. S. Lewis. Unfortunately, she contracted cancer and was about to be deported. Under these delicate circumstances, Professor Lewis agreed to marry her in the hospital, so she could stay in England. They grew to love each other deeply.

Joy's cancer later went into complete remission. After four years, it returned, and Joy Davidman died. Lewis was overwhelmed by grief at his loss. In *A Grief Observed*, he rages against God. Later, he realized that the problem had more to do with his expectations than with what had actually happened.

Fear not; Christ has the keys of death and Hades. He has come back from death eternally alive and brings his convincing presence to all who are willing to feel the impact of his unique overwhelming victory. John saw clearly that Jesus Christ is the Lord of death, as well as the master of life. There is no door he cannot open. The churches were cowering before the last grim mystery—death, and its terrible finality. But Jesus had won the victory, not only for himself. He came back with the keys of death. This was the triumphant message for those in the first century who were facing severe hardship and persecution. It remains the eternal message of the living Christ to each of us.

William L. Self

29

The Angels
and the Churches

The mystery of the seven stars that you saw in my right hand and of the seven golden lampstands is this: The seven stars are the angels of the seven churches, and the seven lampstands are the seven churches.

Revelation 1:20

Scholars have debated whom John had in mind when he talked about the angels of the seven churches. Some have suggested that each church has its own angel. Others have suggested that the word "angel" actually means "messenger," therefore he meant the pastors, or bishops (to use first century language), of the seven churches. I like the idea that the pastors are seen as angels, but I can't find any laymen who feel the same way! We can, however, understand that God has all of his churches in his hands and protects them.

John G. Patton and his wife were missionaries to the New Hebrides Islands. In his book *Angels,* Billy Graham tells a remarkable story about God's response to their intercession. One night, members of the tribe surrounded the mission headquarters, intent on killing the Pattons. The missionaries prayed all through the terror-filled night for the protection and help of God. When daylight came, they watched in amazement as their attackers left.

A year later the chief of the tribe was converted to faith in Christ. Mr. Patton asked him what had happened to make the warriors leave during that ordeal a year before. The chief answered that they had seen many men guarding them, hundreds of big men in shining garments with drawn swords in their hands. They circled the missionaries and protected them all night long. God protects his church and God protects his people. He does indeed answer prayer.

The angels of the seven churches are the guardian angels of these churches. In the second and third chapters of Revelation, the relationship between each angel and its church is close. The letter to each church is addressed to its angel. Both the churches and their angels share equally in the praise and censure of the Christ.

We must never forget that Christ loved the church and gave himself for it. This last word in the Bible is addressed to churches in the first century. No less, however, is it addressed to the whole church of Jesus Christ today. Let us then read and ponder what the Lord of the church is saying to us.

William L. Self

30

1:20

The Unseen Presence

These are the words of him who . . . walks among the seven golden lamp-stands.

Revelation 2:1

Eyes ablaze, feet like bronze, face brilliant as the sun—this is the one who walks in the midst of the churches. The King of Glory! The victor over death and hell! The great I AM! The Alpha and the Omega!

No evidence now of the lowly Galilean, the itinerant preacher and rabbi from Nazareth. Except for one thing—the nail prints. The hands that hold the seven stars, those feet like glowing bronze are scarred. His bearing proclaims him King of kings and Lord of lords. His hands and feet proclaim him the Lamb slain before the foundation of the world.

Who else has the right to walk among the churches observing, commending, and judging? No one. God incarnate alone has that right. Only he who emptied himself of every trace of glory, he who subjected himself to the most savage indignities ever designed by depraved and cruel minds. He alone can observe the churches with perfect insight. He alone can examine them with perfect love. He alone can judge them with perfect fairness.

Could anyone at the temple treasury deny that he observed rightly when he said of the poor widow, "They all gave out of their wealth; but she, out of her poverty, put in everything—all she had to live on" (Mark 12:44)? Could the local merchants deny that Jesus judged them with flawless accuracy that day in the temple when he drove them out with their sheep, their cattle, and their doves saying, "Get these out of here! How dare you turn my Father's house into a market!" (John 2:16)?

As the sovereign King, he walks today among his churches, conferring compliments, delivering encouragement, issuing rebukes and warnings. As the loving Savior, once "despised and rejected by men" (Isa. 53:3), he understands full well the fierce temptations confronting his faithful ones and the cruelty they often suffer at the hands of their unbelieving foes. What does he say to your church and mine? Coming closer still, what does he say to you and to me? In the final outcome, his is the only word that matters.

Richard Allen Bodey

31

What's Your Love Index?

I have this against you, that you have abandoned the love you had at first.

Revelation 2:4 NRSV

By the time this book is published, my wife and I, God willing, shall have celebrated our forty-fifth wedding anniversary. Had anyone told me forty-five years ago that my love for her would deepen and expand over the years, I would have laughed with scorn. "Impossible!" I would have said. "I could never love her more than I do now." But I would have been wrong. My love for her has grown steadily and unfailingly over the years. And it continues to grow. That is one of the wonders of true love. So long as it is healthy, it grows.

Now consider the church at Ephesus. It boasted an unrivaled succession of pastoral superstars. Paul, founder of the church, pastored it for about three years. Afterwards, he ordained Timothy to be its first bishop. In his later years, according to very strong tradition, John himself succeeded Timothy. He also brought Mary the mother of Jesus with him to Ephesus, where both eventually died and were buried.

Who would not assume that a church boasting such proud associations would serve as a model for all congregations across all the centuries? Alas, the Lord of the church uncovered a deadly flaw in it. Many members of the church at Ephesus had abandoned the love they felt for him in the morning of their union. Note that they had not abandoned him, but they had abandoned their ardor and passion for him that sparkled like a crown of diamonds in earlier days.

What about your love for the one who loved you so much that he took your place in judgment on the cross? Does it blaze as brightly today as when first you discovered his boundless love for you? It should. In fact, it should shine more radiantly every passing day. If you keep close to him it will.

> This is my earnest plea,
> More love, O Christ, to Thee.
> More love to Thee,
> More love to Thee.
> Elizabeth Payson Prentiss, 1869

Richard Allen Bodey

About-Face!

Repent and do the things you did at first. If you do not repent, I will come to you and remove your lampstand from its place.

Revelation 2:5b

Repent. The word brings to mind a "sandwich man" I once saw in Philadelphia when I was a boy. Up and down the sidewalk he paraded, his body "sandwiched" between two large poster boards with the warning, "REPENT OR PERISH!"

To many Christians, the word *repent* conjures up the stern, fiery figure of John the Baptist shouting to crowds of the curious in the Judean wilderness, "Repent, for the kingdom of heaven has come near" (Matt. 3:2 NRSV). Now Saint John hears the glorified Christ in his letters to the seven churches of Asia strike the same accent eight times, twice in this letter to the church in Ephesus.

What does this word mean? In the New Testament it usually signifies a radical change of life, a 180° turnaround. Translating it into the vocabulary of an army drill sergeant, it simply means, "About-face!"

Generally, we associate repentance with conversion—the occasion when a person turns deliberately and decisively from sin to Christ for salvation. Rightly so, but that is not the end of the matter. We need to repent again and again every day of our lives, until we take our last breath. We are sinners saved by grace. But, like the Christians at Ephesus, we are sinners still, and shall remain so to the very end. Not a day goes by but we soil ourselves with sin all over again. The good news of the gospel is that whenever we repent, God forgives us anew and washes us clean in the precious blood of Christ.

> With self-accusing voice within
> Our conscience tells of many a sin
> In thought and word and deed:
> O, cleanse that conscience from all stain,
> The penitent restore again,
> From every burden freed.

> Latin, eighth century
> (tr. J. W. Hewett, 1859)

Richard Allen Bodey

33

2:5b

You Can Be a Winner!

To everyone who conquers, I will give permission to eat from the tree of life that is in the paradise of God.

Revelation 2:7b NRSV

One of the most celebrated battles in Christian history was the Battle at the Milvian Bridge over the Tiber River near Rome in A.D. 312. Eusebius, the first Christian historian, records that prior to the battle, Emperor Constantine the Great saw in the sky a flaming cross inscribed with these words, "In this sign you will conquer." Constantine adopted the cross and won the battle, a major turning point in the history of Christianity.

This letter to the church at Ephesus, like the letters to the six other churches of Asia Minor, closes with a promise to "those who conquer." Spiritual defeat seems to be the norm in the lives of many Christians today. God never intended it to be so. The risen Christ, the Lord of the church and the captain of our salvation, is no loser. He is the mighty conqueror of sin, death, Satan, and all the legions of hell. He challenges everyone of us who belongs to him to conquer in the agelong conflict with evil.

What spiritual battle do you face just now? Whatever it is, you don't have to be a loser. The captain of our salvation intends you to be a winner. He has made every provision for you to be a winner. He has baptized you with his Spirit, by whose power he himself faced fierce, more subtle conflicts with the devil than you will ever face. He has equipped you with the weapons of prayer and the sword of the Spirit, which is the Word of God—the very same weapons he himself used to defeat the enemy. The secret of victory lies in steadily keeping close to him, relying on him every moment for the wisdom and strength you need. The battle may be fierce. But victory lies within reach. It will confirm your access to the tree of life that flourishes in the paradise of God.

> I am trusting Thee, Lord Jesus,
>   Never let me fall;
> I am trusting Thee for ever,
>   And for all.
>
> Frances Ridley Havergal, 1874

Richard Allen Bodey

Millionaires Forever!

I know your afflictions and your poverty—yet you are rich.

Revelation 2:9

Over the past several years, Americans in large numbers have tasted prosperity to an extent they never dreamed of, and they want more. Our country now boasts more millionaires than ever before. Contrast this with our Lord's words to the believers at Smyrna, "I know your afflictions and your poverty—yet you are rich!"

Life for the believers in Smyrna was like having the sword of Damocles hanging over your head. Caesar worship was compulsory. Once a year citizens were required to burn a pinch of incense on the altar to the godhead of Caesar. Certificates were issued to those who obeyed. Those who did not were viewed as outlaws. Couple that with the antagonism of the large Jewish population, and the "afflictions and poverty" to which our Lord alludes take on grave form. Christians in Smyrna felt life-threatened.

"Yet you are rich," Jesus says. What "riches" did the believers at Smyrna have of which the pagans knew nothing? The very same ones we possess in the midst of our pagan society. Saint Paul lists some of these "riches" in Ephesians. God has blessed us in the heavenly realms with every spiritual blessing in Christ (1:3). God has chosen us in Christ before the creation of the world (1:4). God has adopted us as his own sons and daughters through Jesus Christ (1:5). God has granted us redemption and forgiveness of sins through the blood of Christ (1:7). God has marked us with the seal of the Holy Spirit, who is the down payment that guarantees our inheritance until our final redemption (1:13–14).

"You are rich," Christ told the believers at Smyrna. Do you want to be a millionaire? If you belong to Christ, you already are one and will be forever—in the currency of Almighty God!

Richard Allen Bodey

35

The Candor of Christ

Do not be afraid of what you are about to suffer. I tell you, the devil will put some of you in prison to test you, and you will suffer persecution for ten days.

Revelation 2:10

In plain language the enthroned Christ in heaven told the believers at Smyrna that they would enter the crucible of suffering. His words are reminiscent of earlier days on earth when he spoke out candidly. As he was sitting on the Mount of Olives his disciples asked him, "What will be the sign of your coming and of the end of the age?" (Matt. 24:3). He answered, "Nation will rise against nation, and kingdom against kingdom. There will be famines and earthquakes in various places. . . . Then you will be handed over to be persecuted and put to death, and you will be hated by all nations because of me" (Matt. 24:7, 9).

With respect to his own approaching death, he was equally honest: "We are going up to Jerusalem, and the Son of Man will be betrayed to the chief priests and the teachers of the law. They will condemn him to death and will turn him over to the Gentiles to be mocked and flogged and crucified" (Matt. 20:18–19a).

"In the world you face persecution" (John 16:33b NRSV). These words of Jesus are as true today as they were twenty centuries ago. In Sudan, China, Indonesia, and elsewhere, Christians are suffering for Christ this very day. Even here in the United States the courts are stripping us who are Christians of our constitutional rights. Where will this growing trend lead? Unthinkable as it seems, some of us may live to suffer even martyrdom for our Lord. He says to us, as he said to the believers in Smyrna two thousand years ago, "Do not be afraid." The final victory belongs to him. All who remain faithful unto death will share that victory with him. They, but no one else!

Richard Allen Bodey

36

Are You Listening?

He who has an ear, let him hear what the Spirit says to the churches.

Revelation 2:11a

In 1798, at the age of twenty-nine, Ludwig von Beethoven began to lose his hearing. By 1820, he was almost totally deaf. In the autumn of 1802, Beethoven wrote a letter to his brothers, which they were not supposed to read until after his death. In it, he described the anguish and heartache he felt because of his physical condition: "What a humiliation for me when someone standing next to me heard a flute in the distance and I *heard nothing,* or someone heard a shepherd singing and I *heard nothing.* Such incidents drove me almost to despair. . . . O Providence—grant me at last but one day of *pure joy*—it is so long since real joy echoed in my heart."[2]

During that very same year, however, in the midst of such suffering, Beethoven composed his wonderfully joyful Second Symphony. For virtually half his life Beethoven wrote his masterful works under those brutally crushing circumstances.

Our Lord knew the precise circumstances of each of these seven churches in Asia Minor. He gave each of them encouragement, advanced solutions to their problems, and—except in the letters to the churches at Smyrna and Philadelphia—issued reprimands. He concluded each letter with this simple command, "He who has an ear, let him hear what the Spirit says to the churches."

Are you living in the midst of adverse circumstances? Are you crying out, "Lord, give me just one day of pure joy"? Don't despair! Through his Word and by his Spirit God will enable you to bear your trials. He is the great enabler. "He who has an ear, let him hear."

Richard Allen Bodey

37

Tried and True

Yet you remain true to my name.
Revelation 2:13b

Before one of his battles to overthrow King Charles I of England, Oliver Cromwell told his soldiers they were "upon an engagement very difficult." The church at Pergamum could have said "Amen" to that statement. It described their plight exactly. Day by day they lived under circumstances most stressful.

After the empire of Alexander the Great was divided in 133 B.C., Rome made Pergamum the capital of the province of Asia. It became renowned for its worship of Aesculapius, the Roman god of healing. R. H. Charles described it as "the Lourdes of the ancient world."

But that was not all. Located on a hill behind the city stood numerous shrines and temples dedicated to various Greek gods. Eclipsing everything else, the massive altar of Zeus stood forty feet high, in front of the renowned Temple of Athena.

Most perilous of all for the Christians at Pergamum, this city, like Smyrna, was a center of Caesar worship, where the citizens considered themselves highly privileged to worship and glorify the emperor of Rome. As a result, Christians bore the name "outlaw," because they refused to burn incense before Caesar's altar. Christians had witnessed firsthand the penalty for nonconformity.

Aware of this and all the other relentless affronts to the worshipers of the only living and true God, Christ commends the believers in Pergamum. "You did not renounce your faith in me, even in the days of Antipas, my faithful witness, who was put to death in your city" (Rev. 2:13c). Nothing certain is known about Antipas. Tradition claims he died an excruciating death, as his enemies slowly roasted him in a bronze kettle.

When fellow workers, friends, or loved ones pressure you to compromise your Christian beliefs and standards, do you remain true to Christ's name? That is when you reveal who you really are. And he sees.

Richard Allen Bodey

38

What's Your Name?

To him who overcomes . . . I will also give him a white stone with a new name written on it, known only to him who receives it.

Revelation 2:17b

Do you recall any time in your childhood, when—inadvertently or deliberately—you discovered one of your Christmas presents before December twenty-fifth? What a letdown on Christmas morning! The element of surprise had evaporated completely.

God's revelation to John abounds with magnificent word pictures depicting what is in store for believers when the final curtain falls on human history and we begin our eternal life in the paradise of God. Splendid and revealing though they are, much remains hidden, which God is keeping for our eternal "Christmas morning." Read once more our verse for today. What is this white stone?

Archbishop Trench likened it to the Urim and Thummim of the Old Testament, which the high priest consulted for divine guidance. He believed the Urim may have been a white stone, a diamond, "bearing the new name of God or of Christ—some revelation of the glory of God, only in that higher state capable of being communicated by him to his people, and which they only can understand who have actually received it."[3] It has also been connected with the twelve stones on the High Priest's breastplate, representing the twelve tribes of Israel. Interpretations, however, are legion.

More intriguing is the new name written on the stone. In Scripture, new names indicate new beginnings: Abram became Abraham, Sarai became Sarah, Jacob became Israel, Simon became Peter, Saul became Paul. New names sometimes also denote character.

Can it be that, as we take up residence in God's presence, we will bear a new name indicating our new status in the "company of the redeemed"? Or, can it be that the way we are living now will determine our new name in heaven? Of this we can be certain: God has many surprises waiting for us when we reach our final destination in his eternal city.

Richard Allen Bodey

39

Time for Plain Talk?

To the angel of the church in Thyatira write: These are the words of the Son of God.

Revelation 2:18a

More than a century ago, Anglican scholar E. W. Bullinger wrote a fascinating book entitled, *The Witness of the Stars.* In it he explains how the constellations proclaim the great truths of the gospel. Many times as we peer up into the dark night sky, however, the Big Dipper, Pleiades, or Orion are obscured from view by low-hanging clouds, or by competing light from the earth.

In his letter to the church at Ephesus, Jesus identified himself as the one who holds the seven stars in his right hand. Addressing the church at Smyrna, he claimed to be the first and the last. In his letter to the church at Pergamum, he called himself the one who wields the sharp two-edged sword. In some respects, each of these descriptions is a veiled indication of his identity. Now, to the church at Thyatira, he discloses himself in plainer language. "These are the words of the Son of God." Why does he speak so plainly?

Thyatira had many guilds comprised of merchants and craftsmen. These guilds honored a local god who was probably fashioned after Apollo. Feasts were held in his honor. Sacrifices and worship were offered to him. Orgies and debauchery polluted the festivities. For Christians, these celebrations posed a dangerous temptation. Forcefully, Christ reminds them who he is—the very Son of God. They needed no further word. His meaning is plain.

How do you conduct yourself in the workplace? In your socializing? Among your unbelieving relatives? Are you staying close enough to your Lord so that even when he veils his identity you recognize who is speaking to you? Or must he remind you plainly, "I am the Son of God"? That should not be necessary. But if it is, be sure you get his message. Be sure, too, that you obey it.

Richard Allen Bodey

40

Compliment
or Reprimand?

I know your deeds, your love and faith, your service and perseverance, and that you are now doing more than you did at first.

Revelation 2:19

Victorian novels of the nineteenth century reflect many bygone customs of that era. People thought it proper, for example, for a woman to blush demurely when paid a compliment. Men responded with a modest look and a simple, "Thank you." Turning back to even earlier times, we learn from literature that the flurry of a fan partially obscured a woman's face when others sang her praises. Men bowed from the waist as they uttered their "Thank you, kind sirs."

Imagine receiving a compliment from our Lord like this: "I know your deeds, your love and faith, your service and perseverance, and that you are doing more than you did at first." "Nevertheless, I have this against you," he adds (Rev. 2:20a).

Compliment! Reprimand! Christ sincerely compliments the Christians at Thyatira, but he also sternly rebukes them. He does not withhold the truth of compliment because of the truth of reprimand. We find a similar instance after Peter's confession, "You are the Christ, the Son of the living God." Jesus replied, "Blessed are you Simon son of Jonah. . . . And I tell you that you are Peter, and on this rock I will build my church" (Matt. 16:16–18). A moment later, however, when Peter refused to accept Jesus' prediction of his impending death, the Lord rebuked him severely, "Get behind me, Satan! You are a stumbling block to me" (Matt. 16:23).

Christ is the Lord of both compliment and reprimand. For those who sincerely seek to follow him, his compliment is what it is meant to be—an expression of praise and commendation. For those who disobey him, his rebuke is exactly that and nothing less.

Christ continues to compliment and reprimand today. Both pronouncements are equally born of love. Both serve the purpose for which they are intended—to help us grow into the fullness of Christ.

Richard Allen Bodey

41

When Tolerance
Goes Too Far

Nevertheless, I have this against you: You tolerate that woman Jezebel, who calls herself a prophetess. By her teaching she misleads my servants into sexual immorality and the eating of food sacrificed to idols.

Revelation 2:20

Have you ever known parents to name their newborn daughter Jezebel? Probably not. The name epitomizes wickedness of the vilest sort. Daughter of Ethbaal, King of Sidon, Jezebel married Ahab the King of Israel. Ahab "did more evil in the eyes of the LORD than any of those [kings] before him" (1 Kings 16:30). It was this Jezebel who stigmatized the name (1 Kings 19:1–2; 21:1–26).

Addressing the Christians at Thyatira, Christ assigned this name to a woman in the congregation. A self-styled prophetess, this first-century Jezebel was enticing Christians to accept some of the most depraved pagan practices, such as sexual immorality and eating food that had been sacrificed to idols. "I have given her time to repent of her immorality, but she is unwilling," Christ declared, so "I will strike her children dead" (Rev. 2:21, 23). Her children included all those who practiced and promulgated her false teaching.

We have our own "Jezebels"—men and women alike—in the twenty-first century church. Their enticements have taken new forms, but we are still confronted by those who are determined to bring the world's allurements and perversions into the church. Christian, be vigilant! These enticements are often deceptively and attractively packaged: "This will demonstrate we're not narrow-minded." "This will show we're inclusive." "This will attract young people." "This will prove we're relevant."

Read with utmost care our Lord's warning to the church at Thyatira lest, too late, your church hears his accusing voice, "You tolerate that woman Jezebel. . . . I have given her time to repent of her immorality, but she is unwilling. So I will cast her on a bed of suffering, and I will make those who commit adultery with her suffer intensely, unless they repent of her ways. I will strike her children dead" (Rev. 2:20–23). Solemn words, indeed!

Richard Allen Bodey

42

Reputation

To the angel of the church in Sardis write: These are the words of him who holds the seven spirits of God and the seven stars. I know your deeds; you have a reputation of being alive, but you are dead.

Revelation 3:1

Reputations are hard to build, but easily destroyed. Your reputation is important because it becomes the currency of your competency and credibility. As Shakespeare observed in *Othello* (act 3, scene 3), "But he that filches from me my good name, robs me of that which not enriches him, and makes me poor indeed."

When reputation does not reflect reality, it breeds disillusionment and cynicism, unless the reality is better than reputation would suggest. Our age has led us to doubt that the reality will match the advertisement, or the product the package.

The church at Sardis appeared to be a fine church with no serious problems, but the outward appearance was deceptive. It was actually in spiritual jeopardy. Although you may appear to be alive, you are actually dead, was the assessment.

Have you ever gone through the motions without being spiritually energized? Others may not have detected any significant difference, but you were aware that all was not well spiritually.

If so, as with the believers in Sardis, you must give attention to that inner reality, strengthening the Spirit's work so that those who observe you will encounter an example of spiritual integrity and vitality.

Luder G. Whitlock

43

Spiritual Vigilance

Remember, therefore, what you have received and heard; obey it, and repent. But if you do not wake up, I will come like a thief, and you will not know at what time I will come to you.

Revelation 3:3

Calamity often arrives unexpectedly: an automobile accident, a heart attack, cancer, or a hurricane. The citizens of Sardis were well aware of that, because Sardis was destroyed by a major earthquake. In addition, the capitol city famed for Croesus and Aesop was twice destroyed by surprise attacks during the middle of the night, when no guards were posted.

Following calamitous experiences, we inevitably second-guess ourselves, thinking about what we might have done to avoid such tragic consequences: drive more carefully, follow the diet, exercise, build stronger and more flexible buildings, and so on.

Then time passes, lots of time, with no problems, and we gradually lapse into complacency, slowly abandoning the protective practices that we established for our well-being and security. When tragedy strikes again, we are unprepared. We learn belatedly that there is no substitute for preparedness and vigilance.

Spiritual vigilance is required because the devil is always looking for an opportunity. That's why the warning to the church at Sardis was so appropriate. Jesus warned all of us to be ready: watching and praying. We can maintain a state of spiritual readiness by reading the Bible, prayer, worship, fellowship with other believers, and earnestness about doing the Lord's will.

Luder G. Whitlock

Overcomer

He who overcomes will, like them, be dressed in white. I will never blot out his name from the book of life, but will acknowledge his name before my Father and his angels.

Revelation 3:5

Christ has overcome the world (John 16:33) and is, therefore, able to offer full and complete redemption to all who trust in him. Now as victor over sin and the grave he sits at the right hand of the Father, with all power and authority.

Because you trust in Christ and endeavor to obey him, you share in his victory. You are an overcomer also. He satisfied the judgment against sin by his death on the cross so that, when you repent and believe in him, you are justified—declared righteous in God's sight. So you will be "dressed in white," symbolic of being clothed in the righteousness of Christ.

When we are facing seemingly insurmountable obstacles or unbearable suffering, his words are a comfort. For we know that, regardless of how impossible the way may appear, he has assured us passage. No matter how painful the adversity, it will not be too much. His grace is sufficient and the victory is assured. He has the power to guarantee it, and he has.

Even our lesser struggles and daily trouble spots, though trying and frustrating, may be seen from a different perspective by faith. It is worth all the effort, too, when we realize that eventually we will be with Jesus and will work with him, dressed in white.

As John put it, those who live with this hope purify themselves, just as Christ is pure (1 John 3:3).

Luder G. Whitlock

45

Anxiety

I will never blot out his name from the book of life, but will acknowledge his name before my Father and his angels.

Revelation 3:5b

We are unable with certainty to predict the future, although we are regularly tempted to speculate about what may occur. Typically, unfolding events further confirm the inscrutability of the future. That could make us anxious, except for the fact that we know that the Lord holds the future in his hands. That realization provides great security, because we know that his promises are sure and no one can nullify them.

When you trust in Jesus as your Savior, your name is written in the Book of Life, and no one else can erase it. He has promised never to erase it, rather, when the appropriate time arrives, to acknowledge us before the Father and all his angels. What could provide greater encouragement or security than these few words? During his earthly ministry, Jesus said, "Do not rejoice that the spirits submit to you, but rejoice that your names are written in heaven" (Luke 10:20).

The believers in Sardis whose walk was worthy of their spiritual calling had no reason to be anxious about the possibility of a surprise judgment arriving like a thief in the night. Nor did they need to be anxious about lesser matters. As long as they maintained their relationship with Christ, everything else would be taken care of.

Be concerned about your relationship with the Lord and don't worry about anything else. Then, when you get to heaven, there will be a place for you at the table, too. You can count on it.

Luder G. Whitlock

Opportunity

To the angel of the church in Philadelphia write: These are the words of him who is holy and true, who holds the key of David. What he opens no one can shut, and what he shuts no one can open.

Revelation 3:7

What is the key of David, mentioned also in Isaiah 22:22? The key is evidently a symbol of trust and authority given to Christ, as the one who is responsible for God's household. The key of David may refer to the temple in Jerusalem. As the symbol of God's presence among his people, the temple ultimately points to the presence of God among his people, the Church. Jesus holds the key that opens the door into his presence. When he opens a door, no one else can close it.

This Scripture passage is not only a wonderful reminder of the door to salvation that God has opened to us, but it is also a reminder of the joy of his presence and the enjoyment of fellowship with him and other believers. The benefits of his presence are immense.

There is also a reminder that God often opens doors of opportunity for us, as he opened a door for Paul to Ephesus (1 Cor. 16:9) as well as Troas (2 Cor. 2:2).

What doors may the Lord be opening for you?

Luder G. Whitlock

47

Strength

I know that you have little strength, yet you have kept my word and have not denied my name.

Revelation 3:8b

Philadelphia was, in the eyes of most people, the smallest and least significant of the seven churches mentioned by John. The city was less prosperous than the others, too. Yet Philadelphia receives the greatest praise from the Lord because they kept his word and endured patiently (3:8, 10). The small band of believers in Philadelphia genuinely loved the Lord, and demonstrated it through their obedient endurance.

They are a poignant reminder that small can be beautiful. Size isn't what counts with God. Through the centuries he has delighted to display his power and grace in small things, like a little boy with a few loaves and fish, a widow's mite, young David with his sling, Gideon's army of three hundred.

How refreshing! What a contrast to the "bigger is better" philosophy that dominates our age. The adulation of the megachurch and the super pastor has blown life out of proportion. God is more interested in your heart than your outward appearance. Genuine faith, though only the size of a tiny mustard seed, is more important to him than earthly riches or power.

No matter how insignificant you may seem to others, no matter how puny your gifts, God can use them to do more than you have begun to imagine.

If he wishes, he can bring the world to our feet. We don't have to be great, because God is great.

Luder G. Whitlock

48

3:8b

Trials

The Black Death, or bubonic plague, decimated the population of the seventeenth century, taking one of every three lives. Epidemics in ancient cities could eliminate as much as two-thirds of the population. The twentieth century was a bloody one, with nearly sixty million lives snuffed out by purges, mass murder, and atrocities of war. Some people wondered if World War II were such an "hour of trial."

None of us is immune from such experiences and, even without them, we have more trouble than we want. We have come to realize that "in this world you will have trouble" (John 16:33). This is a consequence of sin—the cause of human suffering and misery.

Yet we are reminded that such trials strengthen us and develop perseverance (James 1:2–4). Years ago, someone told me, "All sunshine makes a desert." That is true, even though we don't usually think about that. Without storms and rain, you will have a barren situation.

So the Lord sends trials to test us, to strengthen our faith and draw us closer to him. As our weaknesses are exposed, we discover how much we depend on his love and grace.

When the hour of trial comes he will be with you, and the waters will not overflow you.

Luder G. Whitlock

49

Perseverance

I am coming soon. Hold on to what you have, so that no one will take your crown. Him who overcomes I will make a pillar in the temple of my God. Never again will he leave it. I will write on him the name of my God and the name of the city of my God, the new Jerusalem, which is coming down out of heaven from my God; and I will also write on him my new name.

Revelation 3:11–12

Keeping on keeping on is more difficult than it seems. When running a distance race, there comes a point when your body fails you, when it does not seem able to respond. So you push yourself and discover a "second wind."

When discouragement strikes, it is debilitating—like a blow to the solar plexus. You are not ready to quit: You want to quit. You do not want to continue, everything in you resists, squeezing out any desire to continue.

Perseverance as a word is simple. Applied to a challenging situation it is difficult. But it enables you to hold on to what you have, to resist the urge to quit. In adversity, especially, we need the encouragement to hold on.

50

The reward makes it worth the effort. Here we are reminded that we shall become pillars in God's temple. His name shall be written on us, and he promises never to abandon us. We will be with him forever in the delights of the heavenly city, the New Jerusalem. The threefold naming underscores the blessedness of our final reward if we persevere.

Is that sufficient motivation?

Luder G. Whitlock

Surrender

To the angel of the church in Laodicea write: These are the words of the Amen, the faithful and true witness, the ruler of God's creation. I know your deeds, that you are neither cold nor hot. I wish you were either one or the other! So, because you are lukewarm—neither hot nor cold—I am about to spit you out of my mouth.

Revelation 3:14–16

The word *lukewarm* meant something to the Laodiceans, who were aware of the value of hot mineral springs water, as well as cool water from deep mountain cisterns. Since their water was piped from a distance, it was lukewarm, and not appealing. It becomes the perfect illustration to deal with the spiritual deficiency of this congregation—neither hot nor cold.

God detests halfway commitment and halfhearted service. He wants you to love him with all your heart, soul, and mind (Matt. 22:37). Anything less than that is unacceptable. Can you imagine Jesus urging you to trust and obey with care and moderation so that you don't get carried away?

While excess and imprudence have doubtlessly done their damage, and zealots and fanatics have caused more grief than we will ever be able to tabulate, that does not excuse you from your responsibility.

God is looking for disciples who will surrender everything to follow Jesus and, having done so, are on fire with enthusiasm to do his will. What is your spiritual temperature?

Luder G. Whitlock

51

Riches

You say, "I am rich; I have acquired wealth and do not need a thing." But you do not realize that you are wretched, pitiful, poor, blind and naked.

Revelation 3:17

Laodicea was a city of great wealth, possibly the most prosperous city of its day in Asia. Three major transportation routes converged in Laodicea, contributing to its emergence as a commercial and financial capital. It became known for the production of black wool and a notable medical school. Life was privileged in Laodicea. People had everything money could buy.

But money cannot buy everything. Those who have it often learn that the hard way. It does not enrich the inner life or guarantee happiness. The prodigal son is a good example of this.

In this instance, it blinded the Laodiceans in the church. They did not see themselves as they really were—spiritually wretched, pitiful, poor, blind, and naked.

Their prosperity had been enough to delude them into unrealistic spiritual assessment. At most, they had been perfunctory, just going through the motions. They may have had an attractive church with all the usual activities, but spiritual vitality was missing.

What good is it if you gain the world, but lose your soul? "I'd rather have Jesus than silver or gold" is the song that changed George Beverly Shea's life. He got it right.

Luder G. Whitlock

Discipline

Those whom I love I rebuke and discipline. So be earnest, and repent.

Revelation 3:19

Permissiveness breeds selfishness and irresponsibility. It is far less trouble not to correct someone, because when you do, regardless of how careful you may be, there is usually a backlash. During the 1970s, many parents began to realize that their permissiveness was hurting, not helping, their children and society. They discovered the need to correct them for their own good.

In this light we can appreciate "Those whom I love I rebuke and discipline," which is reminiscent of Hebrews 12:5–6: "Do not make light of the Lord's discipline, and do not lose heart when he rebukes you, because the Lord disciplines those he loves, and he punishes everyone he accepts as a son."

God was trying to get the attention of the Laodiceans because he was concerned about their spiritual welfare.

Sometimes the Lord does the same with us to straighten us up. He has our best interests at heart. So don't harden your heart when he tries to get your attention. He loves you; pay attention to him.

Luder G. Whitlock

53

Listening

Here I am! I stand at the door and knock. If anyone hears my voice and opens the door, I will come in and eat with him, and he with me. To him who overcomes, I will give the right to sit with me on my throne, just as I overcame and sat down with my Father on his throne. He who has an ear, let him hear what the Spirit says to the churches.

Revelation 3:20–22

When I was a boy, I could get so involved in reading a book or playing a game that my mother would call and I would not hear. My powers of concentration were remarkable on such occasions. Or the alarm clock would go off early in the morning and I would not hear it. It is remarkable how selective you can be without realizing it. You can screen unwanted things out and not even realize you are doing it. As an adult I have driven past signs and buildings without ever really seeing them.

On the other hand, we are typically tuned in to those things that are important to us. With that in mind, we can appreciate the refrain echoed to each of the churches: "He who has an ear, let him hear what the Spirit says to the churches."

So the Laodiceans were told, "I stand at the door and knock. If anyone hears my voice and opens the door, I will come in and eat with him, and he with me." Obviously some of them were not paying attention. What an opportunity they were missing as a result. It is easy to fault the Laodiceans for their mistakes, but we can make similar mistakes. Are we tuned in to God's communications to us?

God speaks to us through his Word and through others.

Are you listening and looking so that you do not miss what he has to say to you?

Luder G. Whitlock

54

Doors of Death!
Doors of Life!

After this I looked, and there before me was a door standing open in heaven.
And the voice I had first heard speaking to me like a trumpet said, "Come
up here, and I will show you what must take place after this."

Revelation 4:1

In the first verse of chapter four we are invited, through John's vision, to come up and take a look at the place where Christians dream about making their eternal home. There is "a door standing open in heaven." Christ, our Savior who awaits our coming entry through this door, purchased the way for us on Calvary.

A popular poster series pictures a variety of doors from one of the world's great cities. The different shapes, colors, and features of the doors make them appealing to the eye. But I know that not all those doors open to good things. In the course of life, many doors beckon us. We decide whether to enter or pass by. Sometimes the voice on the other side of the door calls us alluringly, like the bait in an animal trap. When we enter, however, pain and destruction ensnare us. We are caught and often scarred forever. These doors lead to destruction and death.

The door Christ opens is not like that. It is the door of promise and hope, the door of eternal life. It leads to a mansion already prepared for us in heaven (see John 14:2).

Make it your resolute aim in Christ's strength to walk through heaven's door and claim your place beside the Lord of life for all eternity.

Barbara M. Holmes

55

Totally in Touch

At once I was in the Spirit, and there before me was a throne in heaven with someone sitting on it.

Revelation 4:2

In Revelation, John mentions being in the Spirit four times. What does it mean to be "in the Spirit"? Here it includes the Holy Spirit giving him the mind of God. He was seeing events and circumstances that he could see only through spiritual eyes. Ordinary human eyesight cannot fully envision the revelation John saw.

To be in the Spirit is to invoke the Holy Spirit to enlighten and direct us as we wait upon the Lord. This is especially important as we seek to discern the message of the Scriptures. Since God inspired the Scriptures, we have no fear about their reliability or authenticity, but we need the Holy Spirit to guide us into a deeper understanding of their truth and application for our daily living.

Some of nineteenth-century author and painter John Ruskin's outstanding paintings were carefully arranged in the order of their production and displayed in Brentwood, his former home. Above each picture were examples of great art masters who had influenced him. Those who came to view Ruskin's work found it easy to see the similarities between the artists he admired and his own canvases. We are all influenced by the lives and work of others.

Who influences us? Are we being influenced by the Spirit's attributes or the world's standards? Is the life of the Holy Spirit evident to those with whom we come in contact?

Get "in the Spirit"! As you pray and read the Scriptures, ask the Spirit to help you understand God's truth and make you more like Jesus day by day. "To this you were called, because Christ suffered for you, leaving you an example, that you should follow in his steps" (1 Peter 2:21).

Barbara M. Holmes

The Promise
of the Rainbow

And the one who sat there had the appearance of jasper and carnelian. A rainbow, resembling an emerald, encircled the throne.

Revelation 4:3

"I have set my rainbow in the clouds, and it will be the sign of the covenant between me and the earth" (Gen. 9:13). The rainbow was given as the sign of God's covenant that he would never again destroy the earth with a flood. It is like his signature upon an agreement, and God never breaks his word.

When a rainbow colors the sky after a storm, its beauty reminds us of God's covenant. Our idea of a covenant and God's are very different. Normally, when we think of a covenant, we get the idea of a pledge between equals. Each party contributes something to the other as an acceptable exchange. But God's covenant requires neither equality nor reciprocity. He provides everything needed to complete it through his Son, Jesus Christ, who died for us on Calvary's cross.

God made promises to us and he keeps them. We also promise him certain things when we accept his Son as our Savior. By making him Savior, we say he will be Lord of our lives. This means that he has access to us anytime he chooses. We should be at his disposal all the time. Our lives belong to Christ. That is foundational to being a Christian.

This Revelation rainbow is one of beauty, vibrancy, and majesty. It is God's reminder to us that he keeps his promises forever. As you live your life for him, ask him to enable you to make it a life of promises kept to him and to others. Let your life flow as a reflection of the beauty, vibrancy, and majesty of God.

Barbara M. Holmes

57

God's Throne Room

Surrounding the throne were twenty-four other thrones, and seated on them were twenty-four elders. They were dressed in white and had crowns of gold on their heads.

Revelation 4:4

As a child in Northern Ireland, I was excited to join in the enthusiastic celebrations for Queen Elizabeth II's coronation. Street parties and commemorative souvenirs for schoolchildren were all part of the festivities of the highlight occasion. Pictures of visiting dignitaries from around the world, all dressed in their ceremonial regalia, each admiring the other until the new queen arrived, accompanied newspaper and television news reports. When the great moment came, a hush fell over the audience. Every eye was upon the new royal leader.

When we think of thrones and crowns today, our minds are often drawn to England's "royals." Sometimes comments made in newspaper editorials question the need for such royalty in today's world, because of the morality, attitude, or excessive demands of potential future monarchs.

The throne in Revelation is different from every earthly throne. God occupies it! Its authority and authenticity are unquestioned. Its King is ever perfect. No wonder the elders revere him!

The picture here is not one of excess but sacrifice. God gave his only Son, Jesus, that we might live. The elders surrounding the throne are said to represent the redeemed of God from every generation in human history. They are seated on their thrones before him. According to Revelation 11:16, they fall on their faces and worship him.

How different from the way today's earthly monarchs are regarded, but then how different this heavenly King! Consider it an honor to be a citizen of his heavenly kingdom, where our perfect King demands no sacrifice from us but, rather, makes the sacrifice of his Son for the sake of his people.

Barbara M. Holmes

Partners
from the Throne!

From the throne came flashes of lightning, rumblings and peals of thunder. Before the throne, seven lamps were blazing. These are the seven spirits of God.

Revelation 4:5

Outside my window lies a winter wonderland. Snow-covered trees and rooftops blend together, and sunshine causes the snow to sparkle on my driveway. It's wintertime in Pittsburgh! The sky above, although blue, shows signs of snow cloud formation, declaring that more snow is on the way. Snow always follows snow clouds. How far different the Mississippi Gulf Coast, where we used to live. There, summer lightning bolts announced the coming of noisy thunder rumbling across the heavens. As in Revelation, lightning always precedes thunder: "From the throne came flashes of lightning, rumblings and peals of thunder." They come to us by the Spirit of God who renews the earth, represented here as "the seven spirits of God" (see Ps. 104:30).

The combination of Pittsburgh's snow clouds and snow, and Mississippi's Gulf Coast lightning and thunder, presents a striking reminder of the relationship between faith and works. One always follows the other. Natural partners, they, too, come "from the throne." When we see summer lightning flash across the sky, we know that thunder's roar will quickly follow, because one accompanies the other. They each go hand-in-hand, reminding us of him who sits on the throne.

"What good is it, my brothers, if a man claims to have faith but has no deeds? Can such faith save him?" (James 2:14). As thunder follows lightning, and snow follows snow clouds, so also works follow faith. This, too, is of God's Spirit. When we have true faith, our actions and thoughts are changed. It makes a complete declaration that the faith is authentic when good deeds follow faith in the life of every Christian.

Barbara M. Holmes

59

Flawed but Saved!

Also before the throne there was what looked like a sea of glass, clear as crystal. In the center, around the throne, were four living creatures, and they were covered with eyes, in front and in back.

Revelation 4:6

The Waterford Crystal factory, near Ireland's southeast corner, is the birthplace of world-famous crystal and a major tourist attraction. On a number of occasions, I have stood in awe watching Waterford artisans create new and unique pieces of crystal. The workmanship that goes into each piece, whether a goblet or Christmas ornament, a table lamp or a trophy for a major sporting event, never ceases to amaze me. The Waterford craftsman examines each piece carefully. When a flaw is found, the piece is destroyed, and the craftsman starts over to re-create his masterpiece.

Our heavenly Father, too, uniquely creates each of us. No two of us are alike. Creation's master craftsman examines us for flaws. When he finds one, rather than destroy us, he saves us and gives us a fresh start. Unlike a flawed piece of Waterford crystal, we are not smashed in a barrel full of useless broken glass. Instead, our Creator himself was broken for our flaws.

The "sea of glass" here highlights both the magnificence and redemptive holiness of God. We are his creation. Through Christ's death on Calvary, he atones for our every flaw.

Next time you lift a glass to take a drink, remember the story of the Waterford craftsman striving for purity and perfection, and casting away every piece that does not meet his standards. Then think of God's gracious willingness to keep us, despite our imperfections, and give thanks.

Barbara M. Holmes

The Four
Living Creatures

In the center, around the throne, were four living creatures, and they were covered with eyes, in front and in back. The first living creature was like a lion, the second was like an ox, the third had a face like a man, the fourth was like a flying eagle.

Revelation 4:6b–7

These words symbolize God's attributes in the appearance of four living creatures: a lion, an ox, a man, and an eagle. The lion symbolizes strength, majesty, and power; the ox—diligence and faithfulness; the man—intelligence; and the eagle—divine sovereignty. Ezekiel saw four similar creatures in one of his visions (Ezek. 1:5–10).

Some scholars say that, taken together, these creatures reveal God's perfect nature, while others say they are the most majestic of all creatures and, therefore, the whole creation. In the early church, they were seen as representing the four Gospels. Matthew is the Gospel of the lion, because it represents Christ as the Lion of Judah. The ox was the great servant of that time; hence, Mark is the Gospel of the ox, picturing Christ as the servant-king. Luke's Gospel speaks of Christ's perfect humanity and was known as the Gospel of the man. In John, the eagle Gospel, we see Christ as the regal Son of God, exalted and divine.

These are the attributes of Christ. What would you answer if someone asked about your attributes? The way we live our lives tells people more about who we are than all the words we can speak. A little ditty goes like this:

> You're writing a gospel
> A chapter each day
> By the things that you do
> And the words that you say
> People read what you write
> Whether faithless or true
> Say what is the gospel
> According to you?
> Author unknown

Today "Let your light shine before men, that they may see your good deeds and praise your Father in heaven" (Matt. 5:16).

Barbara M. Holmes

4:6b–7

Wings like an Eagle

The fourth was like a flying eagle.

Revelation 4:7b

Years ago, in the Allegheny Mountains, a large eagle was shot by a hunter. When he examined the bird, the huntsman was amazed to find that one of its claws was held firmly in a strong steel trap, from which dangled a chain five feet long. Although not heavy enough to prevent the creature from flying, the additional weight had wearied the eagle, and brought it down within reach of the marksman's rifle.

As Christians, we are often encumbered by past sins and failures. We function, but, like the eagle, we cannot soar to the heights God intends for us. Jesus our Savior died on the cross in order that we could be free once and for all from all our sins. It is easy to give our sins to Christ, then take them back upon ourselves. That is not what Christ wants for us. Rather, he wants us to turn all our past failures and wrongs over to him, and to shed all our traps and chains in his name. "Those who hope in the LORD will renew their strength. They will soar on wings like eagles" (Isa. 40:31a).

What keeps you from having the relationship with God and his Son, Jesus, that you need to have? Whatever it is, give it to him today. With your life surrendered totally to Jesus Christ, you are enabled through the Holy Spirit to move forward and soar with wings like the eagle!

Barbara M. Holmes

Eyes All Around

Each of the four living creatures had six wings and was covered with eyes all around, even under his wings. Day and night they never stop saying: "Holy, holy, holy is the Lord God Almighty, who was, and is, and is to come."

Revelation 4:8

I'm sure you have noticed the surveillance cameras that are now so commonplace in our society, scrutinizing so much of our day-to-day existence. There is another kind of observation that has been going on since creation: "The eyes of the LORD range throughout the earth to strengthen those whose hearts are fully committed to him" (2 Chron. 16:9). He protects us, guides us, and loves us! Knowing that our heavenly Father has his eye on us should motivate and encourage us to live in a way that pleases him. It should also make us feel very secure, because he is always watching over us, taking care of us. We need never be afraid. His protecting eye never leaves us.

Here the living creatures use their eyes to observe God's holiness. I heard a visiting speaker say some years ago that Helen Keller, blind and deaf from the age of two, was asked by a young boy, "Isn't it the worst thing in the world to be blind?" Smiling, she replied, "Not half so bad as to have two good eyes and see nothing." She was not speaking about physical sight but the eyes of the heart.

"I pray also that the eyes of your heart may be enlightened in order that you may know the hope to which he has called you, the riches of his glorious inheritance in the saints, and his incomparably great power for us who believe" (Eph. 1:18–19).

Today, look at life through your heart eyes. Look beyond the obvious to see God's holiness present in all things. With the living creatures say, "Holy, holy, holy is the Lord God Almighty, who was, and is, and is to come."

Barbara M. Holmes

Giving God Glory!

Whenever the living creatures give glory, honor and thanks to him who sits on the throne and who lives for ever and ever, the twenty-four elders fall down before him who sits on the throne, and worship him who lives for ever and ever.

Revelation 4:9–10a

Dr. Milton Turney, one of my college teachers, was fond of quoting something he attributed to Norwegian theologian Ole Hallesby. According to Dr. Turney, Hallesby suggested we pray along these lines: "Lord, if it will be to your glory heal suddenly. If it will glorify you more, heal gradually; if it will glorify you even more, may your servant remain sick awhile; and if it will glorify your name still more, take him to yourself in heaven."

The living creatures and elders glorify Christ on his throne. The Westminster Shorter Catechism opens with the question, "What is the chief end of man?" The answer is that, like the living creatures of Revelation, "Man's chief end is to glorify God and enjoy Him forever." How can we do it?

64

The last few years we have seen many people wearing bracelets, necklaces, and pins bearing the logo "WWJD." The logo stands for "What Would Jesus Do?" Some have suggested that the question needs to be adapted to ask, "What would Jesus have me do?" It is a good question to ask ourselves if, like the living creatures and elders, we desire to live in ways that glorify the Lord. When in doubt about an activity, ask yourself the question, "What would Jesus have me do?" Often when we ask it, the answer is obvious, and immediately helps us to determine the right course to take.

As you go about your daily tasks, ask yourself this question each time you face a decision. When the answer comes, act it out. That way, you, too, will glorify God.

Barbara M. Holmes

True Worship?

They lay their crowns before the throne.

Revelation 4:10b

The now-demolished Queen Victoria School in Belfast, Northern Ireland, where I received my early education, had a wall recalling stories from Queen Victoria's life. One told that Dean Frederic Farrar, a personal friend of Queen Victoria of England, once had a conversation with Her Majesty after she had heard one of her chaplains preach on Christ's Second Coming. She said, "Oh, Dean Farrar, how I wish that the Lord would come during my lifetime!" When he asked why she desired this, her countenance brightened, and with deep emotion she replied, "Because I would love to lay my crown at his blessed feet in reverent adoration!" Can you imagine the impact such a statement from a queen had on those of us who were students at that school named in her honor?

Most of us don't have crowns, but what we do possess, we should be willing to give to Christ, our Redeemer.

It's amazing what we have that we don't need. Some years ago, my husband and I, on special assignment, spent a year living in a tiny, one-bedroom, rented apartment across the country. We put most of our furniture in storage, keeping only enough to furnish that little apartment. It was a wonderfully liberating time for us. It taught us a great lesson about possessions. We had just enough to be comfortable, and we were very happy.

Many of us go through life letting our possessions dictate where and how we live. "Naked I came from my mother's womb, and naked I will depart" (Job 1:21). Why do we allow our possessions to possess us in the meantime?

What will you give up in worship of Christ, who gave his life for you? Why not offer it to him freely now? True worship is more than spoken praise. It is being willing to cast our possessions at his feet.

Barbara M. Holmes

65

Worthy of Worship

You are worthy, our Lord and God, to receive glory and honor and power, for you created all things, and by your will they were created and have their being.

Revelation 4:11

In 212 B.C., Rome's citizens gathered in the city streets to worship Scipio Africanus for having defeated Hannibal. As he passed by, cheering throngs shouted tributes to their military hero for defeating an awesome enemy. They thought him worthy of their worship.

Similarly, multitudes lined Christ's route on Palm Sunday. They, too, thought their hero worthy of their worship. But not for long. Four days later they crucified him!

Today, many of us, when we receive Jesus as Savior, join the cheering throngs and give him our worship. Somehow, the joy of new salvation can quickly wear off. We, too, crucify him, not literally, perhaps, but figuratively—by allowing other interests to crowd him out of first place in our lives. True worship means to adore something above all else. That is why God's first commandment is "You shall have no other gods before me" (Exod. 20:3).

Christ is worthy of such worship for two reasons: First, because, as the living creatures' chorus reminds us, he created all things. "Through him all things were made; without him nothing was made that has been made" (John 1:3). Second, because, through his cross, the Father redeemed us from death to life. "He redeemed us in order that the blessing given to Abraham might come to the Gentiles through Christ Jesus, so that by faith we might receive the promise of the Spirit" (Gal. 3:14).

Today, ask yourself if anything keeps Christ from being first in your life. If it does, remove it so that Christ may occupy the throne of your heart. He is worthy of our worship!

Barbara M. Holmes

All Knowledge

Then I saw in the right hand of him who sat on the throne a scroll with writing on both sides and sealed with seven seals.

Revelation 5:1

I recall some years ago, while on holiday in the north of England, going to a theater to watch a play. The friend with whom I went was a drama devotee and seemed to enjoy the experience. The truth, however, is that I hadn't a clue what it was all about.

When we read parts of the Book of Revelation, we could easily come to the same conclusion, that we haven't a clue what it is about. Yet, as we think about it, we see that it is not as difficult to understand as it may seem. In the first verse of Revelation 5 we are told about a scroll with writing on both sides and sealed with seven seals. Naturally our curiosity is aroused about what is written. I suggest that within that scroll lies a secret, and if we knew what that secret was, it would make sense of history and of the world we live in.

Do we need to be reminded that truth and understanding do not rest in the minds of the great leaders, scholars, and academicians of our world? They are not found even within the domain of the world's greatest scientists. They are known only to the One who is the way, the truth, and the life.

Some years ago when our church organ broke down, we found that no one could fix it, until we located the man who had made it. Only the person who made the world, the Creator, and his Son the Redeemer, ultimately know all things.

In a world of uncertainty, take comfort in the One who knows all things and will ultimately make them known to those who know him.

James Rea

67

Highest Honor

And I saw a mighty angel proclaiming in a loud voice, "Who is worthy to break the seals and open the scroll?"

Revelation 5:2

Once a year, in Britain, the government, on behalf of the Queen, publishes an Honors list. It contains the names of hundreds of people who, one way or another, are worthy to be honored. Stars, politicians, and sports achievers are generally recognized, but every year, ordinary men and women are given credit for great work done. These include elderly men and women who have worked tirelessly for little-known charities; also, young men and women who have shown wonderful acts of bravery. The climax of the occasion is a visit to Buckingham Palace to receive an award presented by the Queen.

Acknowledging service in this way is commendable. Some things, however, we will never gain by our own merit, no matter how good we are. We can never gain God's saving grace by our worthiness, nor will we ever receive a place in his kingdom as an honor we have personally achieved. Paul emphasizes this in Ephesians 2:7–9. In verse 9 he says that we have been saved, "not by works, so that no one can boast." Only one person deserves the honor, and his name is Jesus.

In Revelation 5, no one in heaven or on earth or under the earth could open the scroll. At first John found this overwhelming and wept. But his weeping turned into joy when he learned that his Savior Jesus Christ had the power, the authority, and the sinless perfection required to open the scroll.

Remember, unworthy as you are, Jesus will turn your weeping to joy.

James Rea

68

An Impossible Task

Then one of the elders said to me, "Do not weep! See, the Lion of the tribe of Judah, the Root of David, has triumphed. He is able to open the scroll and its seven seals."

Revelation 5:5

On December 3, 1967, Lois Washkansky was given a new heart through the skill of Dr. Christiaan Barnard, the South African surgeon who was the first man to take the heart of one person and transplant it into another. Many at the time described the operation as an impossible task. On July 21, 1969, Neil Armstrong completed another impossible task when he placed his foot on the moon's surface. Since then we have seen many tasks that appeared to be impossible, accomplished.

Some things, however, still remain impossible for any of us to achieve—the magnitude of the task is too great. When John looks at the task of opening the scrolls he weeps. No one is worthy to open these seals to reveal the secrets of life and death. It is almost as if John asks, "Is there anyone who can do this?" And, of course, there is. The Lion of the tribe of Judah—also described as the Lamb (v. 6)—alone can do it, for later he is described as having the keys of death and Hades.

In Revelation 21, John is assured that weeping is unnecessary. What a wonderful thought that there is One who is worthy. And because he is worthy, he makes us *worthy*, too. We gain entry to heaven on the basis of his victory!

James Rea

69

5:5

The True Royal One

Then I saw a Lamb, looking as if it had been slain, standing in the center of the throne, encircled by the four living creatures and the elders. He had seven horns and seven eyes, which are the seven spirits of God sent out into all the earth.

Revelation 5:6

Some years ago, when I was working in East Belfast, we received a visit from the Prince of Wales to one of our church's projects. A few hours before he arrived, we were inundated with VIPs, including the wife of the Secretary of State for Northern Ireland, the Lord Mayor of Belfast, and several other dignitaries. The hundreds of people who waited outside took notice of these interesting people as they arrived. This all stopped, however, when the Prince arrived. No one else was as interesting. He was the center of attraction, the only person that the people of East Belfast wanted to meet.

In Revelation 5 there is one who takes center stage. He is described both as the Lamb, an image that suggests the Old Testament doctrine of sacrifice, and as the Lion, depicting his power and authority. Because of what he has done for us, our gaze is centered on Jesus, for, as always, he is a VIP and a royal dignitary. The word "seven" in the text suggests his perfection.

No wonder he is central to the Christian faith. Some day we will share his splendor and become his royal priests and kings. No other king or royal person can hand his or her lineage on to us. But he can. A Scottish preacher I heard several years ago gave some encouraging words that he attributed to Augustine and that encapsulate this idea for us: "The Son of God became the Son of man so that the sons of men might become the sons of God."

James Rea

The Prayers of the Saints

And when he had taken [the scroll], the four living creatures and the twenty-four elders fell down before the Lamb. Each one had a harp and they were holding golden bowls full of incense, which are the prayers of the saints.

Revelation 5:8

Many years ago a man said to me, "I think there is no point in praying. God has made his mind up already." Sometimes we find it difficult to believe that our prayers are heard by God. The four living creatures and the twenty-four elders mentioned in verse 8, however, are presenting our prayers as they hold up a harp and golden bowls of incense. Significantly, incense is described as a fragrance by the psalmist. "May my prayer be set before you like incense; may the lifting up of my hands be like the evening sacrifice" (Ps. 141:2).

All this suggests that God welcomes our prayers. They are, indeed, a fragrance to him. How wonderful to think that the prayers we offer are not only being heard in heaven today but are being recorded for the final day!

God does hear and answer the prayers of his people. When we pray, we are not just going through some meaningless spiritual exercise but are actively engaged with the One who takes his people into the new future recorded in John's vision.

It is a wonderful future! The elders and the four living creatures present our prayers to Jesus Christ, the One who is our intercessor and mediator. "He always lives to intercede for [us]" (Heb. 7:25). He makes our praying worthwhile, for he alone knows our deepest needs, and as our mediator and Savior, presents them worthily to the Father.

James Rea

71

Singing a New Song

And they sang a new song.

Revelation 5:9a

"I can't tolerate these new songs," said a disgruntled church member. His was just another voice in the divided views we hear over modern worship songs. In contrast to his view, we find the Bible is full of new songs. Mind you, I don't think my friend would ever have taken issue with today's reading: "And they sang a new song."

New songs are usually written for a good reason. Often, it is to rejoice over the new realization someone has about what God has done. The Book of Psalms exhorts us: "O sing to the LORD a new song, for he has done marvelous things" (Ps. 98:1a). It also tells us our new song comes from a deeper walk with God: "He put a new song in my mouth" (Ps. 40:3). The new song in Revelation 5 is there for a similar reason—because of what Jesus did. His sacrifice brings forgiveness and makes us a special people in the service of God, so his people are singing, "Thank you, Lord!"

When I was a lad, we used to sing an old song, "Can you wonder why it is I love him so, when I think of all he has done for me the guilty one, can you wonder why it is I love him so." Once, for me, that old song was a new song. Still, after all these years, singing it brings joy to my heart. I want to sing my song today in anticipation of the new song I will sing someday along with an immeasurable multitude.

James Rea

72

Don't Forget!

"You are worthy to take the scroll and to open its seals, because you were slain . . ."

Revelation 5:9a

In Acts of Remembrance on Armistice Day, the British are repeatedly confronted with the three words, "Lest we forget." They remind us of our need to say "thank you" for human sacrifice given in war. In the death of Jesus on the cross, however, we are confronted with a much more significant sacrifice. When he appeared to his disciples after his resurrection, Jesus invited Thomas to examine his wounds. In this vision in Revelation, John sees a Lamb looking as if it had been slain. Jesus bears the marks of crucifixion, but now he is standing and he is alive. Clearly, death and sin are now defeated.

How can we ever forget what Jesus has done for us? Yet it is easy to become so familiar with the gospel that we take the cross for granted and forget it. The marks of the Lamb remind us of what Jesus has done. Sometimes we sing the old song with its refrain, "I never will forget what he has done for me." We need to continually stand in awe of the Lamb who was slain, through whose blood we are now forgiven men and women with a future beyond our imagination or comprehension.

Several years ago I watched my friend Tommy weep and sob as he came to take the broken bread and wine at an Easter communion service. I became concerned at his obvious distress. "Are you all right?" I remarked, as he left church. "Yes, I am all right," he said. "I was just overcome when I thought about what Jesus did for me." I remembered that Tommy was an alcoholic who had been radically changed by Jesus Christ. He had found forgiveness for the past, strength for the present, and hope for the future. I should have known better. Thanks, Tommy, for that reminder. Jesus is the Lamb slain for all of us.

James Rea

73

All People Everywhere

"With your blood you purchased men for God from every tribe and language and people and nation."

Revelation 5:9b

Because I was brought up in Northern Ireland, I am ever conscious of the divisions of which any visitor will soon become aware. Murals on walls, flags, and emblems tell who is, or is not, welcome in a particular area. In other parts of the world, color, ethnicity, and class divide people. Here in Ireland, religion and politics do. In ancient Judaism, division arose over the acceptance of Gentiles as members of God's kingdom.

What is so attractive about the Christian faith is its inclusiveness. No one is excluded on the basis of birth, color, culture, or upbringing. In verse 9, the four living creatures and the twenty-four elders sing to the people of every nation who have now become, not only members of the kingdom but also priests in the service of God. All sorts of people are part of this new society. It includes everyone who truly loves Jesus Christ.

If you are a Christian and feel excluded in the community where you live, the place where you work, or the family of which you are part, take heart. God has included you in his eternal community.

James Rea

74

Hope for the World

They will reign on the earth.

Revelation 5:10b

In my mind I can still hear my father pray, "Thank you, Lord, that this world is not my home." Interestingly, in the light of this verse in Revelation, that prayer needs to be reconsidered. For here we read that God's people will reign upon the earth. What a promise! God has included us in his plan for the new order.

We must not forget that this earth, despite its imperfections, is part of God's creation. Revelation 21:1, however, speaks of a new heaven and a new earth. We can find this very helpful when we try to perceive what it will be like or what will be happening in the future. While trying to picture heaven can be difficult, the idea of a new, perfect world is more within our understanding. What is important is that, within this perfect world, the promises of Revelation 21:4 will be realized: "He will wipe every tear from their eyes. There will be no more death or mourning or crying or pain, for the old order of things has passed away." Paul speaks in Romans of creation groaning and waiting in eager expectation of this event.

How we long for the day when all hatred and war, suffering and grief, will be no more and God's Son, Jesus, will reign over all creation. If you are struggling with today's world and its problems, take heart. There is great hope for the future ahead and, more thrilling than anything, you will be part of it.

James Rea

75

Who Jesus Is

Worthy is the Lamb, who was slain.
Revelation 5:12a

When I was a boy in Sunday school we often sang the chorus "Everybody Ought to Know Who Jesus Is." We prayed that all people would come to discover Jesus Christ for themselves. John clearly indicates that all people, even those who did not acknowledge Jesus in their lifetime, will acknowledge him at his return. In verse 12 of this chapter, we see the myriads of angels surrounding the heavenly throne with the living creatures and elders, loudly proclaiming the sevenfold attributes of Jesus as they sing of his power and wealth and wisdom and strength and honor and glory and praise.

To him belongs power; therefore, we can say that he is able.

To him belongs wealth; therefore, we can say he owns all things.

To him belongs wisdom; therefore, we can be certain that he has access to God the Father's secrets.

To him belongs strength; therefore, we can believe that he will conquer all the powers of evil.

To him belongs honor; therefore, we can be confident that all people everywhere will acknowledge him.

To him belongs glory; therefore, we know that he shares the Father's divine nature.

To him belongs blessing; therefore, we may experience the power of his love.

Let us not wait until his return but proclaim now in our lives, words, and actions who Jesus is, that people all around us may come to know him. Indeed, let us fervently pray that everybody may come to know now who Jesus is, for, one day, though they will then acknowledge him, it will be too late for them to receive his salvation.

James Rea

5:12a

At the Name of Jesus

Then I heard every creature in heaven and on earth and under the earth and on the sea, and all that is in them, singing: "To him who sits on the throne and to the Lamb be praise and honor and glory and power, for ever and ever!"

Revelation 5:13

In the nineteenth century, a young woman who suffered from poor health, the daughter of an Anglican clergyman, wrote this hymn:

> At the name of Jesus
> Every knee shall bow
> Every tongue confess him
> King of glory now.
>
> Carolyn Maria Noel, 1870

The words are based on Philippians 2:10–11, "At the name of Jesus every knee should bow, in heaven and on earth and under the earth, and every tongue confess that Jesus Christ is Lord, to the glory of God the Father."

The words of Carolyn Maria Noel also affirm the words of Revelation 5:13, which declare that every created being will acknowledge who Jesus is.

We find it almost impossible to comprehend that men and women who rejected Jesus Christ on earth will one day acknowledge him for who he is. Yet, despite theological speculation to the contrary, the text nowhere suggests that, as a result of homage, unbelievers will be saved. It simply signifies God's ultimate power and authority over all things, and proclaims that in that climactic day, even the cynics and skeptics will be so overwhelmed by the glory of Jesus, that they will praise his name.

How sobering that even unbelievers will praise his name and acknowledge who Jesus is! Let us trust him now. Then it will be the most natural experience of all for us to praise him in that great day.

James Rea

Hallelujah

The four living creatures said, "Amen," and the elders fell down and worshiped.

Revelation 5:14

For many of us, the grand highlight of Advent is the opportunity to hear Handel's mighty eighteenth-century oratorio, the *Messiah*. In bygone days, the grandest place to hear it was at London's Royal Albert Hall.

The famous English preacher, Dr. Leslie Weatherhead, reputedly attended the *Messiah* annually at this hall, accompanied by his rather quaint and quite eccentric father-in-law. During the singing of the "Hallelujah Chorus," Weatherhead's father-in-law would stand up in the gallery and conduct the choir, much to his son-in-law's embarrassment! Each time the choir reached the words "He shall reign," the old man would push Weatherhead on the shoulder and ask, "How long, Leslie?" The preacher would respond, "For ever and ever." As the last notes of that grand chorus rang out, the old man would turn to Weatherhead and say, "Hi, Leslie, that is our Jesus they are singing about!"

Yes, it was, indeed, Jesus they were singing about. And it is a glorious piece of music. But how much more glorious will it be when we see him as he is and acknowledge him with praise, adoration, honor, and glory, forever and ever. Yes, the music of composers such as Handel can incite us to spiritual ecstasy in the immediate present, but how much greater will our ecstasy be when one day we join that great choir made up of multitudes no one can number and offer praise to Jesus forever and ever.

The four living creatures said, "Amen." We will shout, "Hallelujah!"

James Rea

Pray for Ability to See

I watched as the Lamb opened the first of the seven seals. Then I heard one of the four living creatures say in a voice like thunder, "Come!" I looked, and there before me was a white horse! Its rider held a bow, and he was given a crown, and he rode out as a conqueror bent on conquest.

Revelation 6:1–2

A young mother in our church painted a large—nine feet square—picture of animals of various kinds, all enjoying the Garden of Eden. They look happy, contented. The painting stands in a busy hallway, where people regularly see it.

One day I asked several people who were passing by what they saw in the picture. One said, "A lion." Another, "A giraffe." But a third saw "Happiness." That third person might have a most important gift for understanding Revelation, the ability "to see."

We can regard the Book of Revelation as a museum, filled with vibrant pictures. John has allowed us to walk with him through the lobby, where we have met the other recipients of the letter, and then on into the atrium with its vast vaulted ceiling.

But now we enter the first gallery of collected pictures; over the entrance archway the words "The First Six Seals" are written. Western Seminary professor Vern Poythress reminds us that Revelation is a picture book, not a puzzle book. We must therefore pray to be good "see-ers" not good "puzzle solvers," as we enter this first room.

John was describing the pictures he was shown. God is their creator. And Jesus is their revealer. We should learn about the language in which they were painted, the words that are their details, and the expressions that are found first in the Old Testament. But primarily, we must look at the pictures—at length, over and over again—as we become responsive "see-ers."

Today, ask God to give you grace to see what he wants you to experience.

George C. Fuller

Recognize the More Important Issues

I watched as the Lamb opened the first of the seven seals. Then I heard one of the four living creatures say in a voice like thunder, "Come!" I looked, and there before me was a white horse! Its rider held a bow, and he was given a crown, and he rode out as a conqueror bent on conquest.

Revelation 6:1–2

What do we see? Awesome power! Armies that overwhelm, crushing cities and their inadequate defenders! Massive tanks roll over the foxholes of soldiers armed with knives and pistols.

Revelation 19:11 also describes a "rider on a white horse." The rider in that passage is Jesus. Many Christians, perhaps correctly, understand that Jesus is also the rider of the white horse in today's passage. These verses can also be seen as describing the ultimate power of Jesus, or the church triumphant, or the conquering impact of the gospel.

We are going to have to make a decision here. The "Four Horsemen of the Apocalypse," as the four living creatures have been called, are appropriately seen as similar to one another. As we will see in the rest of chapter 6, the last three surely represent evils that are to fall on humankind. It seems natural, therefore, to assume that this first horse and its rider do not represent Jesus but rather depict suffering and affliction, as do the other riders.

We remind ourselves of two important lessons. First, our interpretation must be fully subject to review, under our only final authority—God's Word. We may have to learn to be comfortable with saying, "I do not believe the rider represents Jesus, but I am not certain."

Secondly, we want to respect the views of others who also seek to honor and understand God's Word. We can seize the opportunity to reflect on the critical distinction between what we believe the Bible teaches and the Bible's unique authority. And we can affirm the deep fellowship we share with Christians whose understanding of Revelation differs from ours.

Today, thank God for his Word and affirm your commitment to fellowship with brothers and sisters in Christ.

George C. Fuller

Non-signs!

When the Lamb opened the second seal, I heard the second living creature say, "Come!" Then another horse came out, a fiery red one. Its rider was given power to take peace from the earth and to make men slay each other. To him was given a large sword.

Revelation 6:3–4

The year was A.D. 30 (more or less). The disciples asked for "the sign of your coming and of the end of the age" (Matt. 24:3). In response, Jesus told them of wars, struggles, famines, and earthquakes: "You will hear of wars and rumors of wars, but see to it that you are not alarmed. Such things must happen, but the end is still to come. Nation will rise against nation, and kingdom against kingdom. There will be famines and earthquakes in various places. All these are the beginning of birth pangs" (Matt. 24:6–8). The subjects certainly seem similar to those depicted in this second of four pictures.

What did he say about these calamities? "Such things must happen, but the end is still to come. . . . All these are the beginning of birth pangs." Do not be alarmed when such things happen; they are not signs of the end. They are non-signs.

The things Jesus described would occur between A.D. 30 and A.D. 70, at which time Jerusalem was to be destroyed. And they continue to occur throughout history, perhaps growing in intensity, often in tragic combination with one another.

The four riders, then, describe life on earth, at least from A.D. 30 to the time of final judgment. Therefore, Christians ought not to be surprised at pain and suffering in the world.

Today, go forth with confidence that God is on his throne.

George C. Fuller

81

Affirm
the Ultimate Power

When the Lamb opened the second seal, I heard the second living creature say, "Come!" Then another horse came out, a fiery red one. Its rider was given power to take peace from the earth and to make men slay each other. To him was given a large sword.

Revelation 6:3–4

The first four pictures of Revelation 6 do not call forth pleasant responses. You look at them, and "happiness" does not come to mind. This second rider can "make men slay each other." The verb means "slaughter, sacrifice, butcher."

It might appear that everything is out of control and that chaos reigns in this second picture. To affirm that conclusion, however, would be wrong; for God rules. This second rider has no authority, no power, other than what "was given" to him. The riders can spread their havoc only as far as they are granted authority to do so.

We must not be superficial in our affirmation that God reigns even in the midst of tragedy. Jesus' words to Peter (John 18:11) can help us to confront tragedy, including our own: "Put your sword away! Shall I not drink the cup the Father has given me?"

Who killed Jesus? The soldiers, the religious leaders, the unconcerned people, Pilate, Herod, Satan? Who was ultimately responsible for Jesus' death? Jesus said, "the cup the Father has given me." Paul told the Philippians (1:29–30) that the God who grants us faith also grants suffering; how gratefully we accept one—faith—from the hand of a God who has pledged his love to us in Jesus, but not the other—suffering—as coming from the same hand. Job asked his wife, "Shall we accept good from God, and not trouble?" (Job 2:10).

Today, rejoice! God rules, not horsemen or circumstances or tragedy!

George C. Fuller

Worship the Lamb

When the Lamb opened the third seal, I heard the third living creature say, "Come!" I looked, and there before me was a black horse! Its rider was holding a pair of scales in his hand. Then I heard what sounded like a voice among the four living creatures, saying, "A quart of wheat for a day's wages, and three quarts of barley for a day's wages, and do not damage the oil and the wine!"

Revelation 6:5–6

The Lamb opened the first seal; he also opens the second and third, and indeed the last three seals. He seems to be "in charge," like an author who intertwines and unravels his book's characters and events, or like an artist who removes the covers of her six most striking paintings.

In Revelation 6, the Lamb is the Lord of history. Jesus is the Lord of the scroll, the Lord of the book, the paintings. "The Lamb . . . is Lord of lords and King of kings" (17:14).

"Lamb" seems a strange image for the one who alone has the power to open the seals. A popular film might be called *The Lion King*, but not "The Lamb King." Lions are in heavily barred cages to protect people; lambs are in the petting zoo.

John the Baptist fulfilled his pivotal role by pointing to Jesus, "Look, the Lamb of God, who takes away the sin of the world!" (John 1:29). The choirs of heaven affirm that it is precisely because Jesus was the sacrificial Lamb, that he does have authority to open the book: "You are worthy to take the scroll and to open its seals, because you were slain, and with your blood you purchased men for God from every tribe and language and people and nation" (Rev. 5:9).

"Christ Jesus . . . being in very nature God . . . humbled himself and became obedient to death—even death on a cross! Therefore God exalted him to the highest place and gave him the name that is above every name" (Phil. 2:5–9).

Think on these things and worship the Lamb.

George C. Fuller

6:5–6

Seize the
Opportunity to Share

*When the Lamb opened the third seal, I heard the third living creature say,
"Come!" I looked, and there before me was a black horse! Its rider was holding a pair of scales in his hand. Then I heard what sounded like a voice
among the four living creatures, saying, "A quart of wheat for a day's wages,
and three quarts of barley for a day's wages, and do not damage the oil and
the wine!"*

Revelation 6:5–6

The black horse and its rider represent severe food shortage. The
presence of scales indicates that wheat has become increasingly
precious (see Lev. 26:26). A laborer must work for a full day to
earn enough to purchase a daily supply of wheat for one person,
or to buy enough less desirable barley for a family of three. Nothing remains for other expenses.

Jesus had already indicated that the disciples would learn of
famines in many places (Matt. 24:7). Famine did afflict the people of Jerusalem, and the Christians may have suffered further as
an oppressed minority. Food deprivation has been a bitter characteristic of life throughout history. The person now reading these
words may not have much contact with starving people, but ignorance does not change the facts.

The voice says, ". . . do not damage the oil and the wine!" The
severity of the famine is limited. While oil and wine could be
understood as staples of the laborer and his family, perhaps they
are to be regarded as available only on the tables of the wealthy.
The picture then portrays both hunger and luxury, side by side.
The poorer half of the world may live—and die—on the other side
of the street, the other side of the tracks, or on the other side of
the ocean.

Spiritual famine is pandemic. Shriveled souls cry out for living
water and the bread of life. A loaf of bread can feed a starved body,
but only the Bread of Life can feed a hungry soul. The Christian
thanks God for opportunities to offer both.

George C. Fuller

Do Not Ignore Death

When the Lamb opened the fourth seal, I heard the voice of the fourth living creature say, "Come!" I looked, and there before me was a pale horse! Its rider was named Death, and Hades was following close behind him. They were given power over a fourth of the earth to kill by sword, famine and plague, and by the wild beasts of the earth.

Revelation 6:7–8

Death rides a colored horse. What is the color of death? The horse is "pale." The Greek word is *chloros* (think of our word *chlorophyll*), a pasty, yellowish, greenish color. The fourth horseman represents death trampling over the bodies of men and women, boys and girls.

Not all death is in this picture, however. The focus is on violent, ugly, untimely (as we incorrectly say) death. The first recipients of Revelation, especially those in smaller towns and rural areas, would have understood that "the wild beasts of the earth" brought ugly death. Perhaps some of those Christians would be torn to death in the Roman arenas for the sport of the audience. Terrorist bombs, "ethnic cleansings," an unknown virus or a mutated bacterium purposely released—these are the modern weapons of the rider on the pale horse.

But the rider's power is restrained. Clearly subject to a more ultimate authority (power is given him), he exercises his cruel work over a fourth of the earth. Were it not so, he would probably crush all humankind at one time, in one event.

Death, however, is our common future. While the fourth rider claims many lives, death will come in other colors to us all. To ignore that fact is much more than a fatal mistake. The Bible says that "man is destined to die once, and after that to face judgment" (Heb. 9:27).

Have you made preparation if death should come to you today? You can do so by forsaking your sins and trusting Christ Jesus, the Lord who conquered death.

George C. Fuller

85

Praise Jesus for
His Victory over Death

When the Lamb opened the fourth seal, I heard the voice of the fourth liv-
ing creature say, "Come!" I looked, and there before me was a pale horse!
Its rider was named Death, and Hades was following close behind him.
They were given power over a fourth of the earth to kill by sword, famine
and plague, and by the wild beasts of the earth.

Revelation 6:7–8

The Bible's revelation of human history depicts the incredible power of the law, sin, and death. Apart from God's restraint and his direct intervention through his Son, this triumvirate rules in every people and nation. Death comes in varied form, claiming every living person.

Humans are crushed under the hoofs of this fierce horse. So it was in the Roman Empire; so it is now. Christians are hardly exempt and may be special targets of the rider's fury.

The Book of Revelation tells of cosmic struggles, but the ulti-mate victor is never in doubt. In the introductory picture, Jesus says, "Do not be afraid . . . I hold the keys of death and Hades" (1:17–18). The victory accomplished on the cross and in the res-urrection will be finally and fully applied, but in his time. Then, "There will be no more death or mourning or crying or pain, for the old order of things has passed away" (Rev. 21:4). First Cor-inthians 15:26, 55–58 also deserve consideration at this point.

The final victory belongs to his church, his own people. He told Peter, "I will build my church, and the gates of Hades will not over-come it" (Matt. 16:18).

Today and every day, praise Jesus for his victory and ours, even over death.

George C. Fuller

Pray with Expectation

When he opened the fifth seal, I saw under the altar the souls of those who had been slain because of the word of God and the testimony they had maintained. They called out in a loud voice, "How long, Sovereign Lord, holy and true, until you judge the inhabitants of the earth and avenge our blood?"

Revelation 6:9–10

The first four pictures of Revelation 6 depict anguish and suffering on earth. That tribulation was evident during the destruction of Jerusalem (A.D. 70), and under the Roman Empire. The first recipients of Revelation likely lost family members to the riders on the four horses—the riders' fury has often been aimed at Christians. Through this present age the slaughter and anguish continue.

The fifth seal portrays a scene in heaven: Martyrs are joined together in prayer. Surely Stephen (Acts 7) is among them, perhaps also John the Baptist (Matt. 14) and others before him (Heb. 11:32ff.). Their voices call forth from beneath the altar of sacrifice, the place of their ultimate offering to the Lamb.

They ask the Lord to "judge the inhabitants of the earth and avenge our blood." But the martyrs know that vengeance is not an option for the Christian. Recall Stephen's prayer—"Then he fell on his knees and cried out, 'Lord, do not hold this sin against them'" (Acts 7:60)—as he emulated Jesus (Luke 23:34). But they did pray that the Lord would bring proper justice, that he would make things "right."

The fifth picture makes clear their confidence that the Lord is able to do what they ask. They call him "Sovereign" (the Greek is *despotes*), indicating his absolute rule. He is "holy and true," so his ultimate judgments will be in accord with righteousness and truth. And they express confidence that, in his time, he will render judgment. He can and will make right the injustice, the inequity, the agony, and the adversity.

Today, offer your petition with that same confidence.

George C. Fuller

87

Wait with Patience

They called out in a loud voice, "How long, Sovereign Lord, holy and true, until you judge the inhabitants of the earth and avenge our blood?" Then each of them was given a white robe, and they were told to wait a little longer, until the number of their fellow servants and brothers who were to be killed as they had been was completed.

Revelation 6:10–11

The martyrs pray, "How long until you avenge our blood?" They are not angry with God. They are not frustrated with his plan. They do not feel their timing would be better than his. But they are fitted for white robes; white, the color of victory and righteousness, robes washed white in the blood of Jesus (Rev. 7:14). In heaven, they are the church triumphant. So they pray with patient trust.

Such trust may not always be evident among God's people. Can we properly see an element of frustration in similar prayers on earth? "How long, O Lord? Will you forget me forever? How long will you hide your face from me? How long must I wrestle with my thoughts and every day have sorrow in my heart? How long will my enemy triumph over me?" (Ps. 13:1–2). We can see such impatience in our own lives, too. "How long," we ask, "will this or that last? Fix it, but according to our schedule!" We are by nature impatient.

The martyrs are told to wait for God's time; from their perspective, it will not be very long. In the meantime, their number will be made complete. The answer will come, justice will be done, but in God's time. So it is with every prayer for deliverance.

Jesus prayed for those who were yet to believe (John 17:20ff.); he now intercedes for each believer (Heb. 7:25), and will continue to do so until the last one for whom he died is presented to the Father. Then the completed fellowship of martyrs and all his people will no longer need to pray with the words, "How long?"

George C. Fuller

88

Behold! The Greatest Show on Earth

I watched as he opened the sixth seal. There was a great earthquake. The sun turned black like sackcloth made of goat hair, the whole moon turned blood red, and the stars in the sky fell to earth, as late figs drop from a fig tree when shaken by a strong wind. The sky receded like a scroll, rolling up, and every mountain and island was removed from its place.

Revelation 6:12–14

The martyrs' petition for justice continues even beyond death, and they are told to wait patiently. The question is, "When will deliverance come?" The answer is, "It will come."

This picture reveals the Lord's awesome answer to the martyrs' prayers. The first four seals show the riders raining havoc throughout history. This sixth picture brings that history to its end in a scene of cataclysmic confusion. The language of judgment and devastation comes from the Old Testament (e.g., Isa. 34:4). The picture may be emphasizing the extent of the chaos by displaying seven participants: earthquake, sun, moon, stars, sky, every mountain and island.

Will the fulfillment be literal? Of course not! It will be worse. It is not at all sufficient to think in terms of economic, social, or even environmental collapse. God, who created the earth, is seen bringing an end to the death pangs of that same earth, and these will become the birth pangs of his new earth (Matt. 24:8, Rev. 21:1).

In Matthew 24, Jesus closely related this cosmic picture of judgment to the appearance of the Son of Man. He said that no one can know the day or the hour of those events. How then are his disciples to prepare themselves for the coming of the day of judgment and of his appearing? Take to heart what he said, "Keep watch, be ready." Be the wise virgin; use your talent well; give food, drink, and clothes to the hungry, thirsty, and needy.

George C. Fuller

89

Stand Firm in Jesus

Then the kings of the earth, the princes, the generals, the rich, the mighty, and every slave and every free man hid in caves and among the rocks of the mountains. They called to the mountains and the rocks, "Fall on us and hide us from the face of him who sits on the throne and from the wrath of the Lamb! For the great day of their wrath has come, and who can stand?"

Revelation 6:15–17

God confronts seven classes of men and women at the day of reckoning, the day of vindication. No social group is excluded. The bottom portion of the sixth picture shows them fleeing in stark terror. They fulfill Hosea 10:8b, "Then they will say to the mountains, 'Cover us!' and to the hills, 'Fall on us!'"

Perhaps they had worshiped created gods, and now call on those same lifeless gods to deliver them from extreme anguish. They hide in caves and among the rocks, and plead with unresponsive mountains to cover them. But hiding, or even annihilation, are not options in this picture.

Their fear is not of death but of being confronted by God. Isaiah knew that fear in the temple; so did Peter on the sea. And where could Adam hide from God? "Sinners in the Hands of an Angry God" is an unpleasant picture. We know the Lamb to be a sacrifice, and in Revelation we know him as "Lamb/King." But no one wants to experience "the wrath of the Lamb."

With their last breath they cry out, "Who can stand?" They are the world that killed Jesus and slaughtered his disciples. Now the supreme court is imposing the penalty. "Who can stand?" Apparently, no one.

But the martyrs conquer. So do those who stand in grace (Rom. 5:2), and on the gospel (1 Cor. 15:1), who stand firm in the faith (1 Cor. 16:13), and in the Lord (Phil. 4:1), who put on the full armor of God (Eph. 6:13–14). And you will see that the peoples of Revelation 7 do far more than simply survive. Stand firm therefore.

George C. Fuller

God's Possession

After this I saw four angels. . . . Then I saw another angel coming up from the east, having the seal of the living God. He called out in a loud voice to the four angels who had been given power to harm the land and the sea: "Do not harm the land or the sea or the trees until we put a seal on the foreheads of the servants of our God."

Revelation 7:1–3

In a vision, John sees the saints on earth protected by the sealing of God's signet, guaranteeing their divine ownership and entrance into the heavenly city.

This reflects the practice of kings sealing official documents with their signet rings. By placing the signet of the ring upon something, possession was authenticated and secured (Dan. 6:17; Matt. 27:66). In this picture, the seal gives evidence that the church is under God's authority. Later we learn that the mark upon the saints is the Father's name (Rev. 14:1; 22:4).

These servants of God are represented by the mystical figure of 144,000 from all the tribes of Israel. This is a symbolic way of emphasizing that the number of servants here is comprehensive; it is the entire church throughout history. In effect, the church becomes the new Israel.

We find support for this depiction of the church as the new Israel in Jesus' promise that his followers would one day "sit on twelve thrones, judging the twelve tribes of Israel" (Matt. 19:28). Likewise, Paul reminds all Christians that "If you belong to Christ, you are Abraham's seed, and heirs according to the promise" (Gal. 3:29). Moreover, he considers every believer a Jew in the spiritual sense of heart circumcision: "No, a man is a Jew if he is one inwardly; and circumcision is circumcision of the heart, by the Spirit, not by the written code" (Rom. 2:29). James also addresses his church letter to "the twelve tribes scattered among the nations" (James 1:1).

How wonderful to know that those who put their trust in the living God rest secure whatever the future may hold.

Robert E. Coleman

The Completed Church

After this I looked and there before me was a great multitude that no one could count, from every nation, tribe, people and language, standing before the throne and in front of the Lamb.

Revelation 7:9a

What a breathtaking scene! Standing about the throne with the living creatures, the elders, and the angels, the multitude of the redeemed is so vast that it cannot be counted. It streams forth in every direction, as far as the eye can see. Just as God promised Abraham, it is as numberless as the stars of heaven (Gen. 15:5) and the sands of the seashore (Gen. 32:12). All the servants of God, from the foundation of the world, great and small, young and old, stand there before the Lamb.

The Great Commission is fulfilled (Matt. 28:18–20)! The gospel of the kingdom has been preached in all the world (Matt. 24:14), and those who come to Christ are gathered to a great homecoming at the throne. What was in the mind of God before the worlds were made is revealed in the Light that is fairer than day.

How we need this vision in our lives today! It helps us keep our priorities in order, to measure decisions now by what is celebrated in heaven. Any activity that does not contribute to that destiny is an exercise in futility.

While we do not know how it will all come together, we know how it will end. Jesus shall reign upon the throne, and before him every knee shall bow, and every tongue declare his praise. This is reality! This is eternity!

> Eternal are thy mercies Lord;
> Eternal truth attends thy word:
> Thy praise shall sound from shore to shore,
> Till suns shall rise and set no more.
>
> In every land begin the song;
> To every land the strains belong;
> In cheerful sounds all voices raise,
> And fill the world with loudest praise.

Isaac Watts, 1719

Robert E. Coleman

Celebrating the Harvest

There before me was a great multitude. . . . They were . . . holding palm branches in their hands.

Revelation 7:9

Much in this scene is reminiscent of the Feast of the Tabernacles. This joyous holiday at the end of the harvest season expressed thanks for the ingathering of the crops, while also commemorating the miraculous interposition of God bringing his people into the Promised Land (Exod. 23:16; Lev. 23:33–43; Deut. 16:13–17).

The feast lasted a week. Each morning a priest, accompanied by a procession of singing worshipers bearing palm branches, went down to the pool of Siloam, where he drew water into a golden pitcher. Returning to the temple, as his brethren offered the sacrifice, amid a blare of trumpets, he poured the water into a silver basin in the courtyard. As soon as the vessel was emptied, the people, led by the Levites, lifted their voices in praise to God and waved their palm branches toward the altar.

Though the ritual expressed thanks for the showers whereby God had brought the fields to harvest, its deeper spiritual reference pointed to the future outpouring of the Holy Spirit. Recall that it was on the last day of this feast, after the sacrifice and the pouring out of the water, that Jesus startled the multitudes when he punctuated their praises with the shout: "If anyone is thirsty, let him come to me and drink" (John 7:37).

The symbolism of this feast finds its fulfillment in Christ. Palm-bearing multitudes from all nations will celebrate this fulfillment before the throne of heaven, singing the song of salvation. At last the harvest will be gathered. The wanderings of God's people will cease. And the long-awaited day of rejoicing in the land of promise will dawn.

Robert E. Coleman

Magnifying God

Salvation belongs to our God, who sits on the throne, and to the Lamb.

Revelation 7:10

An expanded translation of this shout of the redeemed might read: "Then, our God, sitting in majesty and power upon your throne, together with the Lamb who died in our place, are the cause and the means of our salvation. Without your calling and care, and the blood of your Son, we could not have triumphed over evil or entered into your presence adored in holiness. It is all your doing, and to you belongs all the glory."

Observe that salvation is ascribed to God, for the whole work of redemption is initiated and sustained by him (cf. Luke 3:6; Acts 28:28; Titus 2:11). Neither the celestial hosts in heaven, nor the ransomed souls from earth, no one comes into the presence of the Almighty apart from his divine grace.

This verse expresses our dependence and gratitude. It also conveys a collective feeling of personal possession: He that sits upon the throne is *our* God.

Nothing is more uplifting to the soul than the contemplation of God's glory. This is really what worship is: our adoring response to the infinite majesty of God. While it presupposes submission to him, worship in its highest sense is not supplication for needs, or even thanksgiving for blessings, but the basking of the soul in the presence of God himself.

Whatever the means—preaching and hearing of the Word, celebration of the sacraments, singing of hymns, offering of prayers, quiet meditation—the end of it all is the pure joy of magnifying the One who sits upon the throne.

The hymn writer voiced it well when he wrote:

> Lord, arm me with Thy Spirit's might,
> Since I am called by Thy great name;
> In Thee my wond'ring thoughts unite,
> Of all my works be Thou the aim:
> Thy love attend me all my days.
> And my sole business be Thy praise.

John Wesley, 1751

Robert E. Coleman

Angels Rejoice

All the angels were standing around the throne. . . . They fell down on their faces before the throne and worshiped God.

Revelation 7:11

No sooner has the last line of the multitude's chorus echoed through the celestial realm than the hosts of angels pick up the song. We can feel the intensity of their homage in the expression, "they fell down on their faces," which conveys a strong sense of devotion.

The blood-washed throng attributed salvation to their God, yet he is equally the God of the angels. They, too, have a fascination with the saving work of Christ.

It is not surprising, then, to note that as "ministering spirits sent to serve those who will inherit salvation" (Heb. 1:14), the angels have a special interest in the evangelization of the world (1 Peter 1:12). This role explains why they figure so prominently in the witness of the early church, as message-bearers to and rescuers of the apostles (Acts 5:19; 8:26; 10:3; 12:7–11, 23; 27:23).

Remember that the holy angels never lost their created glory through sin and so do not need redemption. As created ministers of God, however, they have watched the divinely initiated program unfold from the beginning. Though the atoning death of Christ did not alter their own unfallen nature, still the angels share its joy, knowing that by that sacrifice, countless descendants of Adam were liberated from the chains of death, made into a holy and royal priesthood, and destined for a position of privilege higher than their own. There is no jealousy in heaven.

To behold these saints who have been brought out of great trials standing before the throne brings them indescribable joy. If angels rejoice over just one sinner who repents (Luke 15:10), how much more must they celebrate when the whole ransomed church of God comes into its inheritance.

Yet surely the angels' joy cannot compare with the joy of the redeemed. As Charles Wesley put it: "For all your heaven, ye glorious powers, and all your God, are doubly ours!"

Robert E. Coleman

95

Certain Truth

Amen! . . . Amen!

Revelation 7:12

In full agreement with the gratitude of the victorious multitude, the angels preface and conclude their ascription of praise with a resounding "Amen!"

The word means to affirm that which is certain or reliable, that which can be trusted without question. It was a way of identifying with the speaker. By saying "Amen," one not only expressed agreement with the statement of another but also made it binding on oneself.

In the early church, as in Jewish synagogues, it was a common practice to voice this assent after hearing a thanksgiving or an important truth (e.g., 1 Cor. 14:16; Rev. 1:6–7). For this reason, also, prayers customarily close with an "Amen," thereby strengthening their force (Rom. 1:25; Eph. 3:21).

Jesus often introduced his own words with "Amen," or as it is often translated, "truly" or "verily I say to you" (e.g., Matt. 6:2, 16 KJV). Such bold affirmation of the truthfulness of what he said was a majestic expression of his authority.

In its highest form, the word is used of Christ himself (Rev. 3:14), which echoes Isaiah's reference to "the God of truth," or, as it could be stated, "the God of the Amen" (Isa. 65:16). Of course, when we think of the inspired Word, we realize that all the promises of God in Christ are "yes, wherefore also by Him is our Amen" (2 Cor. 1:20 NASB).

This is powerful truth. Do I hear an "Amen"?

Robert E. Coleman

A Sevenfold Doxology

Blessing and glory and wisdom and thanksgiving and honor and power and might, be to our God forever and ever.

Revelation 7:12 NASB

The angels now lift up their own tribute in the familiar sevenfold doxology, which emphasizes completeness. Six of the seven attributes are the same as those expressed before, though the order is different (Rev. 5:12).

"Blessing" is a serendipity of happiness, a spontaneous overflow of worship. It reflects the wonder of the angels before the triumph of God's grace. Whether in creation or redemption, all his works praise him.

"Glory" speaks of majestic radiance, that effulgence of splendor that surrounds the Most High.

"Wisdom" is displayed in his comprehension of all things—the way he understands and orders events for the accomplishment of his purposes, particularly in the salvation of his people.

"Thanksgiving" is offered to God as the only reasonable response to his goodness. He is the giver of every perfect gift.

"Honor" signifies the respect due to God. So exalted is his name that, at its mention, every knee should bow before him.

"Power" describes his capacity to perform whatever is inherent in his nature. Just a word from him, and it is done.

"Might" is that relentless force by which his will prevails, the strength by which the universe is upheld.

To these ascriptions of praise, the angels add, "forever and ever," emphasizing again the eternal character of God.

How wonderful it is to be held in the firm grip of the everlasting arms! Here is security. Our salvation does not rest upon the whimsical notions of well-intentioned men but upon the oath of him who is eternal veracity itself. It is fastened with God's own hand to the unmovable stake of his unchanging nature.

Robert E. Coleman

97

Washed in the Blood

They have washed their robes and made them white in the blood of the Lamb.

Revelation 7:14

Notice that the redeemed are dressed for celebration. They are not bruised and threadbare from the struggles out of which they have come but are wearing white robes. This is the customary dress for a victory celebration. Whether or not they have given their bodies in physical martyrdom, the saints have all shared the spiritual reality of offering their bodies as living sacrifices unto God (Rom. 12:1).

Holding palm branches, indicative of triumphant joy, they laud and magnify him who has triumphed not through force of arms, as kings of the earth, but by giving himself to die for the world.

This blood-washed multitude around the throne brings to mind the children of Israel, who washed their robes in preparation for God's appearance on Mount Sinai (Exod. 19:10–14). The outward cleansing of their garments was a token of their inward sanctification. Still, on that occasion, so awesome was God's holiness—his utter separateness from anything defiled—that the Israelites could not come near the mount, upon pain of death.

What a contrast to this scene at the throne, where the multitude with "clean hands and a pure heart" (Ps. 24:4), as a holy priesthood, in full assurance of faith, have the boldness to enter into the very Holy of Holies!

Have you been to Jesus for the cleansing power?
Are you washed in the blood of the Lamb?

Elisha A. Hoffman, 1878

Robert E. Coleman

98

Clothed to Minister

They have washed their robes and made them white in the blood of the Lamb.

Revelation 7:14

The psalmist asked, "Who may ascend the hill of the LORD? Who may stand in his holy place?" (Ps. 24:3).

The answer was clear: "He who has clean hands and a pure heart" (Ps. 24:4).

Priests in Israel wore robes when they ministered before the altar, as if the robes hid their sin. Interestingly, the Hebrew word for coat has the root meaning "to cover." It is the same word used in Genesis 3:21, which says that God made coats of skin to clothe Adam and Eve. That act, of course, occasioned the first blood sacrifice.

The basic robe worn by all priests offering sacrifice was pure white, representing the purity of God. They were clothed as if with God's own character. To approach God without this covering would bring fearful judgment—death (Exod. 28:43).

The only time in the Bible that a naked priest ever offered a sacrifice acceptable to God was at Calvary. When Jesus was nailed to the cross, he was stripped of his clothes (John 19:23). For the first time in human history, one lived among us who needed no symbolic covering, for he himself was the perfect Lamb of God.

Christ's sacrifice has made a covering by which we can now come before God clothed with "garments of salvation" (Isa. 61:10). With robes washed clean by his blood, we can serve at the throne of heaven. This fulfills God's original plan to have for himself a "kingdom of priests and a holy nation" (Exod. 19:6).

'Twas He that cleansed our foulest sins,
And washed us in His richest blood:
'Tis He that makes us priests and kings,
And brings us rebels near to God.

Isaac Watts, 1720

Robert E. Coleman

99

Follow the Blood

They have washed their robes and made them white in the blood of the Lamb.

Revelation 7:14

God clothes his Word in concepts with which we can identify. One of the most significant of these mediums is the blood. The term appears 460 times in the Bible.

When seen in its ultimate reference—to the poured-out life of Christ on our behalf at the cross—blood represents the very essence of God's redeeming love. Lost in sin, as we all were, and under the judgment of death, it becomes the means by which we can find the way back to our Father's house.

I am reminded of a boy who appeared at a mission hospital in Kenya with a gaping wound in his foot. He had been accidentally injured while cutting grass far out in the jungle. Part of his heel was cut off. Without waiting to inform anyone of the mishap, he and a friend set out across the country to find the mission station where they had heard medical help was available. Every time the little foot touched the sandy earth it left a faint trace of blood. The journey was long and difficult, but at last they arrived.

After a time, the boy's mother appeared. The doctors were surprised that she found the way. There were no well-defined trails, and she had never made the trip before.

"How did you do it?" they asked her. The woman, overjoyed to be with her child, replied, "Oh, it was easy. I just followed the blood."

In a much more profound sense, that is how we come to Jesus. The path is sometimes rough, and may lead through many trials, but we need not fear getting lost. All we have to do is follow his footprints. They are easy to find, for each one is stained with blood. The blood will always lead to the Savior.

> I must needs go on in the blood-sprinkled way,
> The path that the Savior trod,
> If I ever climb to the heights sublime,
> Where the soul is at rest with God.

Jessie Brown Pounds, 1906

Robert E. Coleman

Dwelling with God

Therefore, "they are before the throne of God and serve him day and night
in his temple; and he who sits on the throne will spread his tent over them.
Never again will they hunger; never again will they thirst. The sun will not
beat upon them, nor any scorching heat."

Revelation 7:15–16

Washed perfectly clean by the blood of Christ, and adorned in immaculate robes of holiness, the saints unceasingly serve God in his sanctuary. There is no idleness in heaven. We are not told what this service involves, except that the saints are made "kings and priests" unto God (Rev. 1:6 KJV), certainly occupations of great significance and honor.

Exalting their ministry as an act of worship, "he who sits on the throne will spread his tabernacle over them" (Rev. 7:13 ASV). The phrase could read, "he will make his Shechinah to dwell with them."[4] This reference awakens memories of the tabernacle in the wilderness, where God visibly demonstrated his glory in the sight of all Israel (Lev. 26:11–12; cf. Exod. 40:34–38; 2 Chron. 7:1–3). In its larger sense, the overshadowing heavenly Shechinah is the fulfillment of the promise that God would forever dwell in the midst of his people (e.g., Isa. 4:5–6; Ezek. 37:27; Zech. 2:10).

Salvation introduces the saints to a new life of blessedness. Never again will they suffer from the ravages of hunger or thirst— a blessing especially meaningful to persons who had lived in a land where both food and water were always scarce, even more so for those persecuted for righteousness' sake.

The harassed Christians who were the first recipients of Revelation, many of whom had been driven into desolate wastelands for shelter, would also appreciate the promise that never again will the sun of the desert beat upon them, or any scorching heat.

In a deeper spiritual sense, the longing of the soul will be satisfied, and those who hunger and thirst after righteousness will be filled (Matt. 5:6). As Jesus said, "He who comes to me will never go hungry, and he who believes in me will never be thirsty" (John 6:35).

Robert E. Coleman

101

The Lamb of God

The Lamb at the center of the throne will be their shepherd.

Revelation 7:17

We can never lose sight of the Lamb who was slain. This expression of God's grace is the supreme revelation of the redeeming Word, whereby—through the Spirit—we are brought near to God's throne. To see him this way is to know that God loves us and has taken our sins away.

A story tells of a traveler who looked for unusual things in cities he visited. During a tour of a town one day, he was attracted by a remarkable spire over a public building. Turning to see it better, he noticed, about two-thirds of the way up, a stone figure of a lamb on the wall.

The man stopped a passerby and asked if this lamb had some significance. Told that it marked the place where a workman lost his balance and fell while the building was under construction, the traveler inquired, "Was he killed?"

"No," replied the local resident. "It was a miracle. When friends hurried down, expecting to find his mangled body on the pavement, there he was, shaken and badly bruised, but with hardly a bone broken. Several lambs happened to be on their way to slaughter, and as the mason fell, he landed on the back of one of them. The lamb was killed, of course, but his soft body broke the mason's fall and saved his life. The builder was so impressed with the miracle that he had that stone lamb placed there as a lasting tribute."[5]

We can surmise what must have been in the mind of the mason whose life was spared. Far more profound, however, is the wonder and gratitude of those saved from eternal death through the sacrifice of the Lamb of God.

> Just as I am, without one plea
> But that Thy blood was shed for me,
> And that Thou bidd'st me come to Thee,
> O Lamb of God, I come, I come.
>
> Charlotte Elliott, c. 1834

Robert E. Coleman

Silence before the Lord

When he opened the seventh seal, there was silence in heaven for about half an hour.

Revelation 8:1

Silence does not fit our modern hustle and bustle. However, silence can provide an impressive and reverent ambiance. Here, silence appears to be connected with the offering of the prayers of believers.

In the Bible, silence is often the prelude to the going forth of the Almighty in judgment. "Be silent before the Sovereign Lord, for the day of the Lord is near. The Lord has prepared a sacrifice; he has consecrated those he has invited" (Zeph. 1:7). The following verses in this chapter will unfold, in symbolic language, the awesome judgments of God's retribution.

So the God of the Bible is no buttercup. When we look at the full character of the triune God, we see that he is a God of justice. That essential attribute means that he must deal with sin by means of his wrath. Reverently, we must say that Jesus was a tough customer when he dealt with unrepentant sinners. G. K. Chesterton put it well when he said that Jesus did not hesitate to throw furniture down the front steps of the temple. This is the kind of judgment described in Revelation 8 that is about to be inflicted on the wicked. It is so awesome that all inhabitants of heaven stand spellbound, lost for half an hour in silent amazement. As the Old Testament prophet declares, "But the Lord is in his holy temple; let all the earth be silent before him" (Hab. 2:20).

Set aside a special time for silence before God as part of your daily time with him.

John H. White

Angelic Trumpets

And I saw the seven angels who stand before God, and to them were given seven trumpets.

Revelation 8:2

We commonly do not mix angels and trumpets. After all, angels fly in heaven and are sweet and peaceful, whereas trumpets loudly celebrate triumph or announce warnings.

Here, however, trumpets and angels are necessary twins. The biblical God is both the victorious Lord over evil and, at the same time, the one intimately and lovingly present with his people.

There is much mystery about angels, but one thing is clear—they assist and care for believers. Their special function is to carry the righteous dead into the bosom of Abraham. "The time came when the beggar died and the angels carried him to Abraham's side. The rich man also died and was buried" (Luke 16:22). The wonderful truth is that angels are there to guard believers and to herald Christ's victory.

Wonderful, too, is the relevance of the trumpet, signaling the victorious announcement of the Lord's presence. This eschatological focus (focus on the end times) echoes the use of the trumpet when God spoke with Moses at Mount Sinai (Exod. 19:13ff.), while also signaling the day of Christ's final coming.

"In a flash, in the twinkling of an eye, at the last trumpet. For the trumpet will sound, the dead will be raised imperishable, and we will be changed" (1 Cor. 15:52). "For the Lord himself will come down from heaven, with a loud command, with the voice of the archangel and with the trumpet call of God" (1 Thess. 4:16).

Come, Lord Jesus!

John H. White

104

Incensed Prayer

Another angel, who had a golden censer, came and stood at the altar. He was given much incense to offer, with the prayers of all the saints, on the golden altar before the throne.

Revelation 8:3

Prayer is one of the greatest privileges afforded the believer. But how efficacious are our prayers, especially when we face persecution and the reality of our own sin? They just do not seem to bring justice and grace to the bleak and "unfair" situations of life.

Moreover, our prayers are imperfect, for a sinner offers them, and the words are often incorrect or, at best, inadequate. In our text, the angel has a golden censer and much incense is given to him. Note that it is given to him. The angel does not produce the incense. In the light of the rest of Scripture, it is legitimate to conclude that here is pictured our Savior's intercession on behalf of his church. Also, because of the symbolism of the temple in this passage, and all that it implies concerning the presence of a priest, these prayers are based on the atonement, which in turn sanctifies and purifies the prayers.

Thus made fragrant by the incense of the atonement, the imperfect prayers of God's church are sensed by God as they ascend to him, and are heard. Furthermore, our prayers are precious to the Lord. The depiction of a golden censer and altar points to their value. The answers to these prayers may lie in the future, and we may feel that God does not hear them at all, but he not only hears them, they are also precious to him.

Thus you can be "joyful always; pray continually" (1 Thess. 5:16–17).

John H. White

105

A Weapon for the Battle

The smoke of the incense, together with the prayers of the saints, went up before God from the angel's hand.

Revelation 8:4

Throughout history, Satan has vigorously opposed the plans and purposes of God's kingdom. At various times, and in various nations, ungodly opposition has appeared to be destroying the church. This should not surprise us when we understand the nature of the enmity between Christ's kingdom and Satan's.

"I will put enmity between you and the woman, and between your offspring and hers; he will crush your head, and you will strike his heel" (Gen. 3:15).

Satan unleashes his opposition against God's people at every opportunity. "Our struggle is not against flesh and blood, but against the rulers, against the authorities, against powers of this dark world and against the spiritual forces of evil in the heavenly realms" (Eph. 6:12).

Our weapons, however, are not shrill voices raised against ungodliness nor marches for justice but prayer. Jesus taught us to pray: "your kingdom come, your will be done on earth as it is in heaven" (Matt. 6:10).

In the Lord's Prayer, we ask for the systems and structures of wickedness to be destroyed, for individuals to be transformed by regeneration, and for the final consummation of Christ's kingdom to be hastened. This prayer focuses on the reality of the age to come. We ask God to establish signposts of his kingdom within our present broken reality. Thus the will of Christ will be done in the earth willingly, joyfully, consistently. All prayer with that focus, especially for the church in persecution, goes "up before the Lord from the angel's hand." Our prayers are heard and, in God's timing, produce results.

Pray! Not just for Aunt Suzy's broken toe, nor for a good day, but pray that Christ's church will triumph over evil. That prayer he hears!

John H. White

The Terrible
Speed of Mercy

*Then the angel took the censer, filled it with fire from the altar, and hurled
it on the earth; and there came peals of thunder, rumblings, flashes of lightning and an earthquake.*

Revelation 8:5

We pray for God's reign in his world. God's reign becomes actual
because we personally accept it in our lives, and also as God
imposes it in human affairs.

His call for repentance is reinforced by judgment. Christ's second coming brings final judgment, but in the unfolding of history,
until his coming, there occur a series of crises. As the church prays
for his kingdom to come, God answers, in visitations both of mercy
and of judgment.

This verse portrays the censer as simultaneously a means of
intercession and of judgment on the earth. These two seemingly
contradictory acts by the angel, one act toward God and one toward
the world, are, in reality, perfectly related. When the Lord reigns,
"fire goes before him and consumes his foes on every side . . . the
mountains melt before the Lord" (Ps. 97:3, 5).

Fire is a symbol of purification. John originally saw it in heaven,
but now it makes its appearance on earth. Mercy and judgment
are not two contrasting sides of God's character but are integrally
related. Through our faith in Christ, God's requirement of judgment is satisfied by Christ's atonement, and we receive mercy. But
for those without faith in Christ, judgment is let loose on the earth.

Flannery O'Connor captured this poignant message in *The Violent Bear It Away*, when Francis Tarwater receives the long-awaited
call: "Go warn the children of God of the terrible speed of mercy."[6]

"Your name, O Lord, endures forever, your renown, O Lord,
through all generations. For the Lord will vindicate his people and
have compassion on his servants" (Ps. 135:13–14).

John H. White

107

8:5

Why Hold Back, Lord?

The first angel sounded his trumpet, and there came hail and fire mixed with blood, and it was hurled down upon the earth. A third of the earth was burned up, a third of the trees were burned up, and all the green grass was burned up.

Revelation 8:7

We have all asked: Why does God not act in his world to bring justice? How can a God who is good permit . . . ? "How long will the enemy mock you, O God? Will the foe revile your name forever? Why do you hold back your hand, your right hand? Take it from the folds of your garment and destroy them!" (Ps. 74:10–11).

Even before the consummation of his kingdom, God brings judgment on the earth. This verse and the ones following it picture the priest/king who hears and sees the sighs and suffering of his people. They are in the midst of their tribulation. In the midst of it, Christ hears their cries. So the angel sounds the trumpet of warning. The result is hail and fire mixed with blood, emphasizing the destructive character of the events to come. Throughout the period from Christ's first coming to his second coming, our Lord who reigns in heaven will bring disaster on the earth. These calamities are controlled in heaven.

We remember Jesus' description of this reality. "You will hear of wars. . . . Nation will rise against nation, and kingdom against kingdom. There will be famines and earthquakes in various places. All these are the beginning of birth pains" (Matt. 24:6–8).

These disasters are both judgments and demonstrations of the power and relevance of the gospel. What is our privilege and response as God's people?

"[The] gospel of the kingdom will be preached in the whole world as a testimony to all nations" (Matt. 24:14).

John H. White

The Sea:
Place of Fear or Peace?

*The second angel sounded his trumpet, and something like a huge moun-
tain, all ablaze, was thrown into the sea. A third of the sea turned into
blood, a third of the living creatures in the sea died, and a third of the ships
were destroyed.*

Revelation 8:8–9

For most of us, the sea produces images of relaxation and peace.
In the Bible, the sea is a major means of transportation.

From Patmos, John saw both the sea and a volcanic island
mountain—such a sight could inspire this vision of a blazing mountain hurled into the sea. When Mount Thera erupted in 1573, its
iron oxide tinted the sea orange.[7] Such a phenomenon in John's
time could make the sea seem to turn to blood.

The point of these verses is the terror of God's judgment on the
sea. Not only does God use calamities on the land as an instrument to punish and warn, but he also uses the seas. All sea disasters are to be interpreted in this context; therefore, this judgment
is more severe than that signaled by the trumpet of the first angel.

Frequently the Scripture writers use trumpets as a warning of
impending judgments. Therefore, this angel's trumpet warns that
such events are judgments on the unrepentant and a call to repentance and faith.

God turns that idyllic place for a summer vacation and means
of transportation into a means of judgment and an invitation to
repentance. The message is clear. "God is our refuge and strength,
an ever-present help in trouble. Therefore we will not fear, though
the earth give way and the mountains fall into the heart of the
sea, though its waters roar and foam and the mountains quake
with their surging" (Ps. 46:1–3).

John H. White

109

Water: Means of
Judgment, Call to Faith

The third angel sounded his trumpet, and a great star, blazing like a torch,
fell from the sky on a third of the rivers and on the springs of water.

Revelation 8:10

Water is essential to life. Without water, human beings die quickly. We can often live for days without food, but not without water. That was especially true in the biblical world. Much of the land was desert, and the inhabitants were absolutely dependent on the oasis, the occasional rainfall, or the vital lifeline of the Jordan River.

It is, therefore, understandable that one manifestation of what Paul describes in Romans 1 was a worship of river deities. "They . . . worshiped and served created things rather than the Creator" (Rom. 1:25).

Thus, the source of physical life—water—becomes the object of worship. On the other hand, the Bible uses water as the symbol of spiritual life. The blessed person is "like a tree planted by streams of water" (Ps. 1:3).

"Jesus answered . . . whoever drinks the water I give him will never thirst. Indeed, the water I give him will become in him a spring of water welling up to eternal life" (John 4:13–14).

As the object of worship, water is impotent, so water is both the symbol of new life in Christ and a means of God's judgment. In the floods and epidemics that originate in the marshes it becomes an instrument of his judgment. Furthermore, remember Noah (Gen. 7:11ff.)!

"Then the angel showed me the river of the water of life, as clear as crystal, flowing from the throne of God and of the Lamb. . . . Whoever is thirsty, let him come; and whoever wishes, let him take the free gift of the water of life" (Rev. 22:1, 17b).

Water a call to faith? Yes!

John H. White

110

That Liar!

The name of the star is Wormwood. A third of the waters turned bitter, and many people died from the waters that had become bitter.

Revelation 8:11

In his book, *Screwtape Letters,* C. S. Lewis gave the name Wormwood to the nephew of the infamous Screwtape. Here, the star called Wormwood is no mere satanic agent, but the picture of God's threatened judgment if people worship false idols and listen to false prophets. This worship of idols and adherence to false prophets perverts God's good creation. It makes men and women liable to judgment.

One aspect of C. S. Lewis's character Wormwood captures an element of this verse. Lewis's Wormwood twists truth in order to tempt people to deny God. Water, as part of God's good creation, is a means of beauty meant to slake thirst, to provide cleansing or transportation. Often the things of creation become, in themselves, the object of worship. In our world, we see this subtle perversion of the role of creation in the assumption that we can have mastery over it. A sudden flood, a plague, or violent storms come from God's hand to remind us not to believe that lie. Creation viewed or dealt with apart from God not only creates the lie but also actually opens us to the risk of total spiritual destruction.

"The heavens declare the glory of God; the skies proclaim the work of his hands. Day after day they pour forth speech; night after night they display knowledge. There is no speech or language where their voice is not heard. Their voice goes out into all the earth, their words to the ends of the world" (Ps. 19:1–4).

Do not worship the lie! This is our Father's world.

John H. White

111

Darkness
Reveals the Light

The fourth angel sounded his trumpet, and a third of the sun was struck,
a third of the moon, and a third of the stars, so that a third of them turned
dark. A third of the day was without light, and also a third of the night.

Revelation 8:12

Do you remember the often paralyzing childhood fear of the darkness? Throughout Scripture, darkness is a sign of the withdrawal of the presence of God and an expression of evil.

This verse seems to echo the fourth plague in the Exodus: "Then the LORD said to Moses, 'Stretch out your hand toward the sky so that darkness will spread over Egypt—darkness that can be felt'" (Exod. 10:21).

But our passage does not describe total darkness; only one-third of all light is affected. Does it mean that one-third of the time there was no light at all? We must resist our tendency to harmonize details. John is painting pictures, not writing history or scientific prose. Darkness almost, but not entirely, overcomes the light. "This is the verdict: Light has come into the world, but men loved darkness instead of light because their deeds were evil" (John 3:19).

"Have nothing to do with the fruitless deeds of darkness, but rather expose them. For it is shameful even to mention what the disobedient do in secret" (Eph. 5:11–12).

It is the ugly reality of that darkness that enables us to see the beauty and orderliness of the light. Against the background of the ugliness of the darkness, we can see the beauty of the Savior. "In him was life, and that life was the light of men. The light shines in the darkness" (John 1:4–5).

The manifestation of darkness in verse 12 is a trumpetlike invitation to come to the light. "Wake up, O sleeper, rise from the dead, and Christ will shine on you" (Eph. 5:14).

John H. White

112

The Shout of the Eagle

As I watched, I heard an eagle that was flying in midair call out in a loud voice: "Woe! Woe! Woe to the inhabitants of the earth, because of the trumpet blasts about to be sounded by the other three angels!"

Revelation 8:13

The eagle announces the impending woe because the forces of creation have fallen under divine judgment. It is a warning to the unrepentant.

An eagle is an apt messenger, because of the immense view it sees when it flies at the meridian of the sky. The threefold woe is announced upon those who dwell on the earth, a phrase John uses to refer to rebellious societies and peoples.

Sin has its consequences. It is a taskmaster with servants in its pay. Much modern thinking calls it by other names such as imperfection, disease, and ignorance. We have lost an accurate view of sin, and especially of its terrible consequences.

Although sin is under God's control, it is nevertheless his rival who seeks our service. John's images remind us of sin's power and its consequences.

The stark reality of sin in itself does not lead to repentance. The fear that sin's consequences induces is calculated to give us a vision of the beauty and power of the Lamb who is the source of salvation. Without that stronger influence of the Lamb, sin and its consequences lead to impotence, from which there is no escape.

"For the wages of sin is death, but the gift of God is eternal life in Christ Jesus our Lord" (Rom. 6:23).

113

> Long my imprisoned spirit lay,
> Fast bound in sin and nature's might;
> Thine eye diffused a quickening Day,
> I woke, the dungeon flamed with light;
> My chains fell off, my heart was free,
> I rose; went forth, and followed thee.

Charles Wesley, 1738

John H. White

8:13

A Groaning
Creation Points to God

Woe to the inhabitants of the earth, because of the trumpet blasts about to be sounded by the other three angels!

Revelation 8:13b

This world is not as God intended it to be, for it has been disrupted by sin. "Cursed is the ground because of you; through painful toil you will eat of it all the days of your life. It will produce thorns and thistles for you . . ." (Gen. 3:17–18).

The apostle Paul describes the disruption of creation in a similar way: "The creation was subjected to frustration, not by its own choice, but by the will of the one who subjected it, in hope that the creation itself will be liberated from its bondage to decay and brought into the glorious freedom of the children of God. We know that the whole creation has been groaning as in the pains of childbirth right up to the present time" (Rom. 8:20–22).

It is a reality of our sinful condition that where creation offers no threat to our self-sufficiency, we rarely recognize our dependence on and need for God. That is undoubtedly why Jesus says: "Man does not live on bread alone, but on every word that comes from the mouth of God" (Matt. 4:4).

As believers, we need to echo the prophet Habakkuk's faith: "Though the fig tree does not bud and there are no grapes on the vines, though the olive crop fails and the fields produce no food, though there are no sheep in the pen and no cattle in the stalls, yet I will rejoice in the Lord, I will be joyful in God my Savior" (Hab. 3:17–18).

John H. White

114

Reigning in Judgment

Then the fifth angel sounded: And I saw a star fallen from heaven to the earth. And to him was given the key of the bottomless pit.

Revelation 9:1 NKJV

"Our God Reigns," so claims the title of a contemporary Christian song. The composer echoes the testimony of Scripture: God alone sustains and governs the universe. God has no peers to challenge his rule. "Our God is in heaven; He does whatever He pleases" says the psalmist (Ps. 115:3 NKJV).

We believe the biblical testimony. Yet the tragic landscape of human society and our own experience, coupled with our limited understanding of God's ways, often evoke conflict between the truth we believe and the emotions we feel.

The pain and suffering caused by moral and natural evil tempt us to question God's sovereign control over all things. A mother of five young children is killed by a drunken driver. Someone asks, "Was God in control of the path of that careening car?" Is God in control when evil governments commit brutal atrocities against their citizens? Who really is in charge when abortionists execute helpless babies in the womb? Is God impotent to stop the torture and murder of thousands of Christians around the globe?

Though such questions arise in somber moments and perplex our hearts, the Scriptures affirm again and again: "Our God reigns!" He is harmonizing the events of human history, good and bad, into a glorious mosaic of divine wisdom and providence.

Believers take heart! Though evil appears to run unchecked, God has a short leash on the actions of wicked persons and the power of natural evil. Divine justice will prevail!

And he shall reign forever and ever. Amen!

Emmitte Cornelius

115

Light Prevails

The sun and the air were darkened because of the smoke of the pit.

Revelation 9:2 NKJV

When darkness covered the deep of the young earth, "God said, 'Let there be light'; and there was light" (Gen. 1:3 NKJV). To provide visual testimony that darkness shall not reign in his material creation, God punctuated the deep regions of the cosmos with innumerable light-bearers. In the heavens above he placed two lights: the greater light to rule the day, the lesser light to rule the night. The sun reigns over the day as a fitting testimony to the power of light to overcome darkness, revealing what darkness conceals.

At times, however, dark clouds dim the light of the sun, while even the moon occasionally eclipses its light, though only for a season. When the sun departs to other regions, evening comes. Darkness rushes in to claim a kingdom, only to flee at the dawning of the daystar. God's light prevails over darkness.

Lest darkness should overshadow the rational and spiritual creation, God sent forth his Son—the eternal Daystar—to dispel the darkness reigning in the human heart. When wickedness rises, as if from the pit of hell, to blot out the light of the Lord of glory, he continues to shine unmolested in human hearts, "to give the light of the knowledge of the glory of God in the face of Jesus Christ" (2 Cor. 4:6). God's light prevails over darkness. Sing, O Christian, of the grace of the Father of lights:

> When darkness sought to claim my soul,
> Had shadowed o'er the way;
> The light of glory shone in my heart,
> And changed the night to day.

Emmitte Cornelius

116

Mercy and Malevolence

Then out of the smoke locusts came upon the earth.

Revelation 9:3 NKJV

Hawaii's Mount Kilauea is the largest active volcano in the world. Its eruptions create an awesome display of glowing lava belching up from the bowels of the earth, and cascading over the crater rim into snaking rivers of fire. The red-hot fountain of molten rock seems to leap from an inexhaustible, bottomless pit of boiling fury. Kilauea's inner pit is sometimes called the "House of Everlasting Fire." Moral evil is somewhat like that. It is a seemingly bottomless pit of pernicious, destructive influence, whose depth of malevolence is known only by God.

History records periods when evil reached such levels of destructive influence that many people exclaimed, "It can't possibly get any worse than this!" But evil can get worse and will get worse as we approach the end of the age.

The experiences of succeeding generations prove that evil has not exhausted its malevolent energy. If God in his mercy did not restrain it, life would be unbearable. At times, God mercifully slows its onrushing tide, allowing humankind to enjoy a coveted lull. Great is the mercy of God!

The world has not yet seen the full cup of evil. It is only a matter of time, however, until in divine judgment, God will open the floodgates of unrestrained evil, and unrepentant souls will suffer agonizing pain from the unfathomable depths of the bottomless pit.

But we who are Christians rejoice that, even in judgment, God displays his glory.

Emmitte Cornelius

117

The Seal of Glory

They were commanded not to harm the grass of the earth, or any green thing, or any tree, but only those men who do not have the seal of God on their foreheads.

Revelation 9:4 NKJV

During the Cold War era, when enemy missiles were aimed at our nation, bomb shelters became brisk sellers. Families purchased shelters for protection against the firestorms and deadly radiation of an atomic explosion. In these times of apparent peace, the bomb shelters have been abandoned. But in the Midwest's "Tornado Alley," shelters of a different sort are kept in readiness. Storm shelters provide refuge from the killer tornadoes that form in the region.

There is a far greater threat to human society than atom bombs or killer storms—the coming wrath of God. No man-made shelters can protect from God's wrath. In that awful hour, many will hide in caves and in the rocks of the mountains (Rev. 6:15 NKJV). Only those who have the seal of God will overcome.

118

We who trust in Christ are sealed with the Holy Spirit of promise. Because of his sealing, we have the promise of the Scriptures, "There is therefore now no condemnation to those who are in Christ Jesus, who do not walk according to the flesh, but according to the Spirit" (Rom. 8:1 NKJV). The seal of God is our divine assurance "that he who has begun a good work in [us] will complete it until the day of Jesus Christ" (Phil. 1:6 NKJV).

The seal of God guarantees that believers will not experience the awesome fury of God's wrath. Rather, we shall behold the blazing glory of our Lord's face and be increasingly satisfied in his presence throughout eternity.

Emmitte Cornelius

Pleasure or Pain

Their torment was like the torment of a scorpion.

Revelation 9:5 NKJV

The word "torment" usually evokes thoughts of the future state of the unsaved in the eternal lake of fire. In our Lord's parable of the rich man and Lazarus, the rich man died and entered hell. His plea for help climaxed in an agonizing cry: "I am tormented in this flame" (Luke 16:24 NKJV). It is a fitting picture of the final state of unredeemed souls.

The unsaved, however, experience a measure of torment now. The sinner suffers inner torment, an intense pain resulting from the soul's alienation from the living God. It is an agonizing emptiness of being, a spiritual void where sin dominates like a merciless tyrant, and the inevitability of death spreads an uneasy, sometimes terrifying, pall over all of life. "But," someone protests, "the unsaved appear happy and seem to enjoy life." It is a deceptive sense of well-being. Apart from the constant seeking after pleasures to gratify body and mind, the sinner's life becomes a dark, aching void. When at last the body—the vehicle of sensuous delights—is removed at death, the soul of the sinner descends into a bottomless, eternal abyss—the haunt of indescribable pain and suffering forever.

Not so the believer. Instead of the agony of alienation from God, the believer enjoys the pleasures of sweet fellowship with the Father and the Son. "In your presence is fullness of joy; At your right hand are pleasures forevermore" (Ps. 16:11 NKJV).

Emmitte Cornelius

119

Grace or Wrath

In those days men will seek death and will not find it.

Revelation 9:6 NKJV

The Pharisees listened to the wilderness preacher with curious interest. Perhaps they sought to discover what attracted the common people to him. Seeing them in the throng, the "Baptist" shouted, "Who warned you to flee from the wrath to come?" (Luke 3:7 NKJV). The Pharisees, of course, were not concerned about the wrath of God, for they were the teachers and guardians of the law and the religious "pillars" of the community. Smugly confident in their own self-righteousness, they looked forward to God's favor, not his wrath. But the Pharisees did not realize that the "Baptist" was preparing the way for the One who is the only way of escape from God's wrath—Christ, the Savior.

Multitudes today believe they can choose their own way of escape from the wrath to come. Some echo the self-righteous confidence of the Pharisees. Others are convinced that humanitarian and altruistic endeavors will provide a shelter from divine justice. Those in our text who looked to death as an escape from God's wrath have their modern counterparts. These people reason that the grave destroys the possibility of future punishment. But the Scriptures warn, "It is appointed for men to die once, but after this the judgment" (Heb. 9:27 NKJV).

Who shall escape the wrath to come? Christian, proclaim it to everyone! "Believe on the Lord Jesus Christ, and you will be saved" (Acts 16:31 NKJV).

Emmitte Cornelius

Journey the High Way

They had as king over them the angel of the bottomless pit, whose name in Hebrew is Abaddon, but in Greek he has the name Apollyon.

Revelation 9:11 NKJV

"The Destroyer" is a fitting description of Satan. His diabolical obsession is to ruin and destroy human beings. Satan works to influence the unsaved to continue their journey on the broad way of destruction until it is too late. His ready subjects promote this way as the "good life." They sing of the "good life" in their music, applaud it on talk shows, mimic it in the movies, and sell it in their commercials. The siren sounds of Satan's instruments of destruction—alcohol, addictive drugs, illicit sex, greed, covetousness—play to the ears of sinful inclinations.

We can clearly see the failure of Satan's promises, however. The broad way of destruction is strewn with human wreckage of horrible description. Yet millions remain deceived, clinging to false promises, until at last the "good life" dead-ends in ruin and eternal death.

But the grace of God has introduced a new way—the highway of eternal life. It is the way of Christ who says, "I am the way, the truth, and the life. No one comes to the Father except through me" (John 14:6 NKJV). Those who trust Christ as Savior exit the broad way of destruction, and enter the high way of eternal life to follow him. To follow Christ is to experience the abundant life, and to do so increasingly. On this road we encounter no wrecked lives, false hopes, or unfulfilled promises. The high way of eternal life doesn't dead-end in ruin; it ascends the eternal heights of glory into the joyful presence of God.

Emmitte Cornelius

121

Willing Servants

I heard a voice . . . saying to the sixth angel who had the trumpet, "Release the four angels."

Revelation 9:13–14 NKJV

In John's Revelation, the sixth angel waits for the command of God. At God's word, he releases the angels at the four corners of the earth.

It is the nature of God's servants to live with open ears and ready hearts. Willing servants do not allow the din of the world nor the busyness of the times to drown out the voice of God. Whether on the mount with Moses, amidst the thundering of God's word, or in the cleft of the rock with Elijah, hearing a still small voice, they hear and they obey.

Servants of God have a single passion: to serve the pleasure of God. God finds his pleasure when his glory is both seen and rejoiced in, and when his name and his fame go forth to all the nations. Willing servants strive to model the servant pattern of Christ, who declared his commitment to the Father in these words, "I always do those things that please him" (John 8:29 NKJV).

The angel of Revelation 9 is the servant of God's wrath. Believers today are servants of his grace. The angels are loosed to execute wrath. Believers are set free to go to the four corners of the earth with the gospel of grace. The command has been given: "No more upper room tarrying." We have heard the joyful sound: Jesus saves! Let us go forth with ready hearts to declare the good news to the nations.

Go forth, dear servant, weeping for lost souls, sowing the precious seed of the gospel. Joy comes in the morning when Christ returns, bringing sheaves of the harvest with him.

Emmitte Cornelius

Depths of Mercy

So the four angels . . . were released to kill a third of mankind.

Revelation 9:15 NKJV

We live in times of advancing moral darkness. A sinister mindlessness threatens to engulf more of society. Secular humanism and its companions—materialism and hedonism—roll like juggernauts across the landscape unhindered. The wicked roam like hungry predators seeking their prey.

When many of us who are believers view the rapid advance of social degeneration, we yearn for divine intervention. At times we exclaim with the prophet Habakkuk, "O Lord, how long shall I cry?" (Hab. 1:2 NKJV). But we are reminded that justice delayed is mercy displayed.

When God restrains his wrath in the midst of judgment, his mercy and longsuffering shine brightly. We question how God can be merciful to vessels of wrath. Lest we forget, we need to remind ourselves that when we were yet sinners, Christ died for us. Perhaps it is when God displays mercy and longsuffering in the face of inevitable judgment that we humbly confess, "Oh, the unfathomable depths of the riches of his mercy!"

In times of increasing ungodliness, we must refrain from joining in the chorus of the disciples when they wished to call down judgment on a Christ-rejecting village. Instead, let the words of the hymn writer be our solace:

> The Lord will come and not be slow,
> His footsteps cannot err;
> Before him righteousness shall go,
> His royal harbinger.
>
> Truth from the earth, like to a flow'r,
> Shall bud and blossom then;
> And justice, from her heav'nly bow'r,
> Look down on mortal men.

John Milton, seventeenth century

Until the Lord comes we must zealously proclaim the gospel to those who are perishing.

Emmitte Cornelius

123

Purity by Purging

By these three plagues a third of mankind was killed.

Revelation 9:18 NKJV

Our planet is the crown jewel of God's creative wisdom. Color photos taken from space reveal a ravishingly beautiful globe resplendent with vibrant colors—blues, greens, yellows, browns—sprinkled with puffs of white. Against the backdrop of cosmic darkness, earth shines like a brilliant sapphire, an inviting oasis in the hostile vacuum of space.

From outer space, there is no hint of anything amiss. But the jewel of creation is corrupted. A virulent, evil contagion is rapidly infecting human society. Wickedness is increasing as it did in the days of Noah: "Then the LORD saw that the wickedness of man was great in the earth, and that every intent of the thoughts of his heart was only evil continually. . . . So the LORD said, 'I will destroy man whom I have created from the face of the earth'" (Gen. 6:5, 7 NKJV). God's wrath waxed hot against the earth, but not all perished. Noah found grace in the eyes of the Lord.

The day is approaching when such a plague of unrivaled rebellion against God will again arise, that he must intervene with the severe judgment of wholesale death.

God's zeal for his name demands that he pour out the full cup of his wrath on those who remain unrepentant. In that hour, countless multitudes will experience unmitigated horror. But God's people—like Noah and his family in the ark—will be rejoicing with exceeding joy in the sanctuary of grace.

Emmitte Cornelius

124

By Grace Alone

But the rest of mankind . . . did not repent of the works of their hands.

Revelation 9:20a NKJV

Pain and suffering in the believer's life often produce the sweetest fruits of grace. "Before I was afflicted, I went astray," David confessed, "but now I keep your word" (Ps. 119:67 NKJV). Affliction turned him back from wandering away from God. This, however, is not always the case. Sin can so harden the heart that even in the agony of the most savage suffering, the unsaved do not turn from their ways. Some become still more adamant in their rebellion, railing against God, even mocking his mercy. Others may cry out for help when their suffering becomes unbearable. When relief comes, however, they often resume their former rebellion.

Neither present suffering nor the threat of future suffering in the lake of fire will change a sinner's heart. The Holy Spirit must quicken the heart, enabling the sinner to repent and to exercise faith in Christ. Saving faith comes only by hearing, and hearing by the Word of God.

So let us proclaim the gospel to the unsaved with the steadfast commitment of the psalmist, "My mouth shall tell of your righteousness and your salvation all the day, for I do not know their limits" (Ps. 71:15 NKJV).

Perhaps through your witness, someone heading toward that awful day of wrath will be moved by the Holy Spirit to repent and, through faith, to embrace the Savior. Instead of wrath from heaven, there will be rejoicing in heaven over the wrath-deserving sinner who has received instead the wonderful grace of God.

Emmitte Cornelius

125

Worship Him!

They should not worship demons, and idols.

Revelation 9:20b NKJV

The universe is a magnificent, clear display of God's eternal power and deity. The Creator is not hidden behind a curtain of divine aloofness. Paul says, "What may be known of God is manifest in them, for God has shown it to them. For since the creation of the world his invisible attributes are clearly seen" (Rom. 1:19–20 NKJV). The right response to God's revelation of himself is adoration and worship, while coveting his glory above everything else. When the unsaved reject God as unworthy of exclusive worship, they suppress the knowledge of God in unrighteousness and fail to glorify him as God.

Whoever exchanges the worship of God for the worship of idols commits high treason against the Almighty. The awful results are a downward plunge into idolatry and a life of vile affections and vile behavior: sexual immorality, murder, sorcery, and theft. Against such things God's wrath waxes hot.

The rapids of idolatry and its resulting iniquity are carrying multitudes today ever closer to the unremitting wrath of God. Do we stand on the safe shores of grace, merely observing the condition of those who are swept along? God forbid! The love of Christ constrains us to throw out the lifeline to all who will lay hold. Christ is their only hope.

God will not temper his wrath against those who exchange his truth for a lie. He will uphold and display the infinite worth of his glory—by his grace on the one hand, or by his wrath on the other. In either case, we shall rejoice. For the glory of God is our coveted treasure.

Emmitte Cornelius

Suffering
Becomes a Blessing

Then I . . .

Revelation 10:1

"I" who? John, the apostle of Jesus, was chosen to write a book in which the reader is promised a blessing for reading and hearing its words. "Blessed is the one who reads the words of this prophecy" (Rev. 1:3). John was an old man and a faithful disciple of Jesus Christ. He had witnessed and experienced suffering and tribulations for the cause of Christ. While others were martyred for their faith, John was spared.

However, it appears that the Roman emperor Domitian continued to be irritated with John's life. He banished John to the Isle of Patmos. At that point, the King of kings stepped in. The Lord overruled human intentions. As with Joseph and his brothers, God used the evil actions of one party to advance his good plans in the life of one of his servants. On Patmos, God used John to reveal and to write down a message that will bless its readers for all generations to come. This message gives courage and hope to people.

Believers still experience disappointments and apparent failures. It is encouraging to know that John's God is still in control. He can take what seems to us a failure and turn it into gold to bless others. That is what he did with John. You can trust him to turn your disappointments into blessings.

"We know that in all things God works for the good of those who love him, who have been called according to his purpose" (Rom. 8:28).

Simon Schrock

Walk Close
and See More

Then I saw another mighty angel coming down from heaven. He was robed in a cloud, with a rainbow above his head; his face was like the sun, and his legs were like fiery pillars.

Revelation 10:1

John, who saw these things, was once a young boy trained in Jewish tradition. In manhood he became a fisherman. He heard John the Baptist preach and announce, "Look, the Lamb of God, who takes away the sin of the world!" (John 1:29). With that proclamation, John became a follower of Jesus.

John heard Jesus preach that great Sermon on the Mount. He saw the first of Christ's miracles in Cana of Galilee. He heard Jesus refer to himself as the "living water," the "good shepherd," the "bread of life," and "the way, the truth, and the life." He saw the Lord feed five-thousand people with five rolls and two little fish. He saw Lazarus raised from the dead.

He watched Jesus being the servant and washing his disciples' feet. He was present when the soldiers came to arrest him. He witnessed the phony trial, the cruel hatred, and the condemnation Jesus received. He followed Jesus all the way to the cross. John witnessed Jesus become "obedient unto death, even the death of the cross" (Phil. 2:8 KJV). John's own eyes saw the risen Lord with the scars in his hands.

John was a faithful follower and intimate friend of Jesus Christ. When he was abandoned on the Isle of Patmos, his close fellowship with Christ did not cease. He walked so closely with Jesus that he "saw" much more of him.

That gives us tremendous encouragement. If we walk in an intimate, obedient, loving relationship with Jesus, he will show us greater things about himself.

Right now, commit yourself to obeying God in the things he shows you, and trust him to show you more of himself.

"Walk while ye have the light, lest darkness come upon you" (John 12:35 KJV).

Simon Schrock

Angels Watching
over Me and You

I saw another mighty angel coming down from heaven.

Revelation 10:1

A mighty angel that stands up for God's people! That is indeed a comforting thought. "The angel of the LORD encamps around those who fear him, and he delivers them" (Ps. 34:7).

I'm reminded of something that happened to me after I finished the evening shift at Children's Hospital in Washington, D.C. I started the four-hour drive into the country, where I was staying. In the stillness of the midnight hours, I became sleepy and dozed behind the wheel. Suddenly, I was awakened by a loud, sharp bang.

What was the bang just before I needed to round a curve on the road? Was it a guardian angel? I knew it had to have come from God. Maybe he sent an angel in answer to someone's prayer for me.

I don't know what God used to cause the noise, but I believe he awakened me from sleep in time to make the curve safely.

This reminded me that God wasn't finished with me yet. He had something more for me in his plan. I am persuaded that "an angel of the God whose I am and whom I serve stood beside me" (Acts 27:23).

An angel of the God whose you are and whom you serve stands beside you now. You should be encouraged and comforted to know that God's mighty angels are watching over you.

Simon Schrock

129

Will You Shine like the Sun?

A rainbow was upon his head, and his face was as it were the sun, and his feet as pillars of fire.

Revelation 10:1b KJV

Are God's angels the only ones who shine with glory? The exciting answer from Scripture is that God's saints will also be arrayed with ineffable glory.

The prodigal son took his inheritance and left home. He traveled far away from his father. He spent his money on foolish living. He found a job feeding pigs and ate from their food. He came to himself and went back to his father. He confessed he had sinned and asked to become a servant. His father instructed the servants to get the best robe and put it on his son, to kill the fatted calf and have a banquet. When the prodigal put on that best robe, he was ready for the banquet.

When sinners receive assurance of forgiveness, their sins are covered with a garment of salvation provided by Jesus Christ. When Jesus died on the cross, he provided the robe of salvation.

The angel was clothed with a glorious cloud. The disciples of Jesus will be able to stand before God covered with a robe of righteousness. The scars of sin will not be seen. "He has clothed me with garments of salvation and arrayed me in a robe of righteousness" (Isa. 61:10).

We choose how we will meet God. We can be clothed with a robe of righteousness in Christ, or we can stand before him in nakedness with all our sins exposed.

Today give thanks for Christ's righteousness imputed to you.

Simon Schrock

130

Comforting Friends
or Condemning Foes?

*He was holding a little scroll, which lay open in his hand. He planted his
right foot on the sea and his left foot on the land, and he gave a loud shout
like the roar of a lion. When he shouted, the voices of the seven thunders
spoke.*

Revelation 10:2–3

The angel's right foot on the sea and left foot on the land indicate
that his words of judgment deal with all creation. The voice of a
roaring lion and seven thunders indicate power and might. Think
what it will be like to be found guilty before God, what will happen "when the Lord Jesus is revealed from heaven in blazing fire
with his powerful angels. He will punish those who do not know
God and do not obey the gospel of our Lord Jesus" (2 Thess.
1:7b–8). Guilty humans will be totally helpless before Christ and
his mighty angels. The unprepared will cry for the rocks and for
the mountains, "Fall on us and hide us from . . . the wrath of the
Lamb!" (Rev. 6:16).

For believers, however, Jesus and the mighty angels are good
news. Jesus said, "I tell you, whoever acknowledges me before
men, the Son of Man will also acknowledge him before the angels
of God" (Luke 12:8). Christ promises all who are faithful that he
will represent them to the Father in the presence of those mighty
angels.

The ones who are redeemed by the blood of the Lamb need not
be frightened by the Lord's return with the mighty angels. How
comforting to know that the saints are safe in the arms of Jesus.

O come, angel band, come and around me stand.
O bear me away on your snowy wings, to my immortal home.

Jefferson Hascall, nineteenth century

If this angel with a lion's roar seems scary, take inventory and
be sure you are ready for the coming of the Lord. Then the angels
will be your comforting friends instead of your condemning foes.

Simon Schrock

Do We Have
to Know Everything?

And when the seven thunders spoke, I was about to write; but I heard a voice from heaven say, "Seal up what the seven thunders have said and do not write it down."

Revelation 10:4

There are some things we are better off not knowing. My office is located along Lee Highway. Nearby, Lee Jackson Highway turns west off Lee Highway. Many people miss the turn. They soon realize something is not right and frequently stop to ask for directions. I try to give them simple, easy directions to get back onto Lee Jackson. I do not give them information about streets that do not concern them. That would be distracting.

John was told not to write what the seven thunders said and to keep their words secret. Wouldn't we like to know what those words were? But it is not in our best interest to do a lot of speculating. We do not need to know everything to reach our heavenly home.

I rejoice to know that God did not keep anything secret that we need to know to serve him. He has given us all we need to know in order to become his faithful servants and live godly lives. God's "divine power has given us everything we need for life and godliness through our knowledge of him who called us by his own glory and goodness" (2 Peter 1:3).

We are not told exactly when the Lord Jesus will return because God has determined it is in our best interest not to know everything. God wants us to live in a state of readiness. His Word gives us all we need to know to be ready. Living for God is more important than speculating on the secrets that belong to God.

Simon Schrock

132

Jesus Christ Is King

Then the angel I had seen standing on the sea and on the land raised his right hand to heaven.

Revelation 10:5

This angel serves notice that sovereignty belongs to God. He declares, "This is our sea and our land. My God is the rightful owner. He alone shall reign over it."

Satan wants to establish himself as absolute sovereign. He rages even now to destroy and devour God and his people. We, however, have the blessed assurance that righteousness will reign, in the end, through Jesus Christ. Satan will be brought down and be cast into the lake of fire. Jesus Christ is the King of kings and Lord of lords.

Can you imagine the moment when Pharaoh, who said, "Who is the Lord?" or Herod, who plotted to kill Jesus, or Stalin, who was anti-God, and all the other despots of history will each confess that Jesus Christ is Lord? Imagine the glory and honor that Jesus will receive when every tongue will confess that Jesus is Lord and victor! It is a blessed assurance to know that Jesus is victor, and his children will be victors with him. Those who belong to Jesus Christ will be blessed with his presence throughout eternity. "So we will be with the Lord forever" (1 Thess. 4:17).

When Jesus appears to receive his church to himself, the voice of a mighty angel will accompany him. All the combined powers of earthly kingdoms cannot stop him. Satan will be defeated. The Christian will be under the banner of the King of kings surrounded with his mighty angels. What a comforting thought!

Are you a child of the King, nestled under his wings? Today give thanks that his victory is assured and that you are part of it.

Simon Schrock

133

Hands toward Heaven

Then the angel I had seen . . . raised his right hand to heaven.

Revelation 10:5

This mighty angel reminds me that there is a God in heaven, and that we too can stretch forth our hands.

King David experienced much opposition and frequent threats on his life. In some of those trying times he wrote: "I spread out my hands to you; my soul thirsts for you like a parched land" (Ps. 143:6). David stretched his hands toward God. So can we.

According to a friend of mine, that is what a dear old saint of God did while on an overseas mission, after receiving word that his son was seriously injured in an accident. He came before the Lord with these words from a hymn by Charles Wesley, "Father, I stretch my hands to thee, no other help I know. If thou withdraw thyself from me, ah, whither shall I go?" There are difficult times in life when we just want to reach up toward God.

Life does not come up all roses. There are thorns along the way. I've felt the discomfort of a few myself. My younger brother died the day before my twenty-first birthday. My first wife died when I was twenty-five. Our house was gutted by fire. Folks I thought were faithful friends didn't turn out that way. Yet, God has never failed me.

The angel's hand toward heaven indicates communion with a God who is ever faithful to the raised-hand pleas of his children. Are there hurts and thorns paining you now? Stretch your hands toward God and commit your way to him for healing!

"I want men everywhere to lift up holy hands in prayer, without anger or disputing" (1 Tim. 2:8).

Simon Schrock

The Creator Will Deliver on His Promises

And he swore by him who lives for ever and ever, who created the heavens and all that is in them, the earth and all that is in it, and the sea and all that is in it, and said, "There will be no more delay!"

Revelation 10:6

This detailed designation of God as Creator ties together the mystery of God. The same God who created the heavens, the earth, and the sea will bring to pass the prophecy and judgments of this book.

Step outside on a nice spring day. The earth your feet stand on is God's creation. The radiant sunlight comes by his almighty word. The birds singing in the awesome, blooming fruit tree is his handiwork. The bright colors of the daffodils swaying in the breeze speak of his infinite wisdom and power. The air we breathe, the heart pumping blood through our bodies, and the mind that enjoys his works all demonstrate the wonders of creation. "Great is our Lord and mighty in power" (Ps. 147:5).

The angel's oath declares that creation's God is able to deliver on his promises of judgment and deliverance. The same mighty power of God that brings judgment to the unrighteous need not be dreaded by the righteous. "The Lord will rescue me from every evil attack and will bring me safely to his heavenly kingdom" (2 Tim. 4:18).

We have a God big enough to rule the universe, yet small enough to live within our hearts. The born-again disciple of Jesus Christ can rest with this thought: The almighty God of creation will preserve me unto his heavenly kingdom. I can be assured that, with him, I'm in good hands.

"The LORD will keep you from all harm—he will watch over your life" (Ps. 121:7).

Simon Schrock

When Time
Shall Be No More

There should be time no longer.

Revelation 10:6b KJV

My parents were eating supper in the kitchen. My father asked for the applesauce, then suddenly collapsed and died. For him, time was no longer.

Many people have the erroneous idea that when Jesus comes again, he will come as the loving Savior. There will surely be time to get right with God. At his second coming, however, the Bible says he will come to "judge the living and the dead" (2 Tim. 4:1). Time, as we know it, will be no more.

Modern Western culture has lost respect for God and his creation. We sacrifice our children on the altar of abortion and practice perverseness of the basest kind, of which the Bible says, "God will judge the adulterer and all the sexually immoral" (Heb. 13:4). The Book of Revelation gives ample warnings of God's judgment on such bold ungodliness.

Jesus is preparing a sinless, new heaven for his saints. When he comes to take his children home, there will be no more time for repentance. This is bad news for those who will then answer to Jesus Christ, the judge.

It is, however, good news for the redeemed. They will be rewarded with the awesome presence of Jesus. Make sure you are ready for time to be no more. Do all that you can to help others turn from sin and sure judgment to salvation and sure rewards through Jesus Christ our Lord.

"Now is the accepted time . . . now is the day of salvation" (2 Cor. 6:2 KJV). One day soon there shall be time no longer!

Simon Schrock

136

Exciting
Mysteries Are Ahead

But in the days when the seventh angel is about to sound his trumpet, the mystery of God will be accomplished, just as he announced to his servants the prophets.

Revelation 10:7

A mystery means there is more to be revealed.

My wife enjoys serving guests what she calls a "Mystery Supper." It is a full-course meal with dessert and drink. She prepares a menu, but gives all the items a mysterious name, including the silverware. Corn may be listed as "chicken feed," and a napkin, "something necessary." The guests then check four items for the first course. When the "mysterious plate" arrives, a guest may have ordered: Jell-O, a toothpick, bread, and drink—but no silverware. After several courses are served in mystery, the real menu is revealed. The guests then check whatever revealed entrees they want and continue to enjoy the banquet.

When the seventh angel is ready to blow his trumpet, God's "hidden menu" will be revealed. Here, the mystery is that God has won the victory over evil and Christ will reign forever and ever.

At the mystery supper, the dinner guests wait in anticipation for the revealed meal. There is joyful interaction as their hungry appetites are satisfied. The unfolding of God's mysteries will be exciting for believers. God's Word assures us that when Jesus is revealed from heaven, he will be the victorious King of all kingdoms who will reign forever.

"No eye has seen, no ear has heard, no mind has conceived what God has prepared for those who love him" (1 Cor. 2:9). It will be so glorious that we will need a new body to receive it.

Lord, I commit myself to serve you faithfully as I participate in the mystery of your love now, and anticipate the fully revealed future.

Simon Schrock

137

You've Got a Mission!

I took the little scroll from the angel's hand and ate it. It tasted as sweet as honey in my mouth, but when I had eaten it, my stomach turned sour. Then I was told, "You must prophesy again about many peoples, nations, languages and kings."

Revelation 10:10–11

John was abandoned on Patmos. His testimony for the risen Lord seemed crushed. Instead, God used him to perform a mighty work that would impact every generation.

"You must prophesy again." God was not finished with John. There was yet kingdom work for him to do. John was to prophesy again, and write the Book of Revelation. God has work for every member of the body of Christ. There is a mission for all God's children. All around us are unsaved people, people who are hurting, distressed, and discouraged by grief and disappointments. Orphans, widows, and older people who feel neglected need our ministry. There are people bound to sinful habits who will find release in Christ. This sinful and adulterous generation is discarding God's principles and moving toward the condition of Sodom and Gomorrah.

In this hurting, hopeless world, Jesus has called us to be his "salt and light." "God has arranged the parts in the body, every one of them, just as he wanted them to be" (1 Cor. 12:18). God has placed you where you are to be his ambassador. Whether it is giving a cup of water in his name, or preaching his Word, there is a work for you in his body.

What an awesome thought—I'm part of his body, and I have work to do for him! "Therefore, I urge you, brothers, in view of God's mercy, to offer your bodies as living sacrifices, holy and pleasing to God—this is your spiritual act of worship" (Rom. 12:1).

Simon Schrock

138

Open the Doors and See
What God Is Doing!

*I was given a reed like a measuring rod and was told, "Go and measure the
temple of God and the altar, and count the worshipers there."*

Revelation 11:1

Josef Gabor grew up in communist Czechoslovakia. From his earliest days, he heard the communist lie that religion is for weaklings. Josef's mother, however, was a believer. Each Sunday, Mrs. Gabor arose early and prepared her sons for the three-hour train journey to Prague. From the train station, they walked to the church, where they sat through a two-and-a-half-hour worship service. After worship, they went to a local park where their mother spread a picnic she had prepared before leaving home. Afterwards, there was another worship service. After the second service, the boys accompanied their mother back to the station, where they boarded the train again for the three-hour journey home.

Some people would argue that such an intense Sunday experience would drive children away from church. Not so Josef Gabor! Today he is a Christian leader and missionary in his own country. When he speaks about his childhood Sundays, his eyes often well up with tears of gratitude for a mother who defied all the excuses she might have used and led her boys into the way of Christ.

"Let us not give up meeting together, as some are in the habit of doing, but let us encourage one another—and all the more as you see the Day approaching" (Heb. 10:25). There is no telling what God has in mind for the people who come to his temple for worship. He designed his church as a place for encouragement and spiritual growth. "Go . . . and count the worshipers there," and know that each one is there by grace and that God is at work in each willing heart.

Robert Leslie Holmes

Power to Witness

I will give power to my two witnesses, and they will prophesy for 1,260 days, clothed in sackcloth.

Revelation 11:3

Throughout the Bible, God promises to bless the efforts of those who witness for him with devotion and enthusiasm.

Jonathan Edwards' eyesight was so poor that he had to hold his manuscript close to his face, hiding his malady from his congregation. His voice and pulpit manner were anything but commanding. Yet, his sermons often had a magnetic impact upon those who heard him. His sermon, "Sinners in the Hands of an Angry God," moved hundreds to repent and trust Christ. Some pulpit historians call it the finest sermon ever preached. Some say that one address helped spark America's "Great Awakening" of the eighteenth century.

"'Not by might nor by power, but by my Spirit,' says the Lord Almighty" (Zech. 4:6). From a human standpoint, it is hard to account for such an amazing result from just one sermon, especially when the witness was not known as a dynamic communicator. There was serious spiritual preparation, however, involved in that sermon. For three days before he preached it, Jonathan Edwards neither ate nor slept. Instead he prayed repeatedly, "Lord, give me New England!"

When he arose from his knees to make his way into the pulpit, Edwards was ready, because he had seen God's face. God's Holy Spirit empowered the witness of one some might call unremarkable.

"I will give power to my . . . witnesses." The power of our witness is not ours. God gives it and deserves full credit when good things result.

Bear this in mind today as you witness about God's amazing love in Christ.

Robert Leslie Holmes

140

Fresh Wind!

But after the three and a half days a breath of life from God entered them, and they stood on their feet, and terror struck those who saw them.

Revelation 11:11

After the two witnesses were set upon by the beast from the Abyss (Rev. 11:7–10), they needed a second wind. That is what they received.

It happened the first time at creation: "The LORD God formed the man from the dust of the ground and breathed into his nostrils the breath of life, and the man became a living being" (Gen. 2:7). From that moment on, humanity was different from the rest of creation. The difference was manifold. Principally, however, it was that human beings were born to never die.

It happened, too, when God gave his written Word: "All Scripture is God-breathed" (2 Tim. 3:16). God's breath upon the Bible makes it reliable beyond question, and unlike any other book ever written. Why, after all these centuries, is it still the world's number one seller? It's simple. Reading other books may inform. The Bible alone, because God's breath is in it, can transform.

It happened yet another time: Jesus "breathed on them and said, 'Receive the Holy Spirit'" (John 20:22). The disciples, who only moments before were filled with fear, suddenly came alive as never before. Why? Because the breath of God through his Son, the breath of abundant life, was on them!

No wonder then that "terror struck those who saw them" when the once seemingly defeated prophets stood on their feet!

It happens still! Each time one of God's people feels defeated by life's oppressing circumstances, every time it looks as though the beast may win, God's renewing breath comes in new power and enables us to rise up revived. We shall not be moved! Hallelujah!

Robert Leslie Holmes

141

11:11

Heaven's
Everlasting Song

The seventh angel sounded his trumpet, and there were loud voices in heaven, which said: "The kingdom of the world has become the kingdom of our Lord and of his Christ, and he will reign for ever and ever."

Revelation 11:15

For two thousand years the church has prayed, "Thy kingdom come on earth as it is in heaven." Now, here it is.

The seventh angel's trumpet announces the King's arrival. The early part of this chapter tells the story of preparation and struggle, but now God says, "Time, please!" Suddenly, as the sound of the trumpet echoes into the distance, a great chorus rises up to declare that Christ is the eternal and incomparable Sovereign. His judgment is coming. It will be more severe than any ever seen before, but the heavenly chorus knows that wherever it leads, it will not touch them, for the one who sits on the throne had earlier occupied a cross on their behalf. No wonder they sing so loudly!

Holy God, we praise your name;
Lord of all, we bow before you;
All on earth your scepter claim,
All in heaven above adore you.
Infinite your vast domain,
Everlasting is your reign!

Hark, the loud celestial hymn
Angel choirs above are raising;
Cherubim and seraphim
In unceasing chorus praising,
Fill the heavens with sweet accord:
"Holy, holy, holy, Lord."

Ignaz Franz, 1774

Does something trouble your heart? Are there stresses and pressures that make your life hard to live? Lift up your heart, for one day soon they shall all be gone, and at the end of them all is victory in Jesus!

Robert Leslie Holmes

The Trumpet
Sound of Worship

*And the twenty-four elders, who were seated on their thrones before God,
fell on their faces and worshiped God.*

Revelation 11:16

Three men ascended the Alps. One of them was making the climb
for the first time. The other two were experienced Alpine climbers.
The novice climber ascended the hazardous mountain terrain with
some sense of security, because one guide climbed ahead of him,
paving the way, while the other guide was behind him, watching
his every movement. They climbed the steep mountainside for
hours. As they reached the summit, the guide ahead wanted the
young climber to have the first breathtaking view of the heavens
and earth. He gently moved aside. Ignoring the gale-force winds
that continually blow across the summit, the novice jumped to his
feet. The experienced guides grabbed him down and shouted, "On
your knees, sir! You are never safe except on your knees!"

True worship occurs when we are spiritually on our knees in
awe and praise of the eternal God.

Worship focuses on God. The human soul stares directly on God
with no distraction.

Worship honors God. Humanity can do nothing but honor the
God who loved us so much that redemption was bought by the
sacrifice of the one and only Son of the living deity.

Worship draws God near. His tender gracious love stands beside
us throughout the roller-coaster ride of life.

Worship is our grateful response to our sense that we can reach
upward and touch the Almighty. Through his Word, the living
God raises us above the dark frustration and ambivalence we experience before we know him.

Get out the trumpets and join the twenty-four elders of Revelation.

Derl G. Keefer

143

The Almightiness of God

*We give thanks to you, Lord God Almighty, the One who is and who was,
because you have taken your great power and have begun to reign.*

Revelation 11:17

In 1839 the Sultan of Turkey abolished all Christian representatives from his country. Upon reading his decree, Dr. William Goodell, an American missionary, informed his colleague, Dr. Cyrus Hamlin, president of Robert College in Constantinople. As the two men discussed the situation, Dr. Goodell concluded, "We must leave. The American Consul and the British Ambassador say this violent, vindictive ruler is immoveable." Dr. Hamlin countered with the statement, "The Sultan of the Universe can, in answer to prayer, change the decree of the Sultan of Turkey." Throughout the night, the two men prayed to the "Sultan of the Universe." The following day, the Sultan of Turkey died. His proclamation was no more.[8]

I'm not saying that God killed the Sultan of Turkey in response to the two missionaries' prayer, but one had best be careful to observe that there is only one supreme ruler of the universe. He is Almighty God, the eternal, all-powerful ruler.

He rules the affairs of each of our lives, and conquers all who stand in opposition to his children. What is more, he wants what is best for us. Today you can give him whatever concerns you have, and trust him to lead you.

"Some trust in chariots and some in horses, but we trust in the name of the LORD our God" (Ps. 20:7).

Derl G. Keefer

God's Wrath

The nations were angry; and your wrath has come.

Revelation 11:18a

Mrs. Morris's slight build, short white hair, and grandmotherly appearance betrayed her wrath for the kid who sat in front of me in third grade. He was always getting in trouble. One day, I saw Mrs. Morris coming with a paddle that was at least an inch thick. She pulled Jerry from his desk and began, with what I thought was glee in her eyes, swatting him. After what seemed like hours, the paddle broke as she struck him once again. The defiant Jerry refused to cry. In exasperation, Mrs. Morris returned to her desk and Jerry returned to his. Class resumed, but I thought, "I sure don't want Mrs. Morris mad at me!" The impression has lasted for over four decades.

As a pastor, I get the impression that some people think there is glee in God's eye when he exercises wrath. The truth is that there are only tears, for his heart breaks each time he exercises wrath!

God's wrath is not against people but against sin. Sin is defined as a voluntary transgression against the known law of God. William Barclay tells us that God's wrath reminds us that a person will reap what he/she sows. Escaping the consequences of sin is impossible. That was why Christ took our penalty on Calvary's cross.

Don't be like Jerry; get out of the habit of sin. That is accomplished by asking for God's forgiveness—God's smile of pleasure.

Derl G. Keefer

145

An Eternal
Family Reunion

*The time has come for judging the dead, and for rewarding your servants
the prophets and your saints and those who reverence your name, both small
and great.*

Revelation 11:18b

Something about family reunions cheers the heart. For many of
us, our families are hundreds, if not thousands of miles away, and
we look forward to those rare times when we all get together.

Preparation begins by planning what we stow into the suitcases.
The car goes to the mechanic to ensure it's in proper running condition, and then fueled for the journey. We tuck a map into the
glove compartment in case of detours. The folks on the other end
of the trip are planning enough food and bedding for all.

The reunion site may be a house or a rented hall, but the place
is unimportant. The really important part is all the people we
haven't seen for a long time. Joy will be the emotion of the
moment. Even if this isn't exactly how the reality turns out, this
is how we like to imagine it.

God has planned a fantastic reunion for his family. The place
will be out of this world! But the reunion really isn't about the
geographical place; it is about the people we haven't seen for a
long time who will be there. It is knowing that never again will
we be separated from them.

The One who has provided all of this unabashed joy will be
there—God! Jesus, who died for our sins and provided all this
unleashed joy, will be there! He will be the host at this great family reunion for all believers. Heaven is preparing now for the great
family reunion. Don't be late!

Derl G. Keefer

146

Eternal Destruction—Hell

The time has come . . . for destroying those who destroy the earth.

Revelation 11:18

Many people have foolishly stated, "If I go to hell, I'll have plenty of company." The truth is there are no friends in hell. William S. Deal describes hell as a place where "Everyone will be the eternal enemy of everyone else."

The world feels comfortable hearing about heaven, but hell is not a place most people want to explore. Travel agents offer inviting advertisements to places they describe as "heaven on earth." No travel agent ever advertised a trip to a place like hell. The Bible describes hell as a place of eternal destruction and exclusion from the face of God. If that weren't frightening enough, the other aspects of this eternal place include intense anguish—physical or mental or both, intense loneliness—separation from God and loved ones, intense feelings of permanence, intense fear.

None of this is good news. How can one escape such an eternity? The good news is that "God so loved the world that he gave his one and only Son, that whoever believes in him shall not perish but have eternal life" (John 3:16).

God offers everybody a free ticket out of that awful place. The ticket—faith in Jesus Christ.

Derl G. Keefer

147

Unbreakable Covenant

Then God's temple in heaven was opened, and within his temple was seen the ark of his covenant.

Revelation 11:19

God never loses his covenant, nor does he ever forget it.

During the Vietnam War, the son of a prominent political family did something terribly wrong that would bring disgrace upon his family name. He knew it was only a matter of time before word got back home. Believing his family would be outraged, and rightly so, he determined to tell them. From prison, he sent a letter to his father and told him exactly what had happened. That son was amazed when he received a four sentence, telegrammed response. His father wrote, "I will stand by you no matter what you did. I will be there as soon as I can find a way. Remember who you are and ask God to forgive you. I will always love you."

That's how God's covenant works! His heart may be broken by our misdeeds a thousand times, but he does not forget his covenant. Once God pledges himself to us, as he does through Abraham and Jesus, he stands immovably on his word. He never breaks a promise.

His faithfulness may elude the eyes of unbelievers, or appear to be erased by the storms of doubt, yet, at the proper time, history's veil will be pulled away and the ark of the covenant will be revealed. It will prove true the fullness of grace that is guaranteed to us in Jesus.

Have you fallen short of your commitment to Christ? Have you brought disgrace upon his name? Remember who you are. Ask God to forgive you. He will always love you.

Today, thank God that though you may fail him repeatedly, he will never fail you.

Robert Leslie Holmes

Openness to God

*Then God's temple in heaven was opened, and within his temple was seen
the ark of his covenant. And there came flashes of lightning, rumblings,
peals of thunder, an earthquake and a great hailstorm.*

Revelation 11:19

Children love to play the game "hide-and-seek." Hiding from the
"it" person thrills most boys and girls. The children scatter to various locations, trying not to be seen by the person seeking them.
In such a setting, no one would stand in an open field to be immediately detected by the seeker.

In his book *Fresh Wind, Fresh Fire*, Jim Cymbala writes that
Satan's strategy with the Lord's people seems to be that they don't
call, don't ask, or don't depend on God to do great things in their
lives. It's like playing hide-and-seek from God. He adds, "The truth
of the matter is that the devil is not terribly frightened of human
efforts and credentials. But he knows his kingdom will be damaged when we lift up our hearts to God."[9] When we lift our hurt
towards God—the Lord finds us as though we were hiding in an
open field.

When we seek God, we admit helplessness.

We seek God through prayer. The Christian's source of life
comes through intimate conversation with God.

We develop habits of seeking God through obedience. Oswald
Chambers said, "The best measure of spiritual life is not ecstasies
but obedience."

Seeking God means I desire truth. Truth is the filter that keeps
falsehood out.

Seek God—the Almighty is not hiding!

"Seek the LORD while he may be found; call on him while he is
near" (Isa. 55:6).

Derl G. Keefer

149

The Primeval Battle

A great and wondrous sign appeared in heaven: a woman clothed with the sun, with the moon under her feet and a crown of twelve stars on her head. She was pregnant and cried out in pain as she was about to give birth.

Revelation 12:1–2

Revelation 12 helps us understand the fierce battles that are being waged these days between good and evil.

At Eden's gate, almost immediately after our first parents fell into sin, God announced that a terrifying, history-long struggle had commenced between the serpent's seed and the seed of the woman. "I will put enmity between you and the woman . . . he will crush your head, and you will strike his heel" (Gen. 3:15). Eve could not possibly have understood the meaning of this cryptic prophecy.

Here, in majestic apocalyptic language, is a glorious description of all the people of God of all the centuries. In the first announcement in Paradise, the focus was on the woman as birth-giver; it would be the fruit of her womb that would crush the serpent's head. And in Revelation 12 we see a woman struggling in the pangs of delivery: "She was pregnant and cried out in pain as she was about to give birth."

We must learn to see the fierce struggle between the church and the world in the light of Genesis 3:15 and Revelation 12. Think of our brothers and sisters boldly facing down the persecutor in many lands just now. And what of you? And what of me?

We must be both courageous and resolute. The struggle we endure is part of the greatest struggle of all time. Even in the face of death we say: "Thanks be to God! He gives us the victory through our Lord Jesus Christ" (1 Cor. 15:57).

Joel Nederhood

150

12:1–2

The Flying Red Dragon

Then another sign appeared in heaven: an enormous red dragon with seven heads and ten horns and seven crowns on his heads.

Revelation 12:3

We continue to gasp as technology keeps advancing—television is a marvel and the Internet is a worldwide wizardry. But why is so much of this corrupted and corrupting? Many Internet web sites are pornographic, and those are the slickest, most creative in the world of e-commerce.

Why is this? Well, take a look at the flying red dragon. His seven heads with their seven crowns and ten horns attest to his might. But it is his powerful tail that tells its fullness.

"His tail swept a third of the stars out of the sky and flung them to the earth" (Rev. 12:4b). The might of this ferocious creature spans the earth and the heavens. He plays for keeps.

The flying red dragon heads up the forces that oppose God and ordinary followers of Christ. If Christian believers are going to realize how dreadfully serious their battle with the evil one is, they must take the dragon's picture in Revelation 12 very seriously.

It's no surprise that the forces of evil creep into believers' homes and contaminate them and their children with ideas and temptations that come straight from hell. The flying red dragon respects no one, loves no one, fears no one. His mighty tail whips through the universe and sends the ruined stars crashing onto our earth. He wants to destroy us. He wants to destroy our children.

No wonder the Bible tells Eve's offspring, "Put on the full armor of God so that you can take your stand against the devil's schemes" (Eph. 6:11).

Joel Nederhood

151

Dragon Protection

His tail swept a third of the stars out of the sky and flung them to the earth. The dragon stood in front of the woman who was about to give birth, so that he might devour her child the moment it was born. She gave birth to a son, a male child, who will rule all the nations with an iron scepter. And her child was snatched up to God and to his throne. The woman fled into the desert to a place prepared for her by God, where she might be taken care of for 1,260 days.

Revelation 12:4–6

If my friend's son Joshua had not been born by Caesarian section, he would have been strangled, because the umbilical cord was wrapped around his neck. His watching father will never forget how the doctor saved his son. In delivery rooms, everyone works for the infant's safety.

But the woman who was clothed with the sun—her son was born into a world so hostile, his archenemy was poised to devour him the moment he was born. This is Jesus Christ. We remember King Herod's SWAT team sweeping into Bethlehem at Jesus' birth, destroying little children. Herod was on the side of the flying dragon.

John's language leaps across decades, even centuries, in its precise, yet figurative, description of Jesus' life, death, resurrection, and ascension, as well as of the perfect provision God made for the woman, who represents the church.

At Christmastime, we often celebrate Christ's birth mindlessly, without thinking of his coming, his obedience, and his suffering as an enormous battle with a flying red dragon that would stop at nothing to destroy him.

We seldom think of the way God surrounds his church with his protection. The figure of 1,260 days (three and a half years) is a symbol of God's protection of the church, which the woman's child equipped when he sent it his Holy Spirit.

Jesus likely had all this in mind when he said: "I will build my church, and the gates of Hades will not overcome it" (Matt. 16:18).

Joel Nederhood

The Heaven/Earth Connection

And there was war in heaven. Michael and his angels fought against the dragon, and the dragon and his angels fought back. But he was not strong enough, and they lost their place in heaven. The great dragon was hurled down—that ancient serpent called the devil, or Satan, who leads the whole world astray. He was hurled to the earth, and his angels with him.

Revelation 12:7–9

No question is more vexing than: From where did evil come? We meet evil for the first time when Satan tempted Eve to disobey God (Gen. 3:1–7). From Revelation 12, we learn that Satan came to the place we live because he had been cast out of heaven, where he had lost a war with Michael and his angelic forces.

"The great dragon was hurled down—that ancient serpent called the devil, or Satan, who leads the whole world astray. He was hurled to the earth, and his angels with him."

As John cuts away from our daily warfare to show us its heavenly background, there is no way that our limited minds can begin to grasp what he describes. But his description is a response to our question, "From where did evil come?" Evil originated when Satan, one of God's archangels, rebelled against God. Evil contaminated our world when Satan was expelled from heaven, along with the false angels who had been defeated with him.

Here is yet another indication of the magnitude of the moral struggle we are engaged in: It is not merely an earthly struggle, but it mirrors an even more fundamental struggle between God and his good angels and Satan and his demons.

"Our struggle is . . . against the spiritual forces of evil in the heavenly realms" (Eph. 6:12). No wonder it's often so overwhelming!

Joel Nederhood

153

The Loud Voice
of Victory

Then I heard a loud voice in heaven say: "Now have come the salvation and the power and the kingdom of our God, and the authority of his Christ. For the accuser of our brothers, who accuses them before our God day and night, has been hurled down."

Revelation 12:10

When Satan's power nearly overwhelms us, we need to have good ears. He assaults us at work, through colleagues who try to get us to lie and steal or ask us to accompany them to places where Satan rules. Usually, it's our own nature that makes sin look alluring.

We must surf until we come to the heavenly channel where we hear the loud voice we need to hear. It reminds us that, now that Satan has been hurled out of heaven, we can be saved from hell and from ourselves. Believers do not have to be victimized by Satan.

Listen to what the loud voice says: "Salvation and power and the kingdom of God and the authority of Christ are now in place. They are there to help us when we find ourselves sliding down a slippery slope."

The loud voice tells us that, once you have been saved, you do not have to go on living the same way, for along with salvation we have been given power that "is like the working of his mighty strength, which he exerted in Christ when he raised him from the dead" (Eph. 1:19–20).

The finished work of Christ gives us salvation plus power. His authority is like no one else's. Many corporate executives have the authority, but they don't have the power to make things happen. Jesus' authority is a unique combination of authority and power that accomplishes just what we need to help us in our struggle with Satan.

How good it is that Christ has said: "I am with you always, to the very end of the age" (Matt. 28:20).

Joel Nederhood

154

The Great Accuser

Then I heard a loud voice in heaven say: "Now have come the salvation and the power and the kingdom of our God, and the authority of his Christ. For the accuser of our brothers, who accuses them before our God day and night, has been hurled down."

Revelation 12:10

Zechariah 3, written about six hundred years before these words, presents a drama that helps us understand the high significance of the message heaven's loud voice is announcing. Satan has been hurled down from heaven; never again will he be able to bring his hate-filled accusations against the people of God.

In Zechariah 3, we see Joshua, the high priest of Israel, standing in embarrassed silence as Satan reads off a list of his sins. Joshua represents the entire nation of Israel, and their all too frequent departures from the way of the Lord are openly described in the Bible. As Zechariah put it: "Joshua was dressed in filthy clothes as he stood before the angel" (3:3). He then describes how the Lord's angel commanded that Joshua's filthy clothing be removed, and he be dressed in clean, undefiled garments. The angel then exclaimed: "See, I have taken away your sin, and I will put rich garments on you" (3:4).

Apparently, before Christ vanquished him, Satan would appear before God and remind God of his people's sins "day and night."

Satan's power has not yet been totally neutralized. Yet, he can no longer remind God of our sins. Now that Christ has died, clean garments have been put on all who trust Christ for their salvation.

To all who are embarrassed by their sins, the message comes: "Though your sins are like scarlet, they shall be as white as snow; though they are red as crimson, they shall be like wool" (Isa. 1:18). Hallelujah!

Joel Nederhood

There's Power
in the Blood

They overcame him by the blood of the Lamb and by the word of their tes-
timony; they did not love their lives so much as to shrink from death.

Revelation 12:11

Jesus' blood is the most powerful force in the universe. It affects earth and heaven. Once it was shed on Calvary's cross, Satan was booted out of heaven once for all. He could never appear there again to bring accusations against God's people.

Notice that the loud voice that rejoices because Satan has been banished seems to identify the cause of this event as the action of ordinary believers: "They overcame him." How did weak, sinful human beings cause the Great Accuser to be sent packing?

They accomplished this by believing in Christ and expressing their faith boldly, even to the point of dying for him.

We should not miss the way the loud voice in heaven tells us that the "brothers" themselves were active in this heavenly event. Let there be no mistake: Salvation is by grace alone, accomplished solely by God's initiative and power. But it is a salvation that sweeps believers up into what is happening, and they become so involved that the brothers themselves overcame their accuser.

We can have power if we believe in Christ as our only hope for the forgiveness of sins. When we recognize that the blood he shed is enough to pay for our sins and give us a new life, we become involved in a divine drama that makes it impossible for Satan ever to say a word against us.

Through faith, we can receive the benefits of Jesus' powerful blood. "If you confess with your mouth, 'Jesus is Lord,' and believe in your heart that God raised him from the dead, you will be saved" (Rom. 10:9).

Joel Nederhood

The Heavenly Celebration

Therefore rejoice, you heavens and you who dwell in them! But woe to the earth and the sea, because the devil has gone down to you!

Revelation 12:12a

Christians often comfort each other with reminders that heaven is a better place than where they now live. Yet, as we comfort each other and claim this comfort for ourselves, it is always difficult to describe precisely what it is that makes heaven better.

In Revelation 12:12, we find something specific that we can wrap our minds around as we think about heaven, something that is even more encouraging than the information that the streets there are paved with gold and there will be an eternity of choir singing. We learn that it is a place of jubilant rejoicing, eternal celebration; we can become excited about that.

Some of us are aware each moment that there is something terribly awry here on earth, and those who are spared this in the fullest degree are at least vaguely aware that there is something askew where we live out our days. Even when our circumstances are favorable, we sense our vulnerability and realize that calamity could strike at any time. It's not that way in heaven.

For those who already live in heaven, there is a summons to exuberant celebration. It is a joyful expression of relief at the glorious possibilities that can now arise because every threat of disruption has been removed. Now that the great dragon has been eliminated from the heavenly realms, that environment can be wondrously joy filled and exciting.

We who still linger where the dragon—Satan—continues his dreadful deeds, the prospect of living in a place where he has been vanquished is pleasant indeed. It is even more captivating than the anticipation of walking on gold.

Joel Nederhood

157

The Devil's Deadline

He is filled with fury, because he knows that his time is short.

Revelation 12:12b

Most of us work faster and more efficiently when we have deadlines. It's the same way with the dragon that was cast out of heaven. He is intense and effective in his mission because he knows he doesn't have much time left.

It has been said that nothing focuses your concentration more than knowing that you will be shot tomorrow. Well, Satan knows that it is only a matter of time before he is going to be cast into hell, where he will experience the second and final death forever. He is very focused.

So, the loud voice in heaven announces that those who live in the place where he works so frantically must understand that they are in a cursed place: "Woe to the earth and the sea, because the devil has gone down to you!" Earth and sea pretty much include every square inch of planet Earth.

If only believers and their children could realize the merciless fury of Satan's attacks upon them. The great red dragon is shrewd enough to always appear in disguise. He approaches us with grotesque and pretty lies that promise us the very opposite of what his wretched temptations actually deliver.

The alluring pleasures he holds before us supply the very opposite of pleasure. His temptations are demonically clever. He has so little time.

"Do not gaze at wine when it is red, when it sparkles in the cup, when it goes down smoothly! In the end it bites like a snake and poisons like a viper" (Prov. 23:31–32). Just an example of his tricks!

Joel Nederhood

Déjà Vu—Eden Again

When the dragon saw that he had been hurled to the earth, he pursued the woman who had given birth to the male child.

Revelation 12:13

Commentators generally agree that the woman who dominates Revelation 12 should not be identified with Mary, the mother of Jesus. Rather, she represents the church—all who have ever trusted in the true God for their salvation and all who ever will.

When we think of Satan's action on this planet, we must never forget that it is most intensely directed against the church. Once cast out of heaven, Satan turned his attention to destroying the people of God. In the Old Testament, he did so through Egyptian slavery and Babylonian exile. In the church after Pentecost, Satan sowed false teaching as soon as salvation by grace alone was announced. The Book of Galatians attests to this.

When we think of Satan attacking the church, we should not think first of all of the merciless persecution that rages now—the twentieth century saw more martyrdoms than ever before. This century will likely be the same. Persecution actually makes the church stronger.

Rather, Satan is most effective when he manages to persuade the church to abandon the Scriptures. His tactics today are the same as they were when he first sidled up to Eve and asked her if God really said what he had said. Already then, he realized that if he could get people to doubt God's Word, he would have them in his pocket.

Sometimes Satan allows that the Bible is a fairly good book, but we need more—a supplemental book perhaps, a healthy appreciation of tradition, maybe someone who is receiving divine revelation even now. Sly as he is, he does not abandon the tactics that worked so well in Paradise.

Be warned!

Joel Nederhood

159

The Church in Flight

The woman was given the two wings of a great eagle, so that she might fly to the place prepared for her in the desert, where she would be taken care of for a time, times and half a time, out of the serpent's reach.

Revelation 12:14

The supernatural and fearsome power of the serpent is more than matched by the protection of the church's Lord. Revelation describes the perfection of divine protection with language reminiscent of the Old Testament and is uniquely descriptive of a glorious deed of God that transcends ordinary words.

Once again, we find the time designation found in verse 8; it is a span of time found already in Daniel 7:25, and it is scattered throughout Revelation; in plain English, it's three and a half years. It is usually recognized as the time of dreadful terror when the power of the man of sin will be unleashed with unimaginable fury, just before the end of ordinary human history, prior to the Lord's return. There are strong overtones here of 2 Thessalonians 2:1–12, which tells about the time when the lawless one will be revealed.

The images we confront as Revelation 12 concludes emphasize the effectiveness of divine protection for God's vulnerable people. Here we see the church endowed with the swift mobility of an eagle, remaining just beyond the serpent's outstretched fingers.

There are two things we should not fail to notice here. First, the church must flee when necessary; God gifts it so it can. Second, it must go to a place of isolation—here and in verse 6 the symbol of the desert makes this clear. It is foolhardy for the church to think that it will survive without making use of God's provision for flight and a place to go.

"God is our refuge and our strength, an ever-present help in trouble" (Ps. 46:1).

Joel Nederhood

The Devil's River

Then from his mouth the serpent spewed water like a river, to overtake the woman and sweep her away with the torrent. But the earth helped the woman by opening its mouth and swallowing the river that the dragon had spewed out of his mouth. Then the dragon was enraged at the woman and went off to make war against the rest of her offspring—those who obey God's commandments and hold to the testimony of Jesus.

Revelation 12:15–17

Chapter 12, which began with a nativity scene, has now become a cluster of images challenging us to visualize baffling, terrifying spiritual realities. We see a mighty torrent roaring from the serpent's mouth, rushing to sweep the woman into oblivion.

But—in the nick of time—the earth swallows the river. God's care of his beloved church brings all the forces of nature into play. There is safety only for those who trust in Christ.

Satan has been foiled. But our archenemy, thwarted by nature itself and knowing his time is short, turns to the ordinary, flesh and blood men and women and children who are part of the church on earth. The woman represents the church. Her ultimate safety is certain, but "those who obey God's commandments and hold to the testimony of Jesus"—that's us—continue to be attacked and pummeled by their evil enemy.

Believers in Jesus must never forget their evil enemy—the serpent, the flying red dragon. His hatred of us is so profound he will stop at nothing to destroy us. Often, he makes being a believer exceedingly unpleasant and difficult. He tempts us to abandon the way of Christ and join the forces of darkness. But that would be utterly foolish, for those who join the evil one shall ultimately perish with him in hell. Only when we remain close to our precious Savior is there invincible safety.

"Therefore we will not fear, though the earth give way and the mountains fall into the heart of the sea, though its waters roar and foam and the mountains quake with their surging" (Ps. 46:2–3).

Joel Nederhood

The Scene
at the Seashore

And the dragon stood on the shore of the sea. And I saw a beast coming out of the sea. He had ten horns and seven heads, with ten crowns on his horns, and on each head a blasphemous name.

Revelation 13:1

Chapter 13 continues to trace the malignant character and career of the dragon, or Satan, "who leads the whole world astray" (12:9). "The secret power of lawlessness" has been at work through the ages (2 Thess. 2:7), but will climax at the end of the age with the appearance of the Antichrist (1 John 2:18). Lawlessness will climax in "the man of lawlessness" (2 Thess. 2:8).

The fearsome beast (who appears to be both a system and a person) emerges from the sea under the aegis of Satan. The sea represents the churning and seething restlessness of the nations (cf. Rev. 17:15; Isa. 57:20–21). The raging and defiant nations embody human revolt against God (Ps. 2:1–3).

162

The beast has ten horns, which, in prophetic terms, symbolize power. His seven heads are evidence of his intelligence. His ten horns stand for his rule. On each head is a blasphemous, or exceedingly irreverent, name. The beast is an intimidating and formidable being. He is Satan's masterpiece. Satan is pulling out all the stops.

Martin Luther often said that Satan is God's ape, that is, one of our adversary's strategies is to seek to imitate God. Just as there is a Holy Trinity (Father, Son, and Holy Spirit), there will also be a satanic trinity (the dragon, the beast, and the false prophet). Satan will indeed do the worst, but our God will do the best. We should have a split screen to read Revelation: We need to watch what happens at the seashore, but we must never take our eyes off chapters 4 and 5—"the throne in heaven" from which our great God reigns.

David L. Larsen

The Diabolic Succession

The beast I saw resembled a leopard, but had feet like those of a bear and a mouth like that of a lion. The dragon gave the beast his power and his throne and great authority.

Revelation 13:2

The prophetic Scriptures display varied styles and often contrasting components, yet they are like an exquisite mosaic, fitting together magnificently into a striking whole. In depicting the sway of the satanic colossus at the end of space-time history, the apostle John dips into the vision of Daniel 7, which portrays the rise of four great Gentile powers that will rule in what Jesus called "the times of the Gentiles" (Luke 21:24; cf. Rom. 11:25).

The lion, bear, and leopard, and the fearful horned beast of Daniel 7 set forth the violent, wild nature of Gentile world power across the centuries. The final manifestation of Gentile world power will be the successor to all of the preceding tyrannies. It will be the ultimate composite of "man's inhumanity to man," the cruelty and crass control of a vicious world ruler.

The Antichrist, as endowed by Satan himself, will embody the characteristics of Cain, Lamech, Nimrod, Balaam, Goliath, Antioches Epiphanes (of the intertestamental period), Herod, Nero, Genghis Khan, Napoleon, Hitler, and Stalin. While Satan mounts his climactic challenge to the sovereignty of God ("because he knows that his time is short" 12:12c), we need to remember that "There is no authority except that which God has established" (Rom. 13:1).

Though Satan's dominion is real and ravaging, God's kingdom is greater. It will smite the vain structures of human arrogance and demonic pretension, like a great stone smites the impressive image of Gentile world power: "It will itself endure forever" (Dan. 2:44).

David L. Larsen

163

The Menace
of the Miraculous

One of the heads of the beast seemed to have had a fatal wound, but the fatal wound had been healed. The whole world was astonished and followed the beast. Men worshiped the dragon because he had given authority to the beast, and they also worshiped the beast and asked, "Who is like the beast? Who can make war against him?"

Revelation 13:3–4

We humans crave miraculous signs. Jesus cautioned against seeking such signs. He indicated that even the sign of someone raised from the dead would not be believed (Luke 16:31).

As we see in today's passage, the Antichrist would receive a fatal wound by the sword and would ostensibly be healed. As "God's ape," Satan is seeking to accredit his agent by a pseudo-resurrection. Can the devil actually raise the dead? The Antichrist will come with "all kinds of counterfeit miracles, signs and wonders" (2 Thess. 2:9). The impact will be virtually universal discipleship and worship. How vulnerable we are!

Because there are counterfeit miracles, God's people must always "test the spirits to see whether they are from God, because many false prophets have gone out into the world" (1 John 4:1). The magicians in Egypt could imitate the early plagues up to a point but then were unable to produce the plague of gnats (cf. Exod. 7:22; 8:18).

When confronted with an apparent miracle, we need the maturity and discernment to ask: "Whose miracle is it? God's? Satan's? Just human suggestibility?" While an exaggerated individualism is a peril to our common life in the Christian community, there are dangerous collectivisms that would envelop us in a collapse of critical conviction such as described here—"The whole world was astonished and followed the beast."

David L. Larsen

164

The Time Is Allocated

The beast was given a mouth to utter proud words and blasphemies and to exercise his authority for forty-two months.

Revelation 13:5

The devastating and profane misadventure of the frightful beast is traced through these chapters. The irrationality and insanity of sin and rebellion against God do not impede the despicable designs and efforts of the enemy of our souls. Such is the nature of evil. Our Lord said of this time, "Because of the increase of wickedness, the love of most will grow cold" (Matt. 24:12). Indeed, he also said: "If those days had not been cut short, no one would survive, but for the sake of the elect those days will be shortened" (Matt. 24:22).

The surging crescendo of rebellion will peak during a period of forty-two months when the beast will relish in his arrogant, irreverent schemes. But God will limit his hegemony to a period of forty-two months. The forty-two months, and their equivalent 1,260 days, or three and a half years, figure prominently in the chronologies of both Daniel and Revelation. God allows the beast some line, but only so much line. God allowed Satan to torment Job, but set a limit as to how far he could go (cf. Job 1:12; 2:6). So God allows the beast to strut for a time, but only for a limited and a divinely designated time, after which the folly and futility of the errant being will be manifest.

Jesus our Savior lived on earth in utter confidence in his Father's timing (cf. John 2:4; 7:6; 17:1). God's time is the right time: never too fast nor too slow. As believers, on this day we can rejoice and be glad to say with the psalmist: "My times are in your hands" (Ps. 31:15).

David L. Larsen

165

Pushing the Parameters

He opened his mouth to blaspheme God, and to slander his name and his dwelling place and those who live in heaven.

Revelation 13:6

Of the reckless and disobedient company who determined to challenge God by building a tower that reached to heaven, the Lord said: "If . . . they have begun to do this, then nothing they plan to do will be impossible for them" (Gen. 11:6). The deceit of sin is expansive, and sin is not only irrational, but it also gains momentum and scope. It comes to its sordid climax with the beast's blasphemy against God and his slandering of the holy name of God, of heaven and those who dwell in heaven (as described in Rev. 4–5), including all of the angelic beings and the church itself.

The principle enunciated in Proverbs 29:18 is profound: "Where there is no revelation, the people cast off restraint; but blessed is he who keeps the law." The restless nations (and individuals as well) view the moral restraints of holy God as burdensome chains and fetters, and chafe under divine restriction of any kind (Ps. 2:1–3). Postmodern citizens want all lights to be green and will tolerate no restraint.

This mood reflects the mindset of Satan and his prime puppet, the beast, for whom there is no limit to impiety. He is swept along in the sheer momentum of immorality to the derision of the highest and holiest of all. These are the currents, which are now flowing with immense power in our own culture. We must ask ourselves: "Will I today be caught in these rushing rapids of revolt and rebellion against God, or will I 'not conform any longer to the pattern of this world'?" (Rom. 12:2). Let us remember: "Blessed is he who keeps the law" (Prov. 29:18).

David L. Larsen

166

The
Consummation of Evil

He was given power to make war against the saints and to conquer them.
And he was given authority over every tribe, people, language and nation.

Revelation 13:7

Even though the beast, evil incarnate, carries on what seems to be a successful vendetta against the saints of God, and is manifestly perverse in every respect, his ability to unify the nations and to produce an efficient, powerful coalition makes him seem snug and invulnerable in his tyranny. Dictatorship is always efficient, and character has never counted for much in this world.

Wendell Wilkie's *One World* has come at last. What Plato advocated in his *Republic,* and what Thomas More dreamt of in his *Utopia,* has been achieved. What Tennyson rhapsodized about in "Locksley Hall," and what George Orwell in *1984* and Aldous Huxley in *Brave New World* envisioned as the ultimate shape of human history, has come to pass! But such a concentration of power in depraved hands is a nightmare of oppression. Such an ascendancy by the beast is possible only when the saints are beleaguered and beaten. No nonconformity is allowed.

But all of this is in striking contrast with the ultimate sway of God's heavenly kingdom here upon earth. Daniel sees the rock cut out, "but not by human hands," striking the image of Gentile world power by pulverizing the impressive metal man, until it is "like chaff on a threshing floor in the summer" (Dan. 2:34–35). Indeed, "the God of heaven will set up a kingdom that will never be destroyed" (Dan. 2:44). As citizens of God's kingdom, we Christians pray, "Your kingdom come, your will be done on earth as it is in heaven" (Matt. 6:10). Evil will not have the last word.

David L. Larsen

167

Captive
to Culture . . . Or

All inhabitants of the earth will worship the beast—all whose names have not been written in the book of life belonging to the Lamb that was slain from the creation of the world.

Revelation 13:8

In every age, believers face pressure to conform to a culture that is alien and at odds with God. We think of Daniel and his friends, who courteously and creatively refused to capitulate. They took a firm, unapologetic stand for what God had said in his Word. Even though it might mean the fiery furnace, the three young friends were confident that their God would be faithful to his promises, whether he spared them or not (Dan. 3:17–18).

The Western church today is often caught in the clutches of materialism and secularism. Are we ourselves being swept along in the prevailing currents of conformity? Do we realize the degree to which our thought patterns are being tinctured by the wisdom of this world? John identifies those who resist the worship of the beast as those whose names are written in the Lamb's Book of Life (cf. Luke 10:20). God keeps the roll of those whose hearts are right with him. His "scroll of remembrance," which is written "in his presence," lists those who fear the Lord and honor his name (Mal. 3:16). Are our names there?

But never in Revelation or in any part of Scripture are we ever allowed to forget that being right with God and pleasing him always have reference to the mediating work of the Son of God, and the shedding of his atoning blood. "The Lamb that was slain" and his cross are the moral epicenter of the whole universe. In a world that has lost its moral bearings, and has lost its way so tragically, there is only one answer, "Jesus Christ and him crucified" (1 Cor. 2:2). Only thus can we be counted among his holy ones.

David L. Larsen

A Call to Courage

He who has an ear, let him hear. If anyone is to go into captivity, into captivity he will go. If anyone is to be killed with the sword, with the sword he will be killed. This calls for patient endurance and faithfulness on the part of the saints.

Revelation 13:9–10

The saints embroiled in persecution from every age are now given an important reminder. The Lord says: "Listen!" in the same way he started the letters to the seven churches earlier in Revelation.

Though the power unleashed against us is overwhelming, "the one who is in you is greater than the one who is in the world" (1 John 4:4, referring specifically to "the spirit of the antichrist"). God's decrees of punishment and retribution will be fulfilled.

In a kind of grim gallows humor, some will mock the idea that rebellion against God is folly, but this revisionism does not alter the reality. The dragon and the beast and all their colleagues are losers, and that is an irrefutable fact. Their doom is foretold (cf. Rev. 19:20; 20:10).

In all of this, the people of God are called to exhibit courageous fidelity to God and his truth. We are called to "patient endurance" in the face of the continued assaults of our foe. But it is not sufficient to stand against the evil, to say "no" to what is evil. We must say "yes" and "emphatically yes" to God and his standards. There are those who astutely see the pernicious nature of evil in our times, but who do not surrender to Jesus. We are to be "faithful," that is, unswervingly loyal to our God and his righteousness. Even in our time, when historic Christian faith is being pushed out of the public square and increasingly consigned to the oblivion of the irrelevant and the outdated, we are summoned to courageous faithfulness. In a day when the very idea of truth is scorned, we must seek "patient endurance and faithfulness." Help me, Lord, to live this day for Christ's sake.

David L. Larsen

169

Double Trouble

Then I saw another beast, coming out of the earth. He had two horns like a lamb, but he spoke like a dragon. He exercised all the authority of the first beast on his behalf, and made the earth and its inhabitants worship the first beast, whose fatal wound had been healed.

Revelation 13:11–12

The full picture of the satanic insurgency described in Revelation 13 comes into sharper focus when we see a second beast "coming out of the earth." This monster is exactly like his previously described cohort. He is the dedicated collaborator and agent of the first beast. Clearly, he is a religious figure who enhances his master's political agenda with cunning religious deception. He melds the great false religious system, the great prostitute of Revelation 17, into a vast syncretism in which the prostitute rides the beast until her usefulness is exhausted; then he turns and rends her (17:16).

The first beast was a Gentile from the great restless sea of the nations. The second beast coming from the earth may well be a Jew to catalyze the beast's relationship and covenant with Israel. The earth in Scripture frequently refers to God's ancient covenant people. This second beast is dedicated solely to unifying the constituencies of earth into a gigantic and final idolatry.

He is well qualified to foist this deception on a vulnerable humanity, inasmuch as he appears to be gentle as a lamb. This is a disguise, though. In truth, he speaks like a dragon. His soft-sell approach is appealing in the clamor and cacophony of the end. He is a religious genius, a masterful entrepreneur of popular spirituality. He is subsequently called "the false prophet" and stands in the long succession of those whose purpose has been to delude and to destroy. Here is another Balaam. We must always be on the alert.

We must remember our Lord's much neglected words: "I have come in my Father's name, and you do not accept me; but if someone else comes in his own name, you will accept him" (John 5:43).

David L. Larsen

Popular Religion

And he performed great and miraculous signs, even causing fire to come down from heaven to earth in full view of men. Because of the signs he was given power to do on behalf of the first beast, he deceived the inhabitants of the earth. He ordered them to set up an image in honor of the beast who was wounded by the sword and yet lived.

Revelation 13:13–14

The false prophet uses religion to galvanize human support and loyalty for the beast and his agenda. This religion of the masses is cleverly concocted, but it is horizontal, without divine revelation or redemption. It is worship as spectacle. People watch titillating performances and they are captivated. It is the celebrity syndrome, which has been such a scourge, particularly in recent decades. It is all calculated to cause humankind to give adulation to the first beast.

Massive in design, it is "mega" in every respect. It caters to the carnal love of pleasure and thrills; it is very "soulish" and not spiritual (cf. 1 Cor. 2:14). This religion is sensuous and externally impressive. "Are we having fun yet?" on a bumper sticker expresses the passion for pleasure in our time—we want entertainment everywhere, and that means at church also. Even evangelism at times is done by means of entertainment.

The false prophet uses all of the tricks possible, including an idol to honor the beast. All his machinations scarcely mask the brazen deception being perpetrated. Are we sufficiently awake to see that the flimsiness and shallowness of so-called popular religion in our time, which seems to satisfy so many, is but a soporific that dulls and blunts our higher instincts? We are then left with no appetite for the eternal and the genuinely spiritual. Lord, give us salve to put on our eyes that we may see (Rev. 3:18).

David L. Larsen

The Icon

He was given power to give breath to the image of the first beast, so that it could speak and cause all who refused to worship the image to be killed.

Revelation 13:15

What the Holy Spirit is to the Lord Jesus in the Holy Trinity, the false prophet is to the beast in the unholy, satanic trinity. As the Holy Spirit glorifies the Son and bears witness to him, so the false prophet is dedicated to the magnification of the beast. His ingenious masterstroke involves an icon, the image of the beast, through whom he bedazzles humankind. This crowning impiety is called the "abomination that causes desolation" by Daniel (Dan. 9:27) and by our Lord (Matt. 24:15). It is to be set up in the temple.

The icon, which robotically parrots the party line, is irresistible to the masses. False prophets who disdain doctrine tell the people what their "itching ears want to hear" (2 Tim. 4:3). The puppets of error who ridicule the idea of the second coming of Christ please those who do not want to be disturbed, although they have their own hidden motives (2 Peter 3:3ff.). The widely disseminated greeting card theology of our time, "feel-good" theology, secures an ever-widening following. Many would turn our sanctuaries into spiritual salad bars in which people can choose a bit of this, a bit of that, which tantalizes but is a counterfeit of the true, not the reality.

The stakes are high, and many saints are martyred. Thus many will choose the easy way. Who cares about the first and second commandments? Some will rationalize their craven idolatry by arguing that they are not really worshiping the image but only venerating and reverencing it. John Calvin spoke of the human heart as "an idol-factory." How wary we must be about the intrusion of idols into our heart's worship. Lord, keep me this day from idolatry in every form through your Holy Spirit.

David L. Larsen

172

The Crowd Is Wrong

He also forced everyone, small and great, rich and poor, free and slave, to receive a mark on his right hand or on his forehead, so that no one could buy or sell unless he had the mark, which is the name of the beast or the number of his name.

Revelation 13:16–17

The numbers game is important to us. "Everyone is doing it!" Yet we know truth is not determined by a nose count. How frequently in history the crowd has been wrong! Through the slick maneuvering and clever manipulation of the false prophet, the mass of humankind is coerced into a bland conformity to the new cultural and economic order. So total is this tyranny that physical survival is problematic for those who would march to a different drummer. Without the mark of the beast, existence is not viable. Conform or die!

In the vast syncretisms and pluralism of the end, there will be little tolerance for those who hold to Jesus Christ as the one way. God reveals the truth in his Word, even if only a few acknowledge it. Scripture is clear. Jesus said, "I am the way and the truth and the life. No one comes to the Father except through me" (John 14:6). "Salvation is found in no one else, for there is no other name under heaven given to men by which we must be saved" (Acts 4:12). This dogged insistence runs contrary to the congeniality and collegiality of our culture. It often seems unpleasant and awkward to resist the increasingly prevailing currents of thought in our time.

The question is: Shall we have the mark of the beast on our foreheads, or shall we have the Lamb's name on our foreheads? (Rev. 22:4). We cannot have both. We must make the choice. The movement and clamor of the crowd are massive and impressive, compelling to most. But there are some who will not bend. There is a little flock who resist. Are we among them in our time? Remember, "One with God is a majority!"

David L. Larsen

That Haunting
Horizontalism

This calls for wisdom. If anyone has insight, let him calculate the number of the beast, for it is man's number. His number is 666.

Revelation 13:18

Volumes could be written on the history of the interpretation of this verse. Just about anyone's name can add up to 666. The old saw has it that we try first in Hebrew, then Greek, and then Latin. If none of these works, add a title to the name, and if that does not help, then just don't be too fussy about the spelling. Still, something significant is being advanced here, which calls for wisdom and insight. The number of the beast is meant to be understood. This is the crowning flourish of the description of his nefarious career.

Many have pointed out that the numerical value of the name of Jesus is 888, eight being the number of new things. It is the number of the complete octave. Six is the number of man, since man was created on the sixth day. The text says, "it is man's number." It represents the zenith of human accomplishment, but it is deficient and lacking. Trebling the six means this is humanism with a vengeance. This represents the loss of transcendence; it is the worship of what is created rather than of the Creator.

Much of modern religion is horizontal, with no redeeming sense of the vertical. Theology becomes anthropology. Sermons are stuffed with psychology but bereft of God's transformation. Moralism replaces a genuinely Christian ethic. It avoids the miraculous in Scripture. This is the religion of man as spun by the legions of hell. This is the culmination of idolatry. Self-help religion (the answer is within you!), in effect, deifies humankind and rejects the atonement. It is the triumph of the evolutionary vision in which popular taste is the test of truth. It is 666.

David L. Larsen

The Lamb
and His People

Then I looked, and there before me was the Lamb, standing on Mount Zion, and with him 144,000 who had his name and his Father's name written on their foreheads.

Revelation 14:1

Here the Lamb stands on Mount Zion as the victorious King with his jubilant people. After the troubles of God's people recounted in previous chapters, it is a great relief to read in this chapter of their security and triumph. Someone has said that earlier chapters of Revelation say to the world in general, "Bad news, you lose!" But now the message focuses on the people of God, "Good news, we win!"

If we could see into heaven as John could, we would see that the Lamb of God is there. With him are all those for whom he died. He is not merely the One who was slain, however; he is the one who was victorious.

He shares his victory with us. We are safe and secure with the name of our Father sealed on our foreheads. The sealing protects those who follow the Lamb from their enemies and from the wrath of God.

The Lord, who had compassion for his people during his earthly ministry, continues to care for them after his ascension. He knows their circumstances. He is with them. He protects them.

In John 17 the Lord prayed, "My prayer is not that you take them out of the world but that you protect them from the evil one" (John 17:15). Satan cannot win, and Jesus cannot lose!

Do you fear the future? All those for whom the Lamb of God died will share his victory.

Albert H. Freundt

175

The Throne Room
of the Universe

Then I looked, and there before me was the Lamb, standing on Mount Zion, and with him 144,000 who had his name and his Father's name written on their foreheads.

Revelation 14:1

Zion has been called the throne room or the hub of the universe, the place from whence God rules (Ps. 9:11). It is the heavenly realm into which God raised Christ and has made a place for us (Eph. 1:20; 2:6).

David prophesied Christ's ascension (see Ps. 2:6–8). Peter calls Christ the "cornerstone" placed on Mount Zion, fulfilling the prophecy of Isaiah that those who trust in him "will never be put to shame" (Isa. 28:16; 1 Peter 2:6).

God exalted Christ "and gave him the name that is above every name, that at the name of Jesus every knee should bow, in heaven and on earth and under the earth, and every tongue confess that Jesus Christ is Lord, to the glory of God the Father" (Phil. 2:9–11). When Christ "had offered for all time one sacrifice for sins, he sat down [as a king to reign] at the right hand of God" (Heb. 10:12). "He must reign until [God] has put all his enemies under his feet" (1 Cor. 15:25).

John sees that the course and destiny of all things is determined and controlled by the Lamb. The Lamb who was slain takes on the characteristics of a lion. The world is his stage, and his purpose is being fulfilled in its history. He will conquer and share his victory with his people.

How does it feel to be on the winning side?

Albert H. Freundt

Christe the King

Then I looked, and there before me was the Lamb, standing on Mount Zion, and with him 144,000 who had his name and his Father's name written on their foreheads.

Revelation 14:1

The psalmist knew this truth: "I have installed my King on Zion, my holy hill" (Ps. 2:6).

Evil forces may erect vast superstructures with terrifying proportions, but those structures are built on rotten foundations. In due time they will collapse. Martin Luther said that evil structures were like a balloon upon which was painted an ugly face. The larger the balloon became, the more terrifying was the spectacle. But after the point of maximum expansion is reached, the balloon explodes into nothingness. So are the superstructures of evil. They grow, then God pricks the bubble and they are gone.

When the Turks conquered Greece in the fifteenth century, they took over all Byzantine churches and made them into Muslim mosques. In their domes were beautiful mosaics of Christ looking down upon the people, keeping watch over his own. The Turks plastered over the images, but four hundred years later, when the Greeks won their independence, they returned to their churches and removed the plaster. The mosaics, for the most part, were unharmed. The almighty Christ, although invisible from below, was nevertheless there all the time. So from below, from the time of his triumph of the cross until the decisive manifestation of the victory of the cross in his Second Advent, we may not be able to trace visibly the workings of Christ's rule. Nevertheless, he is still working. The end of the age, when the veil separating us from his visible presence is torn away, will reveal the splendor and the magnificence of his rule, which has never been displaced nor supplanted, nor will it be.

Who is on the Lord's side?
Who will serve the King?
Frances Havergal, 1877

Albert H. Freundt

14:1

God's Holy Hill

Then I looked, and there before me was the Lamb, standing on Mount Zion, and with him 144,000 who had his name and his Father's name written on their foreheads.

Revelation 14:1

The Old Testament calls Zion "the holy place where the Most High dwells" (Ps. 46:4). Just as the old city of Jerusalem was sometimes called Zion, in Hebrews 12:22, Zion is "the heavenly Jerusalem, the city of the living God," occupied by "thousands upon thousands of angels in joyful assembly." In Revelation 14 it is the place where the Lamb of God protects his redeemed people.

As John Newton wrote in 1779:

> Glorious things of thee are spoken,
> Zion, city of our God;
> He whose word cannot be broken
> Formed thee for His own abode.

The Lamb stands "on Mount Zion." Usually, Christ is referred to as being seated at the right hand of God (Heb. 1:3, 13; 10:12). The seated position denotes rule and authority. The reference to standing shows his concern for his people who endure enmity and persecution, as in the vision of Stephen (Acts 7:55–56).

Whatever trials we have to bear in this life, "our citizenship is in heaven." Now we experience trials and have to live by faith, but hard times will not last forever.

Here is a vision to give embattled believers hope and courage! In the worst of times we need to look up and be reminded that God is on the throne. The people of God are in good hands.

"Those who trust in the LORD are like Mount Zion, which cannot be shaken but endures forever. As the mountains surround Jerusalem, so the LORD surrounds his people both now and forevermore" (Ps. 125:1–2).

Albert H. Freundt

178

The Day of Victory

Then I looked, and there before me was the Lamb, standing on Mount Zion, and with him 144,000 who had his name and his Father's name written on their foreheads.

Revelation 14:1

The relation between Christ's resurrection victory and his final triumph has been likened to events in World War II. The decisive battle in Europe was fought on D-Day, June 6, 1944. VE-Day, however, did not dawn until May 8, 1945. Final victory was determined by a battle fought many months earlier. Serious fighting lay ahead, but the outcome was certain after the successful D-Day offensives. D-Day for us fell within the rule of Pontius Pilate, when Christ successfully overcame evil's power. Our VE-Day lies in the future at an hour and time unknown to us. The decisive battle has been fought and won. Each skirmish in which we engage in Christ's name brings us nearer the day of victory.

Evil powers continue to exist, but they now exist as defeated powers. The day will dawn, however, when evil's power will be completely destroyed.

179

From an earthly point of view, it often appears that God's enemies are triumphing and his people are losing. From heaven—as John saw—the truth is otherwise. Christ is now the ruling power, at the right hand of God. Evil forces are waging a losing battle. "Having disarmed the powers and authorities," Paul said of Christ, "he made a public spectacle of them, triumphing over them by the cross" (Col. 2:15).

The church suffers in this age, but the course of history will be brought to a close with Christ, the King of kings and Lord of lords, victorious on his holy mountain.

What a sight to see! What a victory to share!

Albert H. Freundt

A New Song

And they sang a new song before the throne and before the four living creatures and the elders. No one could learn the song except the 144,000 who had been redeemed from the earth.

Revelation 14:3

When God delivered the Israelites from Egypt, Moses led them in this song:

> "I will sing to the LORD,
>   for he is highly exalted.
> The horse and its rider
>   he has hurled into the sea.
> The LORD is my strength and my song;
>   he has become my salvation.
> He is my God, and I will praise him,
>   my father's God, and I will exalt him."

Exodus 15:1–2

When God helped or delivered his people, they exhorted one another, "Sing to the LORD a new song" (Ps. 98:1).

The Book of Revelation contains many praise songs. For example, "We give thanks to you, Lord God Almighty, the One who is and who was, because you have taken your great power and have begun to reign" (Rev. 11:17).

In Revelation 4 and 5, God is praised because he is eternal and holy, and because he has created all things. In Revelation 5:9–10, the redeemed sing what is called "a new song," a song that is based upon redemption by Christ: "You are worthy to take the scroll and to open its seals, because you were slain, and with your blood you purchased men for God from every tribe and language and people and nation. You have made them to be a kingdom and priests to serve our God, and they will reign on the earth."

Whenever we reflect on Christ's sacrifice, that kind of praise is always appropriate.

"Let the word of Christ dwell in you richly as you teach and admonish one another with all wisdom, and as you sing psalms, hymns and spiritual songs with gratitude in your hearts to God" (Col. 3:16).

Albert H. Freundt

180

Followers of the Lamb

These are those who did not defile themselves with women, for they kept themselves pure. They follow the Lamb wherever he goes. They were purchased from among men and offered as firstfruits to God and the Lamb. No lie was found in their mouths; they are blameless.

Revelation 14:4–5

Jesus said, "My sheep listen to my voice; I know them, and they follow me" (John 10:27). Those who follow the Lamb have both his and his Father's name inscribed upon them, an indicator that they follow the Lamb faithfully. Following the Lord is the distinctive mark of a Christian.

Polycarp, a second-century bishop of Smyrna, is typical of those who were faithful even to death. He was carried to the stadium and commanded to deny his faith and pay homage to Caesar for his freedom. He refused, as have others, to deny the Lord.

The first of the harvest was sacred and was dedicated to God. It is fitting that those in the early church who followed the Lord to a martyr's death should be called the firstfruits. They were characterized by truth and purity. They kept themselves free from the influence of a pagan culture. They resisted the pressure to worship the emperor. Consequently, they are glorified with Christ in heaven.

We make a great deal of earthly distinctions such as denominational labels. It is important, we think, to belong to this denomination or the other. But in heaven it does not matter whether we were Baptists, or Presbyterians, or whatever. The only thing that will count is that we belong to Christ and have followed wherever he has led us.

Albert H. Freundt

Fear God

He said in a loud voice, "Fear God and give him glory, because the hour of his judgment has come. Worship him who made the heavens, the earth, the sea and the springs of water."

Revelation 14:7

People fear death, disease, loss, persecution, and punishment. They fear the future and anything unknown. Mary and Joseph and the shepherds feared the angels' appearance. The disciples feared when Christ stilled the storm and again when he walked on water (Mark 4:41; Matt. 14:26). They feared the risen Lord's appearance to them. In the last days, Jesus said, "men will faint from terror" (Luke 21:26).

Jesus gave us this advice about fear: "Do not be afraid of those who kill the body but cannot kill the soul. Rather, be afraid of the One who can destroy both soul and body in hell" (Matt. 10:28). Some fear makes men and women hide from God. Another fear, however, is godly fear: reverence and respect for the God Almighty.

"The fear of the LORD is the beginning of wisdom" (Ps. 111:10; Prov. 9:10). This fear is appropriate. The early church grew in numbers, "living in the fear of the Lord" (Acts 9:31). Paul condemned the heathen world, saying, "There is no fear of God before their eyes" (Rom. 3:18). We fear God in the right sense when we realize that we always live in his sight and that we shall have to give an account to him for what we have done with our lives.

Legend has it that at John Knox's funeral, the Earl of Morton said, "Here lies a man who neither flattered nor feared any flesh." We will never fall prey to other fears if we have a fear of offending God.

Albert H. Freundt

182

The Fall of Babylon

A second angel followed and said, "Fallen! Fallen is Babylon the Great, which made all the nations drink the maddening wine of her adulteries." A third angel followed them and said in a loud voice: "If anyone worships the beast and his image and receives his mark on the forehead or on the hand, he, too, will drink of the wine of God's fury, which has been poured full strength into the cup of his wrath. He will be tormented with burning sulfur in the presence of the holy angels and of the Lamb. And the smoke of their torment rises for ever and ever. There is no rest day or night for those who worship the beast and his image, or for anyone who receives the mark of his name."

Revelation 14:8–11

Babylon is "the great city that rules over the kings of the earth" (Rev. 17:18), the evil world empire that persecuted God's people.

Worship of the emperor was intended to impose a measure of uniformity and solidarity for the diverse peoples in the Roman Empire. While most people had no problem offering incense to the emperor, faithful Christians resisted. They refused to participate in activities that involved homage to the emperor or the pagan deities. Taught that Christ is Lord, they would not give this title to Caesar; consequently, many Christians perished at the stake or in the arena.

But John predicted the overthrow of all that Babylon represents. Just as Babylon "made all the nations drink the maddening wine of her adulteries," so God will make the worshipers of the beast "drink of the wine of God's fury, which has been poured full strength into the cup of his wrath." To drink the wine of God's wrath and to be tormented with fire and brimstone are two ways of saying the same thing.

To compromise your faith or to surrender to the standards and values of this world do not bring rest and peace. They spell doom. "Anyone who chooses to be a friend of the world becomes an enemy of God" (James 4:4).

"The world and its desires pass away, but the man who does the will of God lives forever" (1 John 2:17).

Albert H. Freundt

183

Patient Endurance

This calls for patient endurance on the part of the saints who obey God's commandments and remain faithful to Jesus.

Revelation 14:12

Jesus said his disciples would have trouble in this world (John 16:33). He said to the Ephesian Christians, "You have persevered and have endured hardships for my name" (Rev. 2:3).

The word translated "endurance" denotes the ability to cope with the most trying circumstances: the capacity to persevere no matter how long or how intense the difficulty is. Paul declared, "We also rejoice in our sufferings, because we know that suffering produces perseverance" (Rom. 5:3).

Endurance is not the same as the patience of resignation. It is the spirit that can bear troubles, even persecution, with fortitude and hope. It is constancy under trial. It provides a certain calmness and security in the midst of the worst that enemies and evil can do to us. It can endure hardship because it sees beyond pain to the goal.

George Matheson experienced blindness and awful disappointment. He displayed endurance when he prayed that he might accept God's will, not with dumb resignation but with holy joy.

For years I've heard that Thomas Carlyle asked Bishop Wilberforce if he had a creed, that is, were there beliefs to which he was committed. The bishop replied he had a creed and added, "The one thing that distresses me is the slow progress that my creed appears to be making in the world." Carlyle replied, "A man who has a creed can afford to wait."

"Therefore, since we are surrounded by such a great cloud of witnesses, let us throw off everything that hinders and the sin that so easily entangles, and let us run with perseverance the race marked out for us" (Heb. 12:1).

Albert H. Freundt

The Blessed Dead

Then I heard a voice from heaven say, "Write: Blessed are the dead who die in the Lord from now on." "Yes," says the Spirit, "they will rest from their labor, for their deeds will follow them."

Revelation 14:13

From the world's point of view, death is the most dreaded enemy. But those who die in the Lord are safe; they are free from sin and sorrow and suffering. In Paul's words, "I consider that our present sufferings are not worth comparing with the glory that will be revealed in us" (Rom. 8:18) and, "For to me, to live is Christ and to die is gain" (Phil. 1:21).

There are worse things than death, and there are more important things than life. It is not the persecutors but the persecuted who are truly blessed. If we wish to die in the Lord, we must also live in the Lord.

An old story that I've heard attributed to F. W. Boreham tells us that in the Middle Ages three monks were discussing which aspect of heaven seemed most attractive to them. One, who had seen much sorrow, said his favorite idea of heaven was expressed in the text, "God shall wipe away all tears from their eyes."

Another, who had struggled long and hard against his besetting sin, said his favorite was, "He who overcomes will inherit these things; and I will be his God, and he will be my son."

The youngest of the three said, "My favorite is, 'And his servants shall serve him . . . his name shall be on their foreheads.'"

The blessed dead may be absent from us, but they are present with the Lord (2 Cor. 5:8). Jesus said to Martha, "He who believes in me will live, even though he dies; and whoever lives and believes in me will never die. Do you believe this?" (John 11:25–26).

Do we?

Albert H. Freundt

The Harvest
of the Earth

Then another angel came out of the temple and called in a loud voice to him
who was sitting on the cloud, "Take your sickle and reap, because the time
to reap has come, for the harvest of the earth is ripe." So he who was seated
on the cloud swung his sickle over the earth, and the earth was harvested.

Revelation 14:15–16

The cloud and the sickle give us a vivid picture of the end. Jesus spoke of his return as a time when the Son of Man will be seen "coming on the clouds of heaven" (Matt. 26:64). Revelation 1:7: "Look, he is coming with the clouds, and every eye will see him, even those who pierced him; and all the peoples of the earth will mourn because of him." "The harvest is the end of the age" (Matt. 13:39).

Revelation describes in detail and at length the forces that array themselves against Christ and his people. But evil will not prevail forever. Christ is not only the victorious king; he is also the judge. At his return, he will judge the world and right all wrongs. This means the destruction of all that is evil and unjust. It means the vindication of God's persecuted people and the end of their suffering.

The final destruction of evil is a reality that Scripture never hesitates to emphasize. God's sickle is sharpened. He will cut down all that needs to be cut down. The devastation described in this chapter is almost beyond human comprehension. Judgment and hell are real.

"Since, then, we know what it is to fear the Lord, we try to persuade men" (2 Cor. 5:11).

"The Lord knows how to rescue godly men from trials and to hold the unrighteous for the day of judgment" (2 Peter 2:9).

"Since everything will be destroyed in this way, what kind of people ought you to be? You ought to live holy and godly lives" (2 Peter 3:11).

Albert H. Freundt

Finally!

I saw in heaven another great and marvelous sign: seven angels with the seven last plagues—last, because with them God's wrath is completed.

Revelation 15:1

Things are getting dark. Fire and smoke, judgment and wrath are the order of the day. Last judgment—because God's wrath-cup is full. These are themes we would rather avoid. We prefer "Godstuff" market tested and ready for the shelf. Wrath and judgment don't sell too well these days.

When was the last time your preacher preached the wrath of God? Feel-good church services focus on God's love, our success, and, too often, God's love of our success. Why even think about God's wrath when everything is going so well? When the stock market is soaring, the sun is shining, and the home team is winning, all we want is a God that pats us on the back and says, "Good show!"

But the stock market doesn't always soar, the sun doesn't always shine, and the visitors lose when the home team wins. Cancer steals a mother from her three young children. A police officer, finding a five-year-old boy in the park after midnight, asks, "Where do you live, son?" He replies, "They tell me I live here now."

Perhaps we avoid the subject of God's wrath because we try to inoculate ourselves against facing the injustices of life. "Why is that smelly man pushing a grocery cart?" my son asks. "Quiet!" I hiss, hoping to avoid embarrassment, giving a hard answer and the ugly reality all together.

But the cry of the martyr, the victim, and the oppressed, "How long until you judge the inhabitants of the earth and avenge our blood?" (Rev. 6:10), demands God's righteous wrath. God's wrath-cup is full!

Charles F. Edgar III

187

It Will Not Last Forever

I saw in heaven another great and marvelous sign: seven angels with the seven last plagues—last, because with them God's wrath is completed.

Revelation 15:1

"Are you still mad at me?" my son asked.

I was mad, really mad. Not just because I sometimes get tired and cranky. He really deserved it. Even after being told exactly what he was supposed to do, he deliberately chose to disobey. I was angry with him. And we punished him.

But he is my son. I remember the first time I saw him. I remember how strong and deep my love for him felt. It overwhelmed me. I wept with joy, and I'm no weeper. I remember telling my wife that I couldn't imagine ever being angry with him. But here we were. He deliberately disobeyed, and I got angry.

Now all that was over. "Are you still mad at me?" he asked. "No, son, of course not. I love you."

God made us, and rejoiced over us when he did. He made us because he loved us. Even when our deliberate disobedience kindled his wrath against us, that wrath appeared against the backdrop of his greater love. God's wrath is real, but it is not dominant. It is not eternal. It will end someday.

His love will last forever. Not his wrath. His love creates a way for punishment to be meted out, and our relationship restored.

Revelation paints vivid images of God's wrath against our disobedience, against all of our wickedness and ungodliness. But God pours out his wrath in such a way that it is used up. Completed. His love never ends.

Charles F. Edgar III

Water and Fire

*I saw what looked like a sea of glass mixed with fire and, standing beside
the sea, those who had been victorious over the beast and his image and
over the number of his name.*

Revelation 15:2

All the biblical experiences of water are gathered into the
Christian meditation on baptism: the watery chaos over
which the Spirit of God moved, brooding creation; the cat-
astrophic waters that cleansed the earth of its degeneracy
into continuous evil and carried Noah and his family to salvation; the Red Sea waters that sank the Egyptian horses and
riders and from which Moses marched Israel into freedom;
Solomon's great brass tank [sea] of water used to purify the
priests as they administered the temple worship; the Jordan
waters into which St. John Baptist dipped crowds of repentant sinners and out of which Jesus rose, proclaimed and proclaiming God's kingdom.[10]

God's wrath is real. It is righteous. It is kindled until his wrath-cup
is full. And it will be poured out.

God's holiness and righteousness can't tolerate evil—at all, in
any amount. Evil must be dealt with.

So the heavenly saints and martyrs gather around shining water.
They have been baptized. When they embraced the salvation
offered by the slain Lamb and went down into the waters of baptism, they died to sin and rose to newness of life. In baptism they
encountered God's wrath-cup poured out—poured out not on
them but on the one who at the cross drank the dregs of God's
wrath-cup and offered salvation to all who would believe.

The waters of baptism are the waters of both judgment and salvation. And washed ones are no longer victims but victors through
Jesus Christ our Lord.

Charles F. Edgar III

189

15:2

More than Conquerors

I saw what looked like a sea of glass mixed with fire and, standing beside the sea, those who had been victorious over the beast and his image and over the number of his name.

Revelation 15:2

A friend's father had been a missionary in Africa. Touring a village one day, he came upon a totem pole on the outskirts of town. "That keeps the spirits away," he was told.

"Superstition!" he thought. "I'll show them." So, he grabbed his machete and headed for the pole. He never made it. While still several yards from the totem pole, he was set upon by an invisible mob. Battered and bruised, he crawled back to safety. The pole did come down, of course, but only after much prayer.

The seven sons of Sceva had a similar experience. Trying to cast out a demon, they used an incantation they heard had worked for Paul. "'I command you by Jesus, whom Paul preaches, to come out!' . . . [T]he spirit replied, 'I know Jesus, and I know Paul. But who are you?' And he leaped on them and attacked them with such violence that they fled from the house, naked and badly injured" (Acts 19:13–16 NLT).

Evil often seems unconquerable. The amount and extent of evil in our world overwhelms us. Evil, we think, gets the final word.

But it doesn't. John saw the saints "who had been victorious" gathered at the fiery sea. In Jesus they had overcome evil. Jesus had triumphed. In the New Testament, whenever Jesus and demons met, the demons always fled. Thanks be to God!

Charles F. Edgar III

Not Poor Sports

I saw what looked like a sea of glass mixed with fire and, standing beside the sea, those who had been victorious over the beast and his image and over the number of his name. They held harps given them by God and sang the song of Moses the servant of God and the song of the Lamb.

Revelation 15:2–3

Through the record of the Revelation given to John, we have been privileged to catch glimpses of God's "behind the scenes" activity. More than any other book in the New Testament, Revelation assures us that God is in control, that in "all things God works for the good of those who love him, who have been called according to his purpose" (Rom 8:28). What more comforting word can be offered in the midst of adversity than "God is on the throne" (see Rev. 4:2)?

But let's be honest; nothing is more off-putting than a bad winner. Nothing can hurt the cause of Christ more than a believer who conveys a "holier-than-thou" attitude.

So it seems a bit odd—doesn't it?—that as seven angels prepare to carry out the final dispensation of God's wrath, the martyred saints strike up a song. How colossally inappropriate! What poor taste!

But wait; the saints are standing before baptismal waters. In those waters the wrath of God was poured out. Those baptismal waters of judgment (wherein we died) became the waters of our salvation (because we died in Christ). Eugene Peterson reminds us that "no one standing before the baptismal waters is going to be able to think of judgment exclusively as something that happens to others."[11]

We will rejoice when God avenges the evil done to his creatures and his children, but when we begin to sing the song, we will celebrate God's triumph, not our own.

Charles F. Edgar III

191

Singing the Song
of Moses and the Lamb

They held harps given them by God and sang the song of Moses the servant of God and the song of the Lamb.

Revelation 15:2–3

The people of Israel looked back at the Red Sea through which they had just come. They were safe. Pharaoh and his army, intent on recapturing them and returning them to their life of bondage, had been destroyed. God had delivered his people. And they sang (Exod. 15:1–18).

Years later, while camping on the edge of the Promised Land after forty years of wilderness wandering, an entirely new generation of Israelites waited for their instructions. And Moses sang (Deut. 32:1–43).

The saints and martyrs gather around God's throne on the shore of the fiery sea, having come through great trials. And they sing. The song is always the same (Rev. 15:3–4):

192

> Great and marvelous are your deeds,
>   Lord God Almighty.
> Just and true are your ways,
>   King of the ages.
> Who will not fear you, O Lord,
>   and bring glory to your name?
> For you alone are holy.
> All nations will come
>   and worship before you,
>   for your righteous acts have been revealed.

Our song is the same today. Standing in history between Moses and the martyrs in heaven we, too, sing the song of salvation. Moses' song foreshadowed the salvation the slain Lamb would win. The martyrs' song celebrates its consummation. We join our voices with all the company of heaven and sing praises to our God for our salvation.

May your heart be filled with a song today, as you rejoice in the salvation of our God.

Charles F. Edgar III

Great and Marvelous

They . . . sang the song of Moses the servant of God and the song of the Lamb: "Great and marvelous are your deeds, Lord God Almighty."

Revelation 15:3

As the saints and martyrs begin to sing, we note a striking omission: They never mention themselves. This may seem strange to those of us who have been weaned on contemporary hymns and praise songs: no mention at all of the noble accomplishments of the saints. The focus here is entirely on God and what he has done.

"Great and marvelous are your deeds, Lord God Almighty," sing the martyrs. And they are. Throughout history, God has never failed to work wonders on behalf of his people. No doubt the primary imagery here is the exodus, but Gideon's ragtag army, David's victory over Goliath, the return of the exiles to Jerusalem, Jesus' miraculous birth and his triumph over death, and the explosive impact of the first-century missionary movement are all examples of God's "great and marvelous deeds." They are the object of our reverence.

As John wrote Revelation to the churches of Asia Minor, he sought to inspire faithfulness in the face of persecution. What greater inspiration could there be than the great and marvelous works of God? God had delivered his people before; he could certainly be trusted to do so again.

That is the role of worship in our lives. We gather together as the people of God to focus our attention on his great and marvelous deeds. That we find ourselves strengthened for service, encouraged in hardship, emotionally uplifted—and more—is a by-product, not the goal, of worship.

Charles F. Edgar III

193

Just and True

Just and true are your ways, King of the ages.

Revelation 15:3

One of the greatest speeches in American history was delivered in one of our darkest hours. The country was at war with itself. The battles had been fierce and their toll was staggering. It was too early to tell what the outcome would be, and it was too early to tell what impact the outcome would have on a divided nation, and on the families that had been divided as well.

Abraham Lincoln had just been elected to a second term as president. In that dark and desperate hour he gave his second Inaugural Address. Lincoln may have been the greatest speechmaker in American history. If so, the explanation is that his speaking was marked by humility and simplicity. He engaged in very little political posturing, very little self-aggrandizement. He spoke only what he knew to be true, and let the truth serve as its own assurance.

"The judgments of the LORD are true and righteous altogether," President Lincoln said, quoting Psalm 19:9 (KJV). He knew that neither he, nor anyone else in America, could speak a sure word about what would happen. But he also knew that God could be trusted to do what was right.

Confidence placed in any human being or any earthly thing is misplaced. People are likely to err, to falter, to disappoint. God alone can always be trusted to do that which is just and true. His character is never capricious. Even in our darkest hour, our trust in him is never misplaced.

Charles F. Edgar III

The Worship
of the Nations

Who will not fear you, O Lord, and bring glory to your name? For you alone are holy. All nations will come and worship before you, for your righteous acts have been revealed.

Revelation 15:4

As we stood at the baptismal font on All Saints' Day 1996, I was struck by the fact that these Revelation images were coming to pass right before my eyes. Gathered together in that church, on that day, bringing themselves and their children to be welcomed into the church, was a panoply of the nations: Nigerian, French, Caribbean, Hispanic, and Euro-American.

This was always meant to be. From the first moment that God called Abram to be the father of a great nation, it was made clear that this nation was to bring blessing to all nations (Gen. 12:3). God worked through the remarkable history of a particular people to bring the unique Messiah, his only begotten Son, into the world. But the salvation that Christ Jesus won on the cross was salvation for the whole world.

195

The church's commission is to proclaim the gospel to the ends of the earth. As the gospel has gone out to the ends of the earth, God has called to himself a people. His people are rich in diversity. Members of every race and tribe and tongue and nation call upon the name of the Lord for salvation.

May we, God's people, be filled with the desire to see his mighty acts—the death, resurrection, ascension, and return of our Lord Jesus Christ in great glory—proclaimed to the ends of the earth. And may the coming of his kingdom be hastened by our witness and by our prayers.

Charles F. Edgar III

15:4

The Temple Is Open

After this I looked and in heaven the temple, that is the tabernacle of the Testimony, was opened.

Revelation 15:5

God maintained a distance from his people for a long time. This began during their journey from Egypt to the Promised Land, when he called the people to meet with him on Mount Sinai, but they were afraid.

He had intended that they would be a kingdom of priests, but after their reticence to meet him, they became a kingdom with priests. And only the priests could enter God's presence and mediate between God and his people.

All this changed, of course, on that first Good Friday. When Jesus breathed his last, the gospel writers attest, the veil of the temple, which symbolized the separation of God from his people for nearly two thousand years, was torn in two. The work of atonement was done. We who were once far away were now brought near by the blood of the Lamb. No longer do we need priests to intercede for us. We are again a royal priesthood.

Even in the midst of this awe-inspiring chapter of Revelation, where the judgment of God is about to be meted out, we are reminded that the temple is still open. This knowledge calms our hearts and renews our confidence.

The work that Jesus accomplished on the cross is final. Nothing can ever separate us again from the love of God that is in Christ Jesus our Lord (Rom. 8:31). Even in the darkest hour, the temple is open.

Then let us draw near in faith.

Charles F. Edgar III

196

Vested Angels
and Golden Bowls

Out of the temple came the seven angels with the seven plagues. They were dressed in clean, shining linen and wore golden sashes around their chests. Then one of the four living creatures gave to the seven angels seven golden bowls filled with the wrath of God, who lives for ever and ever.

Revelation 15:6–7

In the Anglican tradition, and in all the churches that emerge from the catholic liturgical tradition, vestments are worn to symbolize holiness and righteousness—not the holiness or the righteousness of the wearer but the holiness and righteousness of God, covering the wearer, as the blood of Christ covers and makes us clean before God.

Gold, too, symbolizes purity. Many churches in our traditions are filled with golden objects, much like the tabernacle and the temple were filled with gold during the time of the Old Testament.

Vestments and gold, combined together in this heavenly scene, serve to illustrate the righteousness and holiness of God's wrath. God's anger over sin and its effects is pure and right. God is not vindictive or arbitrary. God does not get angry over petty matters. God is gracious, slow to anger, and of great kindness. If his wrath has been kindled, we know there is good reason. His judgment is always just and true, and his offer of mercy always precedes his judgment.

Perhaps we fear our own wrath and anger because they are not always—perhaps only rarely—justified. We dare not clothe our wrath in vestments or surround it with objects of gold. But we can always rest certain in the knowledge that God is never angry at those who come to him in faith. We can rest assured, too, that his wrath is kindled only against belligerent evil. Only those who refuse to acknowledge him and his mighty acts of salvation have cause for worry. All who call upon the name of the Lord, however, will be saved.

Charles F. Edgar III

197

Holy Smoke!

The temple was filled with smoke from the glory of God and from his power.

Revelation 15:8

The Chapel of St. Mary the Virgin at Nashotah House Theological Seminary sits nestled in the middle of Wisconsin's cornfields just outside Delafield. It is a lovely place, and, upon entering, one's senses are overwhelmed by the aroma of holiness. But what is that smell?

Throughout the biblical story, God's presence among his people was made manifest through the powerful symbol of smoke. He led the children of Israel through the wilderness with a pillar of smoke. The holy Mount Sinai shook and was covered with smoke when Moses received the Law. The high priest ventured carefully and cautiously into the smoke-filled Holy of Holies on Yom Kippur. When the prophet Isaiah saw the Lord high and lifted up, the temple was filled with smoke.

The people's worship of God also was always accompanied by large quantities of smoke. The altar of incense billowed smoke every morning. The temple courtyard became filled with smoke as burnt offerings and sin offerings were sacrificed to God. Smoke and holiness, smoke and glory, smoke and power, they are intertwined throughout the biblical story. They are here again, as God makes ready the final display of his righteous majesty.

As one enters the Chapel of St. Mary the Virgin, it is the aroma of incense—the lingering effect of smoke absorbed by the varnish on the wood—that palpably conveys the mystery of God's majesty.

Let us offer our lives to God, a sweet-smelling sacrifice of praise and thanksgiving, today and every day.

Charles F. Edgar III

198

When Bad News
Turns Out Good!

Then I heard a loud voice from the temple saying to the seven angels, "Go, pour out the seven bowls of God's wrath on the earth."

Revelation 16:1

When can bad news possibly be good news? Can the news of something that ties your stomach in knots ever be something that makes you shout for joy?

If you are a believer in and follower of Jesus, the answer is a resounding "YES!"

Think about the paradox of the Christian faith. We worship a God who became human. The symbol of our faith is an instrument of capital punishment. Weaknesses are strengths. Death is life. To believe is to see, not the other way around.

So even bad news can be good news, when our faith is firmly rooted in Jesus. The Jewish people came to learn this through their exile to Babylon. Habakkuk told them that defeat was coming (there's the bad news), but they discovered a renewed faith in God in Babylon (there's the good news).

199

To discover that God has a wrathful side cannot be good news to many people. And for the command to pour the "bowls" of his wrath on the earth to be called good news is a stretch.

But it is, or at worst, can be, good news. It means that God is at work and that he is working his purposes out. It means, in a nutshell, that he is beginning the process of drawing things to a close. So while it is bad news immediately, ultimately, it is good news.

The next time someone passes bad news on to you, don't despair. Remember, "he who began a good work in you will carry it on to completion until the day of Christ Jesus" (Phil. 1:6).

Charles W. Roberts

The Face Gives
It Away Every Time

The first angel went and poured out his bowl on the land, and ugly and painful sores broke out on the people who had the mark of the beast and worshiped his image.

Revelation 16:2

I was leading a Bible study with the high school youth group in our church and had made the fatal mistake of asking them what they wanted to study. As anyone who has ever spent time with that age group will tell you, they will always ask to study Revelation.

We were meeting in a local café, gathered in the back room, eating, reading, and discussing. We looked at Revelation 16:2 and were thinking about what it meant.

"Zits!" one boy yelled.

"What?" I asked, trying to make sense of his outburst.

"It's zits," he said. "The sores are zits! We all worship the beast!" And then he started laughing, and everyone joined in.

But it points out the reality that, if we wanted to, we could force our chosen meaning into nearly every verse. That's not what God wants. Rather, he wants us to understand every verse for his sake and our good.

A dermatologist will tell you that your face will give away what you eat and what your life is like.

Pastors can often tell from the look on a person's face during a worship service if they love the Lord or not. It's not the sores or the mark of the beast that gives one away, or even "zits." It depends on the overwhelming love of God. The love shines through every time.

Has that love been allowed to claim you? If it has, it will change the look on your face.

As the old bumper sticker says, "Smile if you love Jesus!"

Charles W. Roberts

Saintly Blood
Is in Your Veins

*For they have shed the blood of your saints and prophets, and you have
given them blood to drink as they deserve.*

Revelation 16:6

Her name was Cassie, and her story has been told thousands of times. Cassie was a student at Columbine High School in Littleton, Colorado, the day two of her classmates went on a rampage, killing many students and wounding others.

As the story is told, Cassie had come to know Christ as her Lord and Savior about a year before. That relationship had transformed her life. The day of the shooting, she was cornered by one of the killers, who pointed his gun at her.

"Do you believe in God?" he asked.

After a brief pause, she said, "Yes!" The gunman pulled the trigger. Cassie died as the word escaped her mouth.[12]

Avoiding here the arguments about gun control, capital punishment, school safety, and the eternal destiny of the two shooters, think instead about that simple phrase, "the blood of the saints and prophets."

How would you have answered the question Cassie answered?

The biblical word "saint" literally means, "one who has been made holy." It does not describe something you have done, or something you hope to be. It describes who you are because of the work of Jesus in your life. So if you have received the Lord in your life, in biblical terms, you are a saint!

Now, don't let that go to your head. Instead, give thanks to God. And know that a life lived in faithful response and service to God will always be honored by the Lord.

Do you believe in God?

Charles W. Roberts

God's Judgments
Are Always True

And I heard the altar respond: "Yes, Lord God Almighty, true and just are your judgments."

Revelation 16:7

"I just believe that the redeemed, and loved, and forgiven people make healthy choices," the speaker said. He sounded sincere, honest, and real.

Yet he was living a lie that caught up with him. He self-destructed. Having lost one marriage to an affair, he was now remarried and entwined in another affair—all this while he claimed to be redeemed, loved, forgiven, and therefore making healthy choices. When the affair became obvious and he confessed it, his second marriage became history.

Too often, we experience the Word of God as something that is restrictive. We do not like being told what to do, or more often, what *not* to do. We want to live life the way we want to and have no outside interference, especially from God.

202

God's judgments, however, are always true and just, even the ones that hurt us. His command to avoid extramarital sex is not to restrict us but to give us freedom and safety within marriage. When we break his laws, we experience his judgment. We resent that, but it is right, and just, and true.

On the other hand, if we obey his laws, we experience the good side of God's judgment. He blesses us and we are protected. His judgments are just and true all over again.

Are you on the good side, or the bad side, of God's judgments? Make sure you live on the good side, today and every day!

Charles W. Roberts

Going for a Good Burn

The fourth angel poured out his bowl on the sun, and the sun was given power to scorch people with fire.

Revelation 16:8

Some people say this verse prophesies the depletion of the ozone layer in the last days. For them, it is evidence that Jesus' return is just around the corner. Some ecologists interpret this verse to support their programs, calling us to stop using aerosols. It is not unusual for people to use the Bible to promote their own causes.

The purpose of the Bible, however, is not to give us ammunition for our pet causes but to give God a medium to get his message across to us and promote his purposes in our lives.

Today's verse says in plain and simple terms that the sun can burn you. Maybe this is God's way of telling us to use sunscreen. More likely, this verse, and all the others that precede it and follow it, is trying to get us to let God's love burn us from the inside out. In short, God desires to set us on fire for his Son, Jesus.

Jeremiah said that if he did not preach, even his bones would burn within him. John Calvin, the great reformer of the church, looked for a "heart on fire for Christ." They both understood that God wants people who are so devoted to him that their hearts burn with passion to serve him.

One thing is certain: If that is our desire too, we won't have to worry about the bowls of God's wrath. They will still be poured out. But for eternity, we will be secure.

Charles W. Roberts

203

16:8

Hardened Hearts

They were seared by the intense heat and they cursed the name of God, who had control over these plagues, but they refused to repent and glorify him.

Revelation 16:9

John Douglas is a former FBI agent. A brilliant man, he investigated serial crimes, and was the man who began to use psychological profiling to be able to identify and apprehend criminals. In one of his books, he reflects on the people he has arrested and studied. Somewhere along the way, he suggests, these people made a conscious choice to commit their crimes. It was not something they had no control over; it was a decision they made.

The last phrase of Revelation 16:9 is a haunting one. "They refused to repent and glorify him." It tells us that there are people who are simply unwilling to let God have his way in them. They make a conscious choice to do evil, even when faced with the consequences of their choices. It's hard to believe, but it is true.

It has happened for generations. Remember Pharaoh, when Moses went to him, asking for the release of the Hebrews? The Bible says his heart was hardened (see Exod. 7:13). He refused to let God be God. Later, when he relented and set the Hebrews free, he changed his mind, and sent his soldiers to kill them. In other words, he "refused to repent."

To make this personal, ask yourself a simple question. Is there something in your life that you know is outside the will of God, but you refuse to repent of it? Do you realize you deny yourself immeasurable blessings? You may not curse the name of God, but you know that your life is not what it could be.

Do the right thing today. Repent!

Charles W. Roberts

204

This Little
Light of Mine

The fifth angel poured out his bowl on the throne of the beast, and his king-
dom was plunged into darkness. Men gnawed their tongues in agony and
cursed the God of heaven because of their pains and their sores, but they
refused to repent of what they had done.

Revelation 16:10–11

It would be hard to find someone who does not think that the world in which we live is a dark world. With rampant corruption everywhere one looks, and school shootings endangering what once was a safe place, it is a dark world everywhere we turn.

In our church last Christmas, something interesting happened at the midnight candlelight service. The light from the Christ candle in the Advent wreath was passed to candles held by young people. They, in turn, passed the light to the candles of people in the pews. We had done this before, and everyone knew how the dark sanctuary became light again, filled with the light of the candles. This year, however, something different happened.

With most people holding their lighted candle in their laps, I asked the congregation to raise their candles as high as they could. Suddenly, the room became even brighter. The result surprised many of us.

The implication is obvious, I hope. If we keep the light of Christ down, its full impact is unseen by the dark world. If we keep it low in our life, far down on the list of our priorities, it helps, but not a lot. Conversely, if we hold Christ high in our lives, his light not only illuminates our life, but it also brightens and dissipates the darkness that surrounds us.

As the old saying goes, better to light a candle than to curse the darkness. Hold Christ's light high in your life that this dark world may see it clearly today!

Charles W. Roberts

205

The Test of Faith

*They are spirits of demons performing miraculous signs, and they go out to
the kings of the whole world, to gather them for the battle on the great day
of God Almighty.*

Revelation 16:14

Many churches claim to have a monopoly on truth. They say they
are the only right church. According to them, they are the only
one with all the right answers. All this is nothing new.

Revelation 16:14 speaks to us when we encounter a church like
that. It reminds us that not everyone is genuine about his or her
profession.

Many things happen in the name of God that may not be from
him. The Bible tells us plainly that some miraculous things are
deceptions, meant to draw us away from the true God.

A day is coming for which Christians have looked for the last
two thousand years, and will continue to look for as long as it
lingers. That day is the great battle that will result in the culmination of history. Tomorrow? Maybe, but one never knows.
Another two thousand years? Maybe. We simply do not know
when the day will come.

One thing we do know: Throughout history, miraculous signs
have been done, and not all by the power of God. Today's passage
reminds us that there are some false teachers in the world whose
ultimate goal is to pull us away from God and his Son, Jesus.

This makes it all the more important that we read the Bible and
pray for discernment in everything related to worship. The early
church's test was whether someone professed Jesus as Lord in
word and in life. That is still the best test. Are those people who
do miraculous works near you living as though Jesus is their Lord?
Are you?

Charles W. Roberts

Prepared for a Surprise

Behold, I come like a thief! Blessed is he who stays awake and keeps his clothes with him, so that he may not go naked and be shamefully exposed.

Revelation 16:15

If you were told that someone was going to break into your house on a certain night, at a certain time, odds are you would be ready and waiting. You would have police officers in your house with you to arrest the thief. You would have moved your family to a safe location. Simply put, you'd be prepared for the criminal's arrival.

Yet, almost all the time, thieves come unexpectedly. That is how Jesus portrays his return. He will come like a thief, at a time when we are not anticipating his arrival. It's not that he will come like a thief and take something away. He will come, and we will be surprised.

The lesson to be learned from this is clear: We have to be ready at all times for Jesus' return. Like a homeowner on a street where his is the only house not already burglarized, the mentality is, "It's not if, but when." A wise homeowner in such a circumstance would be constantly ready to be the next house robbed.

We are called to constant vigilance, to be prepared for the return of our Lord. He *will* come again. It's not a matter of if, but when. This verse calls us to live in a state of constant readiness for Jesus' return. Through prayer, regular worship, and reading God's Word, we make ourselves ready so that when the great day comes we may be surprised, but not caught off guard.

Charles W. Roberts

16:15

Keep Your
Clothes with You

"Behold, I come like a thief! Blessed is he who stays awake and keeps his clothes with him, so that he may not go naked and be shamefully exposed."

Revelation 16:15

The verse we look at again today suggests that when Jesus returns, we need to make sure that we are clothed with the right things. The language offers the imagery of not doing anything that would bring shame to us upon his return. Since we do not know when that will be, we must live lives of moral purity.

The Bible often uses the word "clothing" or its derivatives as an encouragement to be endowed with the right characteristics and qualities. Colossians 3:12 urges Christians to "clothe [the Greek verb literally means 'get dressed'] yourselves with compassion, kindness, humility, gentleness and patience." These are not pieces of clothing but relational characteristics we are to demonstrate towards other people. You will notice that Scripture makes no distinction about whether the others are Christians.

208

Staying awake and keeping your clothes with you does not mean that we never sleep or change clothes until Jesus' return. It does mean that we are called to be aware of what is going on around us, as Christians, and that we are to allow the grace of Jesus to shine through every relationship.

Charles W. Roberts

Where Battles Are Won

Then they gathered the kings together to the place that in Hebrew is called Armageddon.

Revelation 16:16

Armageddon!

It's a name that conjures up many images, isn't it? From cataclysmic battles on earth to cosmic struggles to determine who will win the ultimate battle between good and evil; this word gets our attention. It is also a word that is largely misunderstood and twisted. In the early 1990s, some doomsday prophets thought that, because of its location, the Persian Gulf War was the staging for Armageddon. Time proved that theory wrong.

Revelation says much about life and even more about the life of faith in Jesus Christ. As Christians, when we hear the name *Armageddon,* rather than get upset or frightened, we should find comfort in it.

Whatever transpires in that place, and whenever it happens, it will all fall under God's eternal sovereignty. The Creator of the universe has it all under his control. What's more, he already has the victory. Christ's cross and empty tomb are his war-winning weapons.

What we can do now is trust God. That is all! God is in charge. You can trust him to take care of you in every battle!

Perhaps you respond, "I do trust God, but. . . ." There is no "but" in connection with authentic trust. True trust is absolute. It is based on our conviction that if God is worth trusting for the next life, he is worth trusting for this life also. Whether the battle of Armageddon occurs tomorrow or two thousand years from now, we can rest secure in God. On his cross and through his resurrection victory, Jesus has already overcome the powers of evil. Through that, God's victory is assured for all eternity.

Charles W. Roberts

209

Earthquakes
Are Unsettling

Then there came flashes of lightning, rumblings, peals of thunder and a severe earthquake. No earthquake like it has ever occurred since man has been on earth, so tremendous was the quake.

Revelation 16:18

It's a pun, but it's true: Earthquakes are an unsettling experience! I learned that lesson in college. While I was eating supper in a third-floor cafeteria, the table started shaking. Some people screamed, but it did no good. For a moment, the entire building shuddered and no one could control it!

Later that evening I learned that our school was built on a fault line. That earthquake was relatively minor (just 4.5 on the Richter scale), but it left me with a profound sense of what it means to lose control.

Do you think you are in control of your life? One of the messages of the earthquake John sees in Revelation is that people are never in control of things in this universe. Life earthquakes, whether real earthquakes or unsettling experiences that enter our lives unexpectedly, demonstrate just how little control we do have. John, however, learns that God always is in control of this world's happenings.

The best way to control your life is to surrender it to God through his Son, Jesus, who said, "Whoever wants to save [or control] his life will lose it, but whoever loses his life for me and for the gospel will save it" (Mark 8:35). This God who is in control of the universe will take control of your life, too, if you will invite him.

Have you invited God to take control of your life? Have you asked him to take charge of today's circumstances and schedule? Do it now and see how much better life becomes when God is in control!

Charles W. Roberts

210

Jealous but Patient

*One of the seven angels who had the seven bowls came and said to me,
"Come, I will show you the punishment of the great prostitute, who sits on
many waters. With her the kings of the earth committed adultery and the
inhabitants of the earth were intoxicated with the wine of her adulteries."*

Revelation 17:1–2

Marriage is one place where physical intimacy is heralded by God.
It is the proper and sacred place for fleshly desire and covenant
love to dance in ecstasy. God has willed and created marriage to
be so. In its purity, the intimacy enjoyed in the growing love and
desire between husband and wife is probably the closest a man
and a woman will ever come to experiencing the joy of heaven
without leaving this earth.

Over and over again, the Old Testament describes God's relationship with Israel in the metaphor of marriage. The God of Abraham, Isaac, Jacob, and Joseph is a jealous God who wooed his
spouse out of Egypt and established an everlasting covenant. Yahweh and Israel: together forever, and a blessing to all nations.

But unfaithful Israel spurned her spouse. She preferred the intimacy of false gods, and the close companionship of wooden or
stone idols. She laid with others in shame, and danced to the hal-
lucinating tune of earthly ecstasy. Israel searched for joy, but found
only instant gratification and humiliation as an abused creature.
God's jealousy burned, and God's heart ached. Yet, in that pain
and jealousy, patience rose from within Yahweh's heart, produc-
ing a great desire to restore the lost intimacy. For God, it was a
love to die for. The nations of the world have been blessed because
of this great redeeming love, whether they know it or not.

Listen carefully, for God is calling. With whom does your heart
rest tonight?

Roger L. Steiner

211

Let's Get Carried Away

Then the angel carried me away in the Spirit into a desert.

Revelation 17:3a

Joseph interpreted dreams. We are not Joseph. John of Patmos recorded visions. We are not John of Patmos. But even though we are neither Joseph nor John, God gives us dreams and visions in the quieter moments of life. They are the supporting strength for the busyness of today, and the hope of our tomorrow.

Our present builds on foundational visions and dreams of the past. By grace, God made us partners in the ongoing work of creation through the revelations and revolutions of our minds. Together we experiment, create, manufacture, build, and, in some cases, destroy our way into the future. Together we fulfill the destiny of dominion over all the earth, pushing and being pushed to the outer and inner limits of human capabilities. To go beyond those limits is to court death. It is to dare to touch the hem of God's royal robe with dirty fingers, or to look upon the fullness of God's face without proper respect. Only in sacramental worship does God establish proper bounds for such longing and intimacy.

212

We can get carried away in our domination of the world and nature, but it pales in comparison to being swept off our feet in the free-flowing winds of dreams and visions of the Spirit. Compare it to the exhilaration and liberation of stepping naked from a pool of water into a stiff, cool breeze. Birth. Baptism. The genesis of a new creation. Our visions and dreams are the stuff of life begun in the heart and mind of the One whose Spirit moved over the face of the churning waters and spoke us into being.

So, let's get carried away!

Roger L. Steiner

True Wealth

The woman was dressed in purple and scarlet, and was glittering with gold, precious stones and pearls. She held a golden cup in her hand, filled with abominable things and the filth of her adulteries.

Revelation 17:4

Wealth. On the one hand, it is the reward of fruitful living. Unfortunately, many devote their lives to the pursuit of gold and jewels and pearls. Kings and queens of private kingdoms, these self-ordained priests of mammon surround themselves with glitz and glitter so everyone will notice them. They are walking showrooms for the ritzy citadels of commerce. Opulence radiates from their clothes and cars and jewelry, commanding an aura of respect built on worldly terms and conditions. Forget about the other guy or gal.

On the other hand, Jesus teaches us that true wealth comes through our investments in human relationships. As we lose our life for the sake of his gospel, we gain it. When we sacrifice our own good for the good of another, the tears of joy and the hugs from a new friend display God's storehouse of love and grace. This, Jesus says, is greater than all the wealth of the world put together in one place. To take this analogy seriously is to realize that the whole world is ours, including its wealth, because God first gave it to us. God invested in us and called us to wise stewardship. To cut up the wealth of creation into parcels, giving most to a few and a little to the rest, is not gospel.

Thus the overindulgence of the woman completes the anti-gospel vision for us. She is the object of God's jealous rage unveiled before us. Look upon this idolatry, but beware of its power to lure you away from God.

Roger L. Steiner

213

Revealed Mystery

This title was written on her forehead: MYSTERY, BABYLON THE GREAT, THE MOTHER OF PROSTITUTES AND OF THE ABOMINATIONS OF THE EARTH.

Revelation 17:5

Many people like a good mystery book. In such a story, clues are revealed throughout, and then tied together in the end for proper resolution. The reader is often surprised by the solution because of missing or misinterpreted clues along the way.

Our journey of faith is a mystery, which will some day be fully revealed. Paul says in 1 Corinthians 13:12: "Now we see but a poor reflection as in a mirror; then we shall see face to face. Now I know in part; then I shall know fully, even as I am fully known." Like teenagers swimming the rapids of physical, spiritual, and emotional identity, so is the life of the person bearing the cross of Christ and waiting for his coming again. We receive only bits and pieces of insight and vision from God. Some of us may or may not be pleasantly surprised by the final outcome, because we may have missed or misinterpreted clues along the way.

Revealing the mother of prostitutes and of earth's abominations puts our lives in greater perspective. That is to say, we can be thankful that God is mindful of us, even in the midst of the larger dilemma of sin and evil (Ps. 18). And whereas we have clues to our future glory in Christ, the mother of prostitutes is clueless for what awaits her.

Roger L. Steiner

214

Blood
of the Overcomers

*I saw that the woman was drunk with the blood of the saints, the blood of
those who bore testimony to Jesus. When I saw her, I was greatly astonished.*

Revelation 17:6

The traditional Inuit preparation to catch a wolf is amazing. The
hunter takes a razor-sharp knife, dips it in blood, and lets it freeze.
He repeats this procedure of dipping and freezing several times,
until the knife has a thick enough coating to hide the blade. When
ready, he sticks the knife in the ground with the blade up. The
wolf smells the blood and begins licking. Soon its tongue is sliced,
and, not knowing the difference between its own blood and the
blood on the knife, the wolf licks in a more frenzied manner, only
to slice its tongue further. Eventually, the wolf bleeds to death.

The woman drunk with the blood of the faithful saints is indeed
an astonishing sight. To understand this vision is to understand
the suffering and death of the countless multitudes of saints
throughout the ages. Many have willingly died for Christ at the
hands of oppressive or indifferent governments. In their frenzied
thirst for more power, the world's courts and gallows prey upon
the seemingly weak and humble Christians, accusing them of being
troublemakers and revolutionaries.

But the razor-sharp sword of the Spirit is neatly hidden in the
testimony to Jesus. As each Christian faithfully bears witness to
the risen Christ in word and deed, dying in many ways for the
world's salvation, the power and authority of God's kingdom is
strengthened. The woman may be drunk with the blood of the
saints now, but one day it will be her undoing.

Pray for perseverance in faithful testimony and in seeking justice.

Roger L. Steiner

The Trick Candle

*The beast, which you saw, once was, now is not, and will come up out of
the Abyss and go to his destruction. The inhabitants of the earth whose
names have not been written in the book of life from the creation of the
world will be astonished when they see the beast, because he once was, now
is not, and yet will come.*

Revelation 17:8

Trick candles are fun at younger ages. Older persons short on
breath find them a cruel joke. Blowing them out just to have them
come to life again frustrates even the most patient person.

Like a trick candle, evil (the beast) persists. It was, is not, and
is about to ascend. Satan pops up at the least expected times,
wreaks havoc, then disappears. We never see his coming, just his
departure. By that time, our hands are dirty and guilt wraps around
our hearts. Children unknowingly have fun in this way, at least
until punished, while older people find Satan to be a constantly
cruel joke.

So how is a trick candle finally extinguished? You wet it or pinch
it. Pinching it could get you burned if you're not careful. Therefore, the safest way to deal with a trick candle is to smother it in
water.

But rather than soaking Satan, God drowns us to protect us
from the smoldering wrath of the beast. We are baptized in the
cool refreshing waters of true life. Even so, this does not guarantee complete safety. Our call is to return daily to the river of life
in Christ Jesus. There our daily sin is washed away, even as we
learn obedience and love at the foot of the cross. Without this daily
attentiveness to God and the Word made flesh, we will find ourselves short on breath in the race against time and the devil.

Satan might be like a trick candle. But with God, we have the
last laugh for all eternity. Let us praise the One who was, who is,
and who is to come.

Roger L. Steiner

216

The Cup of
Wisdom Is Never Full

This calls for a mind with wisdom.

Revelation 17:9a

Wisdom comes from our experience of life. It is born and bred through our encounters with people, events, and the natural wonders surrounding us. A farmer breeds wisdom much differently from the city dweller. First graders see the world in a much different light than senior citizens. Each positive or negative experience adds to our collective wisdom, combining it with ideas and beliefs for a worldview unique to each of us. This worldview motivates us to act in certain ways.

A mind that has wisdom is open to new possibilities and impossibilities. It has the ability to think, and to perceive what is and is not true. Indeed, the mind that has wisdom hungers for God to reveal the wonders of creation and life. Abraham and Moses, David and Elijah, Mary and Paul, and countless others have all grown in wisdom because they were open to the words of angels and prophets and God.

Surfing the Internet or flipping through channels can stimulate thought. But we gain wisdom elsewhere: in the street, in the barn, at school, in the factory, sitting at the coffee counter in the local donut shop, kneeling at the altar rail.

Where might God be revealing life to you, so that you may gain wisdom and insight about creation, life, and salvation? Is your mind open or closed to new possibilities or impossibilities? Surely your cup of wisdom is not yet filled.

Roger L. Steiner

In Defense of Rome

The seven heads are seven hills on which the woman sits.

Revelation 17:9b

Seven is a good biblical number, standing beside ten and twelve as a number of perfection or wholeness. Add to this the image of the mountain as God's place of revelation: Sinai, Horeb, Zion, and the Mount of Transfiguration. Taken together, "seven hills" intimates yet another direction from which God battles the anarchy of chaos.

A city of history and culture, Rome sits on seven hills. Readers of the Revelation would have known this.

Rome crafted an empire of roads and aqueducts dedicated to uniting and ordering the then known world. Its stability brought peace and tolerance, allowing growth in education and commerce. Could it be that as the world's superpower, Rome was of God's making, so the message of salvation in Christ Jesus could be spread easily?

218

Yes, Rome could very well have been an instrument of God's peace. In fact, Paul's letter to the Romans highlights the importance of government in ordering creation, so long as it does not claim for itself the place of God. Whether Roman authorities acknowledged it or not, they served the living God by providing for the needs of their citizens and promoting peace and tolerance. In this environment, the seed of the Word sprouted and grew.

In this third millennium of Christ's reign on earth, let us pray for the present governments of the seven continents, sitting on the seven seas, that they will fulfill the purposes of God by maintaining peace and order, so that the Word may be spread.

Roger L. Steiner

The Victorious Lamb

They will make war against the Lamb, but the Lamb will overcome them because he is Lord of lords and King of kings—and with him will be his called, chosen, and faithful followers.

Revelation 17:14

War exists because evil exists. Evil likes power—corrupt power. It attaches itself like a leech and sucks the lifeblood out of one originally created good. Unchecked, it abuses and dominates in its own twisted way, slowly killing its unwary victim.

In the massive halls of government, evil anchors itself for a feeding frenzy. Power and glory are sweet nectars to a godlike thirst. Never assuaged, the system seeks ways to survive and grow. The "what is" of the status quo is perpetuated under the guise of political correctness and secularism. Taxes support the addicting habit, while war machinery are the toys and tools of force and destruction. The environment is ripe for the subtle tyrant of evil to breed corruption, and to try winning a war already over.

But who has won? The Lamb of God, who is Lord of lords and King of kings, has won. Plowshares are his tools to feed a hungry world. Humility, self-sacrifice, service, and love are his trademarks to build the individual. His innocence and truth bled freely on the cross, winning the prize of salvation for all who trust and believe in him. The throne is Christ's. He alone is worthy of perpetual worship and adoration. Christ, the Lamb of God, is God's response to evil. Thanks be to God for the victory!

Roger L. Steiner

219

We Are in This Together

Then the angel said to me, "The waters you saw, where the prostitute sits, are peoples, multitudes, nations and languages."

Revelation 17:15

The earth is a living organism of enormous complexity. Each person, animal, plant, mineral, or substance exists and interacts according to its nature as created by God. The fun of biology class rests in learning plant and animal categories, food chains, and interrelated systems of living. The joy of faith is acknowledging everything as the handiwork of God. Unfortunately, many people unwisely think they understand this complexity, so ecosystems and rainforests are indiscriminately destroyed, and the long-term effects remain a mystery or are ignored.

All relationships, good or bad, intertwine into one fabric called "life on earth." This reality is inescapable. Revelation 17:15 ties us all to the abominations of the prostitute who sits over the multitudes. Her power far surpasses ours, dominating the landscape. She represents the overarching system that governs all people in the world, unchecked and seemingly invincible.

Now this is a scary thought: No individual can tear down or destroy this abomination. Why not? Because by complacency, indifference, or weariness we have already contributed to the power and the abominations of this prostitute. There are no innocent bystanders. Together, we build this image of Revelation 17:15, and God is the only one who can shatter it.

Thanks and praise be to God whose kingdom and power and authority are greater than that which overshadows our existence. Let us worship God who alone sits on the throne of eternal truth and salvation.

Roger L. Steiner

220

Nothing Lasts Forever

The beast and the ten horns you saw will hate the prostitute. They will bring her to ruin and leave her naked; they will eat her flesh and burn her with fire.

Revelation 17:16

"Nothing lasts forever" is a flippant phrase. Easier said than believed, particularly for those suffering injustice, it has caused us to tolerate many abuses throughout the ages. But rape victims never totally overcome the fear and indignation from their trauma. Government-sanctioned torture affects a nation's conscience. Even a young child's untimely death imprisons loving parents in unresolved grief. To say that "nothing lasts forever" is a form of comfort may actually be a slap in the face.

However, the vision and promise revealed through John is that nothing lasts forever except God's reign. Easier said than believed because we suffer in various ways on earth, this Scripture clearly establishes hope. This hope does not disappoint us, as Paul writes in Romans 5:5. In fact, this hope enables us to press on toward our heavenly goal, despite any injustice we experience.

At the same time, we should not forget another source of hope for the future: the promise of Holy Baptism, when God forgives sin and claims you as his child, making you an inheritor of eternal life. That is to say, the power and grace of God allow the true believer to participate *now* in the eternal kingdom of heaven, by faith in the risen Christ.

Reminiscent of Moses long ago (Deut. 30:11–20), this passage challenges us to choose whom to follow: the abominations of this world, which will ultimately be destroyed, or God, who gives freely the gift of eternal life to all who believe. This really is a "no brainer."

Roger L. Steiner

221

God's Will Is Done

For God has put it into their hearts to accomplish his purpose by agreeing to give the beast their power to rule, until God's words are fulfilled.

Revelation 17:17

A force exists in the universe upon which all is centered. It is a truth permeating the outer boundaries of space and plumbing the depths of our souls' inner sanctums. Good and evil surround this magnetic spectrum in varying degrees of obedience and choice. Where we lie depends upon our faith in the Son of God, who sits on the throne.

All that exists must eventually submit to this truth, willingly or unwillingly. The beast, the governments, the people, the animals, the stars, the planets, and everything else we could ever imagine or think of must ultimately bow down before the throne of God. God (who was, who is, and who is to come) is the author and giver of life. The Almighty gave Christ "the keys of death and Hades" as "the Living One" who once was dead but is now alive forever and ever (Rev. 1:18). Nothing of spiritual or physical substance can exist apart from this reality.

In the beginning was God's will, and in the end it will be God's will that continues to rule and govern. All that is necessary for this to happen has happened in Jesus. His death and resurrection have sealed this reign and authority forever. What joy is ours in the precious thought that evil will not ultimately triumph! What joy will be ours in the fulfillment of revelation when God lays the final living stone in the kingdom of heaven! Until then, let us wait patiently, focusing on him who is our salvation, Jesus Christ our Lord. Amen.

Roger L. Steiner

Holy, Holy, Holy!
Lord God Almighty!

After this I saw another angel coming down from heaven. He had great authority, and the earth was illuminated by his splendor. With a mighty voice he shouted: "Fallen! Fallen is Babylon the Great!"

Revelation 18:1–2

The judgment of Babylon reminds us of God's majestic and awesome holiness. God will not allow sin to go unpunished. God's people are to reflect his holiness, and are therefore to avoid the lifestyle and sins characteristic of Babylon's inhabitants. Christians are a called-out, chosen people, a holy people set apart for God and his love to use to change the world.

Babylon was the greatest city that was ever built. In fact, it was so marvelous that for centuries it was considered to be fictitious. Scholars proclaimed that a place with hanging gardens rising four hundred feet, the tower of Babel, and huge walls fourteen miles long on each side was all fable and myth.

In 1899, Robert Koldewey uncovered Babylon! For fourteen years, he and thousands of workers labored to uncover a portion of the wall of Babylon. As majestic as she was, God declared in Jeremiah 51:37, "See, I will stir up the spirit of a destroyer against Babylon and the people of Leb Kamai."

One day, God will call the world, which is attempting to live without him, to account for herself. The judgment will be harsh, in line with God's hatred of sin. Destruction is the price that one pays for rebellion.

The words of this great hymn of the church remind us of God's holiness.

Holy, holy, holy! Though the darkness hide Thee,
Though the eye of sinful man Thy glory may not see;
Only Thou art holy—there is none beside Thee,
Perfect in pow'r, in love and purity.

Reginald Heber, 1826

William M. Flannagan

Rescue the Perishing

Fallen! Fallen is Babylon the Great! She has become a home for demons and a haunt for every evil spirit, a haunt for every unclean and detestable bird. For all the nations have drunk the maddening wine of her adulteries.

Revelation 18:2–3

When we attempt to function apart from God, divine judgment is the only possible outcome. Regardless of our possessions, status, or accomplishments, God wants us to acknowledge him and recognize that he is the only sustaining presence in the world.

Babylon, the jewel of the ancient world, was a city dripping with arrogance. Excavations revealed that Babylon's walls were 136 feet thick and 350 feet high. The gold-plated buildings of the city of Babylon could be seen over the walls, gleaming in the sunlight. The main city gate was an arch 630 feet tall. It was the most massive city of its time.

Babylon's evil influences spread worldwide, causing nations, kings, and merchants to fall into her beguiling trap of godless materialism, humanism, and infidelity. We should never forget that materialism is the central aspect of this ancient destruction of Babylon.

God so utterly destroyed the city of Babylon that, for centuries, it was not even thought to have existed. Now, the oldest part of Babylon has sunk beneath the river, while the rest of it lies in total desolation, inhabited by scorpions, snakes, and scavenging birds.

In spite of the impending judgment of God, he still faithfully offers his salvation to all those who repent.

Rescue the perishing, care for the dying,
Snatch them in pity from sin and the grave;
Weep o'er the erring one; lift up the fallen,
Tell them of Jesus, the mighty to save.

Fanny J. Crosby, 1869

William M. Flannagan

We Are God's People

Then I heard another voice from heaven say: "Come out of her, my people,
so that you will not share in her sins, so that you will not receive any of her
plagues; for her sins are piled up to heaven, and God has remembered her
crimes."

Revelation 18:4–5

This voice from heaven, which calls God's people to come out of Babylon, is evidently the voice of Jesus calling to "my people." He does not want his people partaking in the sinful indulgences and self-gratification of the Babylonians.

Babylon's iniquity grew over a period of time. It eventually became the world center for occultism and wickedness. It was demon controlled, and the city became a haven for astrology, witchcraft, and a multitude of satanic indulgences. Her influences spread to many other nations and rulers.

The fall into sin is more often gradual than instantaneous. Many people in our generation have drifted into immoral behavior. Slowly, but surely, a plague of immorality and lawlessness has gradually infected us, and it has such a grip on us that many people in society are afraid to speak out on the need for moral living. Our culture, like the culture of Babylon, has gradually grown into a generation that longs to deify itself and live by its own rules.

God calls his people to be different, to be godly, holy, and faithful to him, and loving to each other. The Christian church is literally "the called-out ones." God calls us out of the self-serving, sin-seeking ways of the society in which we live and into a new way of life through the Lord Jesus. In the words of hymn writer Bryan Jeffery Leech: "We are God's people . . . , And strong in Him we stand."

William M. Flannagan

225

18:4–5

The Line That Marks the Difference

Give her as much torture and grief as the glory and luxury she gave herself. In her heart she boasts, "I sit as queen; I am not a widow, and I will never mourn." Therefore in one day her plagues will overtake her: death, mourning and famine. She will be consumed by fire, for mighty is the Lord God who judges her.

Revelation 18:7–8

Babylon is being judged here because of her spiritual infidelity. Her people had exchanged the true God of heaven for an earthly god of their own design and making. They grew comfortable and confident in their pride. The city's heart reflects an attitude of invincibility and immortality. It was sin run amok.

God hates sin with an everlasting, implacable hatred. The destruction that is pronounced upon Babylon is proof that God does not tolerate evil and will pronounce judgment upon it.

The same is true in our generation. Divorce has become a convenient way to slip away from commitment and responsibility. Homes and families lie in ruins because of self-centered, indulgent living. Teenage pregnancies and a rapidly increasing rate of illegitimate births plague many nations around the world.

In times like these, Christians are to make a recognizable difference in their culture. By our lifestyle, we are to demonstrate the way of godly excellence in the name of Christ, who died to set us free from sin's presence, power, and penalty. God is a great and mighty God. A God of justice? Yes! Yet also a God of grace and mercy! Isaiah's invitation echoes for the ears of our generation. Today let them echo in your heart: "Seek the LORD while he may be found; call on him while he is near" (Isa. 55:6).

Let us remember the resounding truth of these words by an unknown poet:

> There is a hidden line unseen that crosses every path.
> The line that marks the difference between God's patience
> and God's wrath.

On which side of God's line will you stand?

William M. Flannagan

God's Image

The merchants of the earth will weep and mourn over her because no one buys their cargoes any more—cargoes of gold, silver, precious stones and pearls; fine linen, purple, silk and scarlet cloth; every sort of citron wood, and articles of every kind made of ivory, costly wood, bronze, iron and marble; cargoes of cinnamon and spice, of incense, myrrh and frankincense, of wine and olive oil, of fine flour and wheat; cattle and sheep; horses and carriages; and bodies and souls of men.

Revelation 18:11–13

Babylon, covering 196 square miles, was the greatest city of its time. There were one hundred bronze gates and houses three and four stories high. The city spread across the Euphrates River. An amazing bridge, 3,240 feet long, joined it. A tunnel under the river connected the royal palace, which was wider than the river.

Babylon was New York, Paris, Rome, or London to the world of its time. It was the commercial and financial center of the entire world. Yet despite its great wealth, accumulations, and accomplishments, God destroyed Babylon because of the way its people regarded human life. Humanity was considered of no more value than precious stones, pearls, cloth, wood, marble, and spices. People were traded and bartered at whim. Human life was completely devalued.

Much that happens around our world reflects this mindset. We see the evidence in abortion, infanticide, abusive relationships, disrespect between persons, and in other ways that people act towards others.

In a world like ours, God calls his people to make a difference, to emphasize the value of human life, to uphold and defend the dignity of every man, woman, and child, and to see his image in everyone. "I tell you the truth, whatever you did not do for one of the least of these, you did not do for me" (Matt. 25:45).

Today, look for the image of God in every person you meet and remember that you, too, are made in God's image.

William M. Flannagan

Be Prepared!

The merchants who sold these things and gained their wealth from her will stand far off, terrified at her torment. They will weep and mourn and cry out: "Woe! Woe, O great city, dressed in fine linen, purple and scarlet, and glittering with gold, precious stones and pearls! In one hour such great wealth has been brought to ruin! Every sea captain, and all who travel by ship, the sailors, and all who earn their living from the sea, will stand far off."

Revelation 18:15–17

On May 18, 1980, at 8:31 in the morning, Washington State's Mount Saint Helens exploded. In milliseconds, the concussive waves, traveling faster than the speed of sound, ruined everything within one hundred fifty square miles. Tons of rock disintegrated and disappeared into a cloud reaching ten miles into the sky. A wall of mud and ash, fifty feet high, buried cars, cabins, and people. This mountain erupted with a force five hundred times greater than the nuclear bomb that leveled Hiroshima. For days to come, the Mount Saint Helens aftermath impacted much of the United States, Canada, and other parts of the world.

Today's Scripture reveals that the great city of Babylon was brought to ruin in just one hour. God revealed his sovereign majesty and power by bringing instantaneous destruction upon the people of Babylon because of their disobedience and rebellion. The suddenness and completeness of the destruction terrified kings, merchants, and sea captains. The loss of their possessions startled them more than the loss of lives. They did not even consider the loss of their own souls as a possibility.

We need to bring this message to the attention of many people today: God does not allow sin to go unpunished. As Christians, we have an awesome opportunity to share with society that the only hope for the future is found in Jesus Christ and that we must live our lives in a state of constant readiness.

John assures us: "I tell you the truth, he who believes has everlasting life" (John 6:47).

William M. Flannagan

228

Profit for Many!
Affection from None!

"When they see the smoke of her burning, they will exclaim, 'Was there ever a city like this great city?' They will throw dust on their heads, and with weeping and mourning cry out: 'Woe! Woe, O great city, where all who had ships on the sea became rich through her wealth! In one hour she has been brought to ruin!' "

Revelation 18:18–19

The sea merchants who had traversed the globe and brought their wares to this Middle Eastern port gazed in horror at the terrible and swift destruction of Babylon. They had lived well from Babylon's activities, yet not one of them stretched out a hand to help. The great city brought profit to many, but affection to none.

A few years ago, California experienced the worst winter season since records were kept. High seas washed away highways, piers, parks, and houses. Rain, which continued night and day, flooded roads, washed away hillsides, dislodged bridges. Howling winds felled power lines and plunged city after city into darkness. It was in the middle of this catastrophe that the scientists at the California Institute of Technology sent out a warning for the entire state of California to prepare for an earthquake of major proportions. The poor Californian wading through the flooded ruins of his home was now being warned that soon an earthquake would shake everything else into the sea.

The bad news for Babylonians was that God's judgment was being poured out upon them because of blatant sinful rebellion. Their sinfulness had spread and infected the entire known world. Not one of them would escape the impending doom.

The good news for Christians today is to know that God has a plan for the redemption of the world. We can overcome the present sin in our own lives, and in the life of our nation, through Christ, who comes to us at our point of despair and says, "I am Lord! There is no circumstance beyond my power, and you can trust me."

William M. Flannagan

229

Rejoice,
the Lord Is King

Rejoice over her, O heaven! Rejoice, saints and apostles and prophets! God has judged her for the way she treated you.

Revelation 18:20

The call to *rejoice* at Babylon's destruction does not reflect a vindictive spirit. It is a recognition that justice prevails in a sinful world. God will have his way. We can stake our lives on his truth revealed in Scripture.

This rejoicing emphasizes that there is a God behind creation, and that he is in control from beginning to end. Wrongs done to the saints of God are now put right. The Revelation of Jesus Christ is carefully calculated to restore and renew hope in every true believer. You can trust your life and future to God, because he alone knows and controls the future. You can trust him because he loves you and sent his Son to redeem you from your sins.

In 1845, James Russell Lowell wrote, "Once to Every Man and Nation." The fourth stanza of this marvelous hymn clarifies the truth of today's verse:

230

Tho' the cause of evil prosper, Yet the truth alone is strong;
Tho' her portion be the scaffold, And upon the throne be wrong,
Yet that scaffold sways the future, And, behind the dim
  unknown,
Standeth God, within the shadow, Keeping watch above His
  own.

William M. Flannagan

They Shall
Overcome Him

The light of a lamp will never shine in you again. The voice of bridegroom and bride will never be heard in you again. Your merchants were the world's great men. By your magic spell all the nations were led astray.

Revelation 18:23

April 20, 1999, is one of the most tragic dates in American history. Gunmen Eric Harris and Dylan Klebold massacred twelve students and a teacher before committing suicide at Columbine High School in Littleton, Colorado. Dressed in black, with hearts enveloped in Satan worship, Harris and Klebold apparently intended on killing even more students before they were stopped.

Today's verse reminds us that Satanism and witchcraft were rampant in Babylon. Researchers tell us that in today's Black Masses, participants try to reverse everything they know about Christianity. The crucifix is hung upside down. The altar is covered in black instead of white. When the names of God or Jesus Christ are mentioned, the "priest" spits on the altar. To make this blasphemy more despicable, sometimes a child is slain. Worshippers renounce their faith in anyone but Satan as lord. Regardless of how evil and repulsive this may sound to us, thousands of people worship in this manner.

But Christians need not fear nor be anxious about this kind of spiritual battle. In the midst of trials and sufferings, God will provide his peace, joy, and fellowship. Even though evil and the things of Satan are real, Jesus Christ and the power of the living God are even more real. Here is our hope for today and every day: "They overcame him [Satan] by the blood of the Lamb and by the word of their testimony; they did not love their lives so much as to shrink from death" (Rev. 12:11).

William M. Flannagan

231

God Leads Us Along

In her was found the blood of prophets and of the saints, and of all who have been killed on the earth.

Revelation 18:24

The first persecution of the Christian church took place in the year 67, during the reign of Roman Emperor Nero. Thousands of men, women, and children were brutally murdered because of their faith in Jesus Christ. These believers were exposed to all manner of punishments and tortures.

At a seminar many years ago, I heard it said that the lives of the early Christians consisted of "persecution above ground and prayer below ground." Skeletons unearthed from Christian graves in Rome tell their own horrible story. Heads are severed from bodies, and ribs and bones are crushed apart and often charred black from fire. In spite of the tortures, suffering, and death, some of the inscriptions reveal peace, joy, and triumph: *"Carried away by the sweet hand of God," "At rest in peace with Christ," "Receive my soul, Lord Jesus."*

Christian symbols carved on the catacombs join this chorus of victory under persecution. They include the good shepherd displayed with a lamb on his shoulder, and images of angels with harps and crowns. We can also find the symbol of the fish, which denotes strong faith in Jesus Christ. Together, the inscriptions and carving should inspire us when we are tempted to renounce our faith in tough times.

As this chapter is closed, we can almost hear the voices of the saints joining in the glorious words of G. A. Young's hymn, "God Leads Us Along":

> Some thro' the waters, some thro' the flood,
> Some thro' the fire, but all thro' the blood.
> Some thro' great sorrow, but God gives a song
> In the night season and all the day long.

William M. Flannagan

232

A Time to Rejoice

After this I heard what sounded like the roar of a great multitude in heaven shouting: "Hallelujah! Salvation and glory and power belong to our God, for true and just are his judgments."

Revelation 19:1–2a

We could appropriately call this the "Hallelujah Chapter" of Holy Scripture. The divine revelation granted to the apostle John prior to this chapter is marked by judgment and pain, plagues and woes. Now, suddenly, the heavens open and the glory of God is revealed in all its majesty and wonder. We realize that all that has come before is only a prelude, preparing us for the climactic moment of God's ultimate and eternal victory.

In the face of such glory, we can offer no more worthy response than the shout of "Hallelujah!" which literally means, "Praise be to God!" As common as the word *hallelujah* has become in the language of the church, this chapter is the only place in the New Testament where it is found.

Praise naturally springs from our recognition of God as he truly is. When we understand that God is the author of our salvation, the fountain of true glory, and the source of all power, we can do no less than join in the heavenly chorus of praise.

Yet God deserves our praise not only because of who he is but also because of what he is like—because of his nature. His nature is marked by truth and justice, characteristics that flow from him alone.

What a privilege we enjoy to join the angels in proclaiming the praise of which God alone is worthy. Hallelujah!

Michael Duduit

233

A Thanksgiving
for Judgment

*After this I heard what sounded like the roar of a great multitude in heaven
shouting: "Hallelujah! Salvation and glory and power belong to our God,
for true and just are his judgments. He has condemned the great prostitute
who corrupted the earth by her adulteries. He has avenged on her the blood
of his servants." And again they shouted: "Hallelujah! The smoke from her
goes up for ever and ever." The twenty-four elders and the four living creatures fell down and worshiped God, who was seated on the throne. And
they cried: "Amen, Hallelujah!" Then a voice came from the throne, saying: "Praise our God, all you his servants, you who fear him, both small
and great!"*

Revelation 19:1–5

In chapter 18, the destruction of the great prostitute is foretold.
Now in chapter 19, the angelic choir erupts in an anthem of praise,
celebrating God's righteous judgment. Why is this divine action
so praiseworthy?

234   The great prostitute—identified as Babylon (see 17:4–5)—has
seduced the kings of the earth (17:18) and drawn many away from
God. While some interpreters identify the prostitute (Babylon) as
Rome, there is a deeper significance. The prostitute represents a
godless system or culture that establishes itself as an alternative to
God's righteous kingdom. This satanic counterfeit offers luxury
and comfort but in truth can ultimately produce only destruction
for those who are drawn into her trap.

The return of Christ, however, represents the final destruction
of the prostitute. His coming represents the decisive divine victory
over the worldly culture that stands opposed to the ways of God.
So long as the prostitute remains entrenched among the peoples
of the earth, God's kingdom will not be fully and finally established in human history. When Christ comes again to establish his
reign in history, those forces that have stood in opposition to God's
truth and righteousness will be swept away in judgment.

Michael Duduit

The Marriage
of the Lamb

Then I heard what sounded like a great multitude, like the roar of rushing waters and like loud peals of thunder, shouting: "Hallelujah! For our Lord God Almighty reigns. Let us rejoice and be glad and give him glory! For the wedding of the Lamb has come, and his bride has made herself ready. Fine linen, bright and clean, was given her to wear." (Fine linen stands for the righteous acts of the saints.)

Revelation 19:6–8

Although the NIV translates the phrase in verse 6, "For our Lord God Almighty reigns," a better translation is found in the New English Bible: "The Lord our God, sovereign over all, has entered on his reign!" The process is not yet complete, but it has begun.

The coming of Christ is represented by the image of a marriage. Christ is the Lamb and the church is his bride. The image is not new. Hosea represented God's relationship with his rebellious people in terms of a marriage to an adulterous wife (Hosea 2:2). Jesus used the language of the bridegroom in describing himself (Mark 2:19–20), and Paul compared the church to the wife of Christ (Eph. 5:32).

The most direct connection to our present passage is Jesus' use of the wedding feast metaphor in Matthew 22 to point to the future coming of God's kingdom. The church is the bride of Christ and awaits his arrival so that the celebration of the wedding feast can commence. Yet even as she awaits her groom, the church-bride must make preparation, donning the beautiful wedding garments provided by the bridegroom. These garments consist of a righteous and godly life. Even this is available only as a gift of God. We are called to live a life that honors Christ, and he enables us to live this life through the empowerment of his Spirit.

It is impossible to look at the culture in which we live and fail to see evidence of an evil influence behind it all: from the celebration of materialism and greed to the delight in violence, promiscuity, and excess. Our culture has indeed become like a prostitute who calls us to a moment of pleasure, no matter what the cost.

The day is coming, however, when Christ will return and establish God's kingdom in history. Even as the heavenly choir will praise God on that day, so we praise him now as we anticipate that glorious triumph.

Michael Duduit

235

19:6–8

The Greatest Invitation

Then the angel said to me, "Write: 'Blessed are those who are invited to the wedding supper of the Lamb!'" And he added, "These are the true words of God." At this I fell at his feet to worship him. But he said to me, "Do not do it! I am a fellow servant with you and with your brothers who hold to the testimony of Jesus. Worship God! For the testimony of Jesus is the spirit of prophecy."

Revelation 19:9–10

The image is a familiar one: a joyous banquet celebrating the union of a bride and groom. Family and friends gather to rejoice and make merry. We are glad when we are invited to such a festive event.

The focus of the metaphor has changed from the bride to the wedding guests, but the people of God remain the subject. The message is clear: Invitation to share in this eschatological wedding supper is a source of great joy. Note the word "invited." No one walks in off the street to "crash" this celebration. Admittance is by invitation only. That invitation comes from God alone. None of us can gain admittance by our own initiative or merit.

The next phrase is intriguing, as the angel adds this assurance: "These are the true words of God." There is an important assurance here, particularly for a first-century church undergoing increasing persecution—and for Christians through the ages who have experienced similar struggles: God will bring about the ultimate victory and vindication of his people. No matter what our present circumstances may appear to be, we can rest in the confidence that God will accomplish his purpose in history and in our own individual lives as well.

Perhaps mistaking the angelic messenger for Christ himself, John falls at his feet to worship him. But the angel corrects him. Like John, the angel is a servant of God. What a remarkable idea: men and women united with the angelic host in a partnership of praise to almighty God! This is a wedding feast you do not want to miss!

Michael Duduit

236

The Testimony of Jesus

For the testimony of Jesus is the spirit of prophecy.
Revelation 19:10b

In the first portion of this verse, John mistakenly begins to worship the angelic messenger, who quickly corrects him. The angel informs John that he himself, like the apostle, is merely a servant of the God who alone is worthy of worship.

Then follows this intriguing little sentence. The NIV translates it as part of the angel's message. But the Revised Standard Version more appropriately identifies it as John's own explanation of the angel's reminder. What do the words "The testimony of Jesus is the spirit of prophecy" mean?

Primarily, they mean that every prophetic message must be rooted in the work and words of Jesus Christ. Apart from him we have no message to proclaim. Before a preacher has a word to share, he must go to the cross. Before a teacher has a message to offer, she must go to the cross. Before the church formulates doctrine or practice, it must stand before the cross. In Jesus Christ crucified alone do we find the substance of our faith. There is no prophetic message apart from the redeeming Christ.

Perhaps these words convey a further meaning as well. Not only is Jesus the source of our prophetic messages, he is also the one who empowers and inspires our proclamation of the gospel. His life and ministry produce the dynamic energy and inspiration that compel us to go forth and share the good news in his name.

Because of who Jesus is, we have a message to proclaim.

Michael Duduit

237

The Names
of Christ (Part One)

I saw heaven standing open and there before me was a white horse, whose rider is called Faithful and True. With justice he judges and makes war. His eyes are like blazing fire, and on his head are many crowns. He has a name written on him that no one knows but he himself.

Revelation 19:11–12

In this portion of chapter 19, John uses four different names to identify Christ at the moment of his glorious return.

The first name is "Faithful and True." The Greek word translated "faithful" refers to one who can be relied upon absolutely. That, certainly, is true of our Lord Jesus Christ. No matter what our need or challenge or circumstance, he is the one on whom we can rely completely. Christ is also "true." No falsehood or deception resides in him. What he tells us, we can accept. As we might say of a trustworthy human friend who promises something, "You can take it to the bank!" Without question, we may trust whatever Christ says, for his very nature is truth.

Christ also has a secret name—"a name written on him that no one knows but he himself." Perhaps these words suggest the Old Testament idea that to know the name of another is somehow to command power over that person. Recall the story of Jacob's wrestling match with the divine combatant who refused to reveal his name (Gen. 32:29).

Or maybe this unknown name represents some part of the nature of Christ, which we, as humans, simply cannot know. This much is certain: Our knowledge of God will never be complete until we gather around his throne in the age to come.

Michael Duduit

The Names
of Christ (Part Two)

He is dressed in a robe dipped in blood, and his name is the Word of God. . . .
On his robe and on his thigh he has this name written: KING OF KINGS AND
LORD OF LORDS.

Revelation 19:13, 16

The third name given to the conquering Christ in this chapter is
"the Word of God" (v. 13). In Jewish thought, a word was not simply a sound or a visual representation of an idea. A word was an
active, dynamic force in its own right. Never could that be more
true than when speaking of the Word of God. As the prophet Jeremiah recorded: "'Is not my word like fire,' declares the LORD, 'and
like a hammer that breaks a rock in pieces?'" (Jer. 23:29). In Christ,
the Word of God acts with power and might to accomplish the
divine purpose.

We find a fourth name of Christ in these verses—one of the
most famous: "King of kings and Lord of lords." Even as we read
the words, we hear the majestic strains of Handel's *Messiah* thundering this awesome name in praise and celebration.

He is King of kings—above all human authority. He is Lord of
lords—sovereign over all of creation. He is the transcendent power
in the cosmos, beyond anything we can imagine. To our utter
amazement, he is also a God who loves us all the way to a cross.
Heaven's ruler became earth's redeemer. We can never comprehend such love. But we can accept it, celebrate it, and serve the
One who loves us so.

Michael Duduit

239

The Conquering Christ

I saw heaven standing open and there before me was a white horse, whose rider is called Faithful and True. With justice he judges and makes war. His eyes are like blazing fire, and on his head are many crowns. He has a name written on him that no one knows but he himself. He is dressed in a robe dipped in blood, and his name is the Word of God.

Revelation 19:11–13

Using highly symbolic language, John draws us into a remarkable scene: the revealing of the victorious Christ as he emerges from heaven and prepares to inaugurate his reign in human history.

The rider of the horse is clearly the Lord Jesus Christ, for he is "Faithful and True"—that is, he is the One who keeps his covenant with his people—and "his name is the Word of God." He sits astride a white horse. White represents victory. Here Christ rides forth to accomplish his final victory over the forces of evil.

He "judges and makes war" on the satanic powers that have so long opposed the purposes and people of God. Yet even in battle he acts "with justice," that is, he acts righteously and in faithfulness to the nature of God. He goes into battle with eyes "like blazing fire"—the same description used of Christ in Revelation 1:14 and 2:18—for nothing can be hidden from his gaze. "On his head are many crowns," representing the sovereignty and authority with which he engages in this climactic battle. He bears an additional "name written on him that no one knows but he himself," demonstrating that human understanding alone cannot grasp the awesome mystery of this messianic Lord.

This conquering Christ is stained with the blood of battle and conflict, a reminder to believers that nothing less than Christ's own blood could purchase our redemption. The One who rules the cosmos is the very One whose love drew him to a cross for you and for me.

Michael Duduit

240

The King Is Coming

I saw heaven standing open and there before me was a white horse, whose rider is called Faithful and True. With justice he judges and makes war. His eyes are like blazing fire, and on his head are many crowns. He has a name written on him that no one knows but he himself. He is dressed in a robe dipped in blood, and his name is the Word of God.

Revelation 19:11–13

One of the most popular songs in many churches has been "The King Is Coming," a musical celebration of the second coming of Christ. In our text we see the moment to which the song points: the king of heaven, Christ Jesus, is revealed as he initiates his climactic return.

If the New Testament was a novel, we could think of the nativity as the beginning of the story, where the action commences. The cross and resurrection would be the crucial event, the turning point that determines the ultimate outcome. This passage in Revelation 19 would be the culmination of the action, as the outcome of the earlier events unfolds to provide a final resolution to the story. The New Testament, however, is not a novel. It is a cosmic history in which God works through his Son to accomplish his purpose. In the second coming, that ultimate, eternal purpose becomes a reality in all of its glory and majesty.

The second coming of Christ is an event of cosmic significance, yet it also has enormous meaning for you and me, as we benefit from the redemptive work of Christ. "In his cross and resurrection," writes George Ladd, "Christ won a great victory over the powers of evil; by his second coming, he will execute that victory."[13]

Michael Duduit

241

The Coming Judgment

The armies of heaven were following him, riding on white horses and dressed in fine linen, white and clean. Out of his mouth comes a sharp sword with which to strike down the nations. "He will rule them with an iron scepter." He treads the winepress of the fury of the wrath of God Almighty. On his robe and on his thigh he has this name written: KING OF KINGS AND LORD OF LORDS.

Revelation 19:14–16

John's description of the conquering Christ continues. He is surrounded by the heavenly host, an army of angels also dressed in the white garments that represent victory. No weapons of warfare on their part, however, are mentioned. This is the Lord's battle, and he comes to the field with the weapon of his word.

The "sharp sword" that comes from his mouth is his word. Just as God brought the created order into being by the power of his word, so the final victory over evil will be accomplished by the word of Christ. The author of Hebrews observed: "The word of God is living and active. Sharper than any double-edged sword, it penetrates even to dividing soul and spirit, joints and marrow; it judges the thoughts and attitudes of the heart" (Heb. 4:12). Christ's word is the creative and sustaining force in our world. It is also the power by which he judges sin and establishes his righteous kingdom.

The image of judgment continues with the picture of the warrior Christ pressing out the wine of destruction that will be served to the enemies of God. How can we be sure of this judgment? Christ bears supreme authority and ultimate sovereignty. He is "King of kings and Lord of lords." No one is above him. No one is greater. What he will do, he will do.

Michael Duduit

242

Christy and Antichrist

And I saw an angel standing in the sun, who cried in a loud voice to all the birds flying in midair, "Come, gather together for the great supper of God, so that you may eat the flesh of kings, generals, and mighty men, of horses and their riders, and the flesh of all people, free and slave, small and great."

Revelation 19:17–18

The Book of Revelation reaches its climactic moments as the warrior Messiah-King emerges from heaven, surrounded by the heavenly host, to do battle with the Antichrist and his minions, then to accomplish his final victory over Satan and the forces of evil.

In apocalyptic language, an angelic messenger calls to the birds, inviting them to come, share in a feast. The menu? The remains of those who, having allied themselves with the Antichrist, are now about to be left dead on the battlefield of Armageddon. "All people" refers to those who bear the mark of the beast, that is, those who have chosen to serve the Antichrist rather than to accept the lordship of Christ. Because of their foolish alliance, they will be destroyed in Christ's total victory over the forces of sin and evil.

Have you ever read an exciting story and, eager with anticipation, flipped over to the final pages to find out how the story ends? Here in the final pages of Scripture, we learn the thrilling conclusion of the divine-human drama. Christ is victor! Though, through the years, the power of evil often seemed too great, God is far greater still, and he will ultimately destroy all those powers and forces that oppose his sovereignty.

Christ will be victorious! This is all that matters in your life and mine. Let us then live as those who walk with the coming King.

Michael Duduit

243

The Final Battle

Then I saw the beast and the kings of the earth and their armies gathered together to make war against the rider on the horse and his army. But the beast was captured, and with him the false prophet who had performed the miraculous signs on his behalf. With these signs he had deluded those who had received the mark of the beast and worshiped his image. The two of them were thrown alive into the fiery lake of burning sulfur. The rest of them were killed with the sword that came out of the mouth of the rider on the horse, and all the birds gorged themselves on their flesh.

Revelation 19:19–21

The idea of "Armageddon" has fascinated and intrigued people for centuries. Books, movies, and songs have depicted this great final battle between the forces of light and the forces of darkness. Curiously, Scripture describes nothing of this great battle except its outcome. In verse 19, John sees the two armies arrayed against each other. In the very next verse the noise of battle ceases, because the beast (Antichrist) and the false prophet have been captured.

The beast and the false prophet are then "thrown alive into the fiery lake of burning sulfur." This lake of fire is Gehenna, although the word itself nowhere appears in Revelation. Much apocalyptic literature identifies Gehenna (the Valley of Hinnom) as the place where final judgment takes place. In chapter 20, Satan himself is cast into Gehenna forever.

As our chapter closes, John again relates the destiny of those who gave their allegiance to the Antichrist. They are utterly destroyed, their bodies left to feed the birds. What a gruesome reminder of the ultimate destruction that awaits those who refuse God's grace and choose evil instead!

To the very last moment of history, some will not respond to the outstretched hand of Jesus. Unmoved by his sacrificial love, they will mock him and turn away to their own pursuits. But the message of Revelation is clear: Apart from Christ, only death and destruction await us all. This day, let us choose to serve in the armies of the Lord, eagerly awaiting the coming King.

Michael Duduit

The Messenger
from Heaven

And I saw an angel coming down out of heaven, having the key to the Abyss and holding in his hand a great chain. He seized the dragon, that ancient serpent, who is the devil, or Satan, and bound him for a thousand years. He threw him into the Abyss, and locked and sealed it over him, to keep him from deceiving the nations anymore until the thousand years were ended. After that, he must be set free for a short time.

Revelation 20:1–3

We are now in the midst of the minefield of controversy mentioned previously. But there is guidance through it from Revelation 1. There, what starts out as an encounter with an angel ends up as an encounter with Christ: "Do not be afraid. I am the First and the Last. I am the Living One; I was dead, and behold I am alive forever and ever! And I hold the keys of death and Hades" (1:17b–18). In chapter 20, the angel (literally, "messenger") from heaven is said to hold the keys to the Abyss into which Satan is thrown. The One who holds the keys to hell and death in the first chapter would seem to be the One who still holds the keys in this chapter.

What John is revealing is that the Son of God meant it in Matthew 28:18 when he said, "All authority in heaven and on earth has been given to me." The sovereignty of Christ is the theme of our text. If we reject the sovereignty of God, we end up worshiping a deity who is helpless to do anything about earth's events. Thus we comfort ourselves with this revelation: He not only ultimately controls the events of this life but also of the life to come. Those keys can not only lock the evil one in hell but also blessedly lock us out of there, thereby assuring that our destiny is heaven with the Lord Jesus. Our experience of the first resurrection, through faith in the finished work of Christ, qualifies us to bathe our souls in this blessed assurance.

Lane Adams

1,000 Years:
Literal or Symbolic

And I saw an angel coming down out of heaven, having the key to the Abyss and holding in his hand a great chain. He seized the dragon, that ancient serpent, who is the devil, or Satan, and bound him for a thousand years. He threw him into the Abyss, and locked and sealed it over him, to keep him from deceiving the nations anymore until the thousand years were ended. After that, he must be set free for a short time. I saw thrones on which were seated those who had been given authority to judge. And I saw the souls of those who had been beheaded because of their testimony for Jesus and because of the word of God. They had not worshiped the beast or his image and had not received his mark on their foreheads or their hands. They came to life and reigned with Christ a thousand years. (The rest of the dead did not come to life until the thousand years were ended.) This is the first resurrection. Blessed and holy are those who have part in the first resurrection. The second death has no power over them, but they will be priests of God and of Christ and will reign with him for a thousand years.

Revelation 20:1–6

In the short span of only six verses, a time period of one thousand years is mentioned five times. It encapsulates the incarceration of Satan, the reign of Christ and those martyred for their faith, and the reign with Christ of all those who participated in "the first resurrection" by their new birth experience. Over the centuries, multiple volumes have been written as to whether this is to be taken literally or symbolically. If literally, we're anticipating an event yet to come. The question then arises: Who is ruling the world now? What shall we do with John 13:3: "Jesus knew that the Father had put all things under his power, and that he had come from God and was returning to God"? His victory over our sins on the cross, his triumphant resurrection, and his ascension to the glorious right hand of the Father are proof of his sovereign rule now.

It takes eyes of faith to see beyond our millennial squabbles into the blessed eternity that awaits those who have experienced the first resurrection. Our Lord Jesus Christ will one day return in visible glory with all the Father's holy angels. Until then, in the midst of the storms of life we have this assurance, "For he must reign until he has put all his enemies under his feet. The last enemy to be destroyed is death. For he 'has put everything under his feet'" (1 Cor. 15:25–27).

Lane Adams

20:1–6

Taking Responsibility!
Claiming Victory!

He seized the dragon, that ancient serpent, who is the devil, or Satan, and bound him for a thousand years.

Revelation 20:2

Some Christians maintain that Satan is in charge of this world with powers nearly equivalent to those of our Lord. When they fail they deny personal responsibility and give Satan credit for having overwhelmed them. It's a victim mentality, akin to comedian Flip Wilson's Geraldine character's excuse, "The devil made me do it!" Yet, God's Word says, "The one who is in you is greater than the one who is in the world" (1 John 4:4b).

Jesus says, "If I drive out demons by the Spirit of God, then the kingdom of God has come upon you. Or again, how can anyone enter a strong man's house and carry off his possessions unless he first ties up the strong man? Then he can rob his house" (Matt. 12:28–29).

Today's verse says the strong man, Satan, has been bound until just prior to Christ's return. How then do we explain rampant wickedness in our world? What we have lost sight of is the depth of fallen human nature.

Many people, including many Christians, consider humans to be basically good with a slight tendency to evil. The Bible, however, says, "As for you, you were dead in your transgressions and sins" (Eph. 2:1). Yet the good news is that all who receive Christ are enabled by him to live victoriously and overcome sin's power. How? "He has given us his very great and precious promises, so that through them you may participate in the divine nature and escape the corruption in the world caused by evil desires" (2 Peter 1:4).

Stand tall in Christ, who won the victory for you on Calvary.

Lane Adams

247

The First Resurrection

Blessed and holy are those who have part in the first resurrection. The second death has no power over them, but they will be priests of God and of Christ and will reign with him for a thousand years.

Revelation 20:6

John, in exile on the Isle of Patmos, wrote Revelation in apocalyptic code, drawing on Daniel, Ezekiel, and other parts of the Old Testament to encourage the churches. Naturally, this created some confusion—then and now. But much of the confusion can be clarified by applying the rule for interpretation found in the Westminster Confession of Faith. It says: "The infallible rule of interpretation of Scripture, is the Scripture itself." What is meant, then, by "Blessed and holy are those who have part in the first resurrection"?

The apostle Paul gives us these clarifying words, "You were dead in your transgressions and sins. . . . And God raised us up with Christ and seated us with him in the heavenly realms in Christ Jesus" (Eph. 2:1, 6).

Our experience of coming into new life in Christ is likened to our being raised from the dead. It is there that we die to sin in order that we might live unto righteousness. What is the assurance of our text? "The second death (our physical death when we die) has no power over [us], but [we] will be priests of God and of Christ and will reign with him."

As we face a rising tide of both verbal and legal persecution of Christians, what a blessed comfort it is to remember: "Hallelujah! For our Lord God Almighty reigns" (Rev. 19:6).

Lane Adams

248

God Doesn't Have
a Killer Instinct

When the thousand years are over, Satan will be released from his prison.

Revelation 20:7

In the year immediately following the Houston Rockets' second world championship season, they still had the nucleus of a great team. Basketball fans were calling for a "three-peat." Unfortunately, however, the season was far from over before even casual fans began to recognize that the Rockets had a fatal flaw: The team lacked the killer instinct.

Like so many good teams, they could get off to a good start. Once they were comfortably in front, however, they could not capitalize on their advantage and deliver the knockout punch. Inevitably, their opponents would gradually even the score and, in the closing seconds of the contest, win the game.

In verse 7 of Revelation 20, God, who has subdued the old adversary, Satan, releases him. Why didn't God press his advantage and take the devil out? Why didn't God end pain, evil, and death forever?

There are multitudes of people who have not made up their minds about Jesus Christ. If God entirely eliminated evil, they would lose their freedom to choose. What a gracious God he is, to offer humankind one more chance, even at the eleventh hour, another opportunity to say "yes" to Jesus Christ!

Hell is real eternal separation from God. An old camp meeting song describes a Christian's attitude toward hell: "Wait a little longer, please, Jesus. There are still so many wandering out in sin."

Our God doesn't have the killer instinct. He is redemptive to the end. If we insist on going to hell, we'll have to climb over his Son's outstretched, crucified body.

William H. Hinson

249

Enough!

They marched across the breadth of the earth and surrounded the camp of God's people, the city he loves. But fire came down from heaven and devoured them.

Revelation 20:9

The forces of evil gather for battle. Their number is like the sand on the seashore. They surround the camp of the saints and the beloved city. The expected titanic battle between God and evil does not, however, take place. When God's "enough" is reached, there is no contest. Fire destroys the armies of evil and the devil is thrown into the lake of fire with his chief servants, the beast and the false prophet.

The late Pierce Harris, longtime pastor of the First United Methodist Church of Atlanta, had an unforgettable way of describing the coming of God at the end of time. Harris said that Almighty God would come striding down a stairway of stars, rattling some keys in his hands and saying, "It's closing time, folks."

There will be an end to history as we know it, according to the teaching of Revelation. On that climactic day, evil will be forever defeated and destroyed. In Jesus Christ, through his life, death, and resurrection, a mortal blow has already been struck against all the powers of darkness. Finally, our deliverer will defeat all foes, and the last great enemy will be vanquished. That's good news for every believer who struggles to be faithful in a world filled with temptation.

No matter how tough things become, we can hang on a little longer. We know that we are on the winning side. We are not like so many hamsters running on an exercise wheel; we are going somewhere. We have a glorious future, and evil will not survive.

William H. Hinson

Gog and Magog

When the thousand years are over, Satan will be released from his prison and will go out to deceive the nations in the four corners of the earth—Gog and Magog—to gather them for battle. In number they are like the sand on the seashore. They marched across the breadth of the earth and surrounded the camp of God's people, the city he loves. But fire came down from heaven and devoured them.

Revelation 20:7–9

Gog and Magog, the epitome of evil, are aligned against God and the people of God. The evil forces described in Revelation are numerous and powerful. They do their malevolent work in the world and in our hearts.

A rebellious little boy insisted that his mother tell him why he had to go to Sunday school. His mother responded, "So you'll grow up to be a good little boy." "But mother," the boy replied, "I already know how to be a better little boy than I want to be."

All of us can relate to that little boy. We are in desperate need of someone who can, to use words I once heard Carlisle Marney say, "fix our wanter." Alone, the power of evil that surrounds and threatens is too much for us.

Each day's headlines underscore the existence of racial prejudice, strife, and injustice. Nations, feeling threatened by other countries, take up arms. World peace continues to elude us. Economic prosperity and a decent standard of living depend upon our ability to live harmoniously with each other. Malignant powers intrude, however, and we are tempted to despair.

Surely our world, and each of us, sometimes feels under siege by evil. Revelation tells us that our deliverance comes from a power outside of ourselves. We must pray for the same faith that Elisha asked God to give his servant—a faith that opens our eyes to the hosts of God that shield and protect us from evil.

William H. Hinson

251

All People
Great and Small

And I saw the dead, great and small, standing before the throne, and books were opened. Another book was opened, which is the book of life. The dead were judged according to what they had done as recorded in the books.

Revelation 20:12

At the end of the day, there is accountability. The one who gave us life will inquire as to how we invested ourselves, and will examine the fruit of our years.

The concept of judgment, of accountability, is at the heart of our faith. William Temple said that God would be immoral if, on the day we appeared before him, he said, "Never mind." God asserts his sovereignty by judgment, which follows our neglect of his law. All of those who stand before the great throne will be stripped of earthly status and distinction. Both the great and small will stand on level ground. Death is the great equalizer.

Once, I was praying with a wealthy church member in the closing moments of her life. As I sat beside her bed, I could visualize the numerous gifts she and her husband had made to our city. Those monumental gifts, some huge buildings, would soon be memorials to her. In the minutes preceding her death, however, she steadily declared that all of her faith was in Jesus. In that moment, she joined the rest of God's creation in our collective need for grace. On the day when the books are opened and we must render an account for all of the things we have done, we will stand on level ground.

Before the judgment day, hopefully we will have stood at another level place; that is, at the foot of Christ's cross. No amount of good works will suffice to atone for our sins. We need a redeemer and an advocate, Jesus Christ the righteous.

William H. Hinson

So Deep You
Can't Get under It

The sea gave up the dead that were in it, and death and Hades gave up the dead that were in them, and each person was judged according to what he had done.

Revelation 20:13

Did you ever sing the children's song that goes like this? "So high you can't get over it, so low you can't get under it, so wide you can't get around it, so you'd better come in at the door." That little song reminds us there is no place too deep for God's power to work. Ultimately, even the depths of the sea and the depths of the earth must yield their dead. What a comfort that must have been for first-century Christians in Asia Minor who were dying for their faith! What a comfort these words are to us today. We can never fly too high or fall too low that the Savior's strong arm cannot reach us.

A young professional shared his story with me recently. His addiction to drugs and alcohol rendered him so ineffective he lost his license to practice his profession. Eventually, he lost his home, and his wife and children left him. His friends no longer associated with him. When he finally admitted himself to an institution where he could receive treatment, the first Sunday there he staggered, still in a stupor, to the television room. He watched a church service and heard a preacher say that Jesus, our great Deliverer, can set us free. The next Sunday he returned. Soon, he was gloriously saved and set free from his addictions. That young man has regained his license, is reunited with his wife, and has the respect of his children again. He testifies that Jesus descended into hell to save him.

Someone we love may be sinking into a chaotic place. Even there, Jesus has power to save.

William H. Hinson

253

We Only Die Once

Then death and Hades were thrown into the lake of fire. The lake of fire is the second death. If anyone's name was not found written in the book of life, he was thrown into the lake of fire.

Revelation 20:14–15

The *Wall Street Journal*'s lead editorial on February 25, 2000, described how many members of the Baby Boomer generation are turning their attentions from the "good life" to the "good death." Such a shift, the writer explained, is normal as we become older.

The editorial declared that our greatest fears of death are often physical pain and being alone. The writer described alternative practices and places to ensure that those who sign up for "good death services" will not suffer needlessly, and that they will have friends and family physically present.

Thanks to modern medical science, our fears can be calmed about the wrenching, agonizing pain that often accompanied dying just a generation or so ago. Being alone, however, still represents a challenge. In the deepest sense, death is a very personal experience. None of your family and friends can walk through the experience of death with you. Each of us must walk that lonesome valley alone.

Those who have been born anew in Christ, however, understand that while death is a personal experience, we need not be alone. Jesus has promised that he will never leave us or forsake us. Indeed, he has promised that he will personally come and take the faithful home to the Father's house. Death has no dominion over a Christian.

Remember the saying, "Born once, die twice; born twice, die once." Those who put their faith in the atoning work of Christ need not fear the first death, and the second death isn't even in the picture for those who believe in Christ.

William H. Hinson

254

Nothing like It!

I saw a new heaven and a new earth, for the first heaven and the first earth had passed away.

Revelation 21:1a

All of us blessed with the gift of sight agree with the writer of Ecclesiastes, "He has made everything beautiful in its time" (Eccles. 3:11). Some people travel the circumference of the globe to feast their eyes on a mountain range, a waterfall, or a rock formation. Astronauts report that the view of earth from outer space is awesome. All this magnificent beauty in a fallen world!

Now God has brought his creation full circle. "God saw all that he had made, and it was very good" (Gen. 1:31). "Then I saw a new heaven and a new earth for the first heaven and the first earth had passed away" (Rev. 21:1).

The old adage, "New is always better," has been challenged by many who claim, "New is not always better." When God is the creator there is no doubt: The new heavens and the new earth will be incomparably more splendid than the most spectacular wonders our eyes have ever seen.

The New Testament writers use two different words for *new*. The first, *neos,* refers to something new in terms of time. The object may be exactly like a lot of other things of its kind, but it is a newly made copy. When our Lord refers to new wine in old wineskins, the Gospel writers use the word *neos* (Matt. 9:17; Mark 2:22; Luke 5:37–38).

The other Greek word is *kainos.* This designates something that is new in terms of both time and quality. In other words, it is not only newly made, but nothing like it has ever been made before. Not surprisingly, *kainos* is the word for *new* that we find throughout the Book of Revelation.

Saint John has chosen some of the most graphic symbolism known to us to describe the wonders of the new heavens and the new earth. Think about it! The blueprint is ready! On God's appointed day, our eternal home will be newly created and ready for all of us whose names are written in "the Lamb's book of life" (Rev. 21:27). Hallelujah!

Richard Allen Bodey

255

21:1a

When the Sea Is History

There was no longer any sea.

Revelation 21:1b

From "The Spirit of God was hovering over the waters" (Gen. 1:2) to "There was no longer any sea," waves crash somewhere in the background of Scripture.

The sea's passing means mystery is history. As a lad growing up in Ireland, I often stood on the shore, looking at the horizon and puzzling what life might be like across the water. When the sea disappears, all our questions will be answered to our satisfaction. What don't you understand that you really want to know? One day you will see it clearly.

The sea's disappearance also promises that unruliness will cease. I've stood on the same shores and licked the briny water from my lips as the sea crashed with fury. I have conducted memorials for young people lost at sea and noted that the ocean, like an unchained tyrant, has an unquenchable and unpredictable appetite for human life. No one but Christ can control its fury. "Even the wind and the waves obey him!" (Mark 4:41). One day, however, the sea will claim its last victim. One day, the sea will give up the dead that were in it (see Rev. 20:13). One day, the sea will rule no more. One day, tyranny will be history. One day, perfect peace will come.

The precursor of that day can be today when we give our questions, our troubles, and our unrest over to the Christ who controls all our seas.

256

When peace, like a river, attendeth my way,
When sorrows like sea billows roll;
Whatever my lot, thou hast taught me to say,
"It is well, it is well, with my soul."

Horatio Spafford, 1873

Robert Leslie Holmes

Ready for the Wedding?

I saw the Holy City, the new Jerusalem, coming down out of heaven from God, prepared as a bride beautifully dressed for her husband.

Revelation 21:2

The morning of my wedding day, my mother brought me breakfast in bed, serving it on the new china and with the new silver I had been given as wedding gifts. After breakfast, I stayed in my bedclothes, resting and taking it easy, so I would be fresh for the service and the reception that would follow that evening. Several hours before I was to leave the house to go to the church, I began to get ready.

I started with my makeup, carefully applying it in order to enhance any physical beauty I might have and hide the many flaws I did have! I worked on my hair, sweeping it up so it would stay under the veil, yet be visible enough to frame my face. Finally my mother came to my room and helped me get into my wedding gown, fastening the dozens of small buttons up the back and adjusting the chapel-length veil. When I had done everything I knew to do to get myself ready, I just stood in front of the full-length mirror and gazed at the young woman enveloped in ivory silk and lace who was reflected in it. I was tense and eager as I wondered, after six and a half months of preparation, if I would be beautiful and desirable to my husband.

As elaborate as my preparations were as a bride seeking to be beautiful for my husband, they were feeble in comparison with the Lord God's preparation for his bride for that greatest wedding day of all.

What will you do to make ready today for that great wedding day God is planning for you? Do it with all your heart!

Anne Graham Lotz

257

The Best Company!

I heard a great voice out of heaven saying, Behold, the tabernacle of God is with men, and he will dwell with them, and they shall be his people, and God himself shall be with them, and be their God.

Revelation 21:3 KJV

A pastor from China told me about a young convert named Lo, who, with some apprehension about leaving home, prepared to study in England. To help his language skills, Lo began to read the Bible in English. He found his fears relieved when he encountered Matthew 28:20: "Lo, I am with you alway, even unto the end of the world" (KJV). Aglow with the joy of his newly discovered companion, he exclaimed, "Look, pastor, Jesus says he will be with Lo always!"

It happened once before, not just for Lo but also for us. God came near at Bethlehem when Christ was born. John reminds us, "The Word became flesh and made his dwelling among us" (John 1:14).

It happens now, every day. The whole of Scripture is a continuing promise of Jesus' presence among his people.

It will happen again in the New Jerusalem. God will come among his people in a significantly different way. He will come among us for all eternity. What does this mean? It means joy, security, peace, and love. It means that we can go out to strange places, even difficult ones, and know that we are not alone.

Today, rejoice in the assurance that this New Jerusalem promise is already being fulfilled for you. You will go through this day in the best of company, for God, by his Holy Spirit, is with you now.

Robert Leslie Holmes

258

Tears Forever Gone

He will wipe every tear from their eyes.

Revelation 21:4a

Probably few other sentences in Scripture tug at our heartstrings as does this verse from the pen of Saint John. Even the most stoical believer must admit to experiences in life that cause tears to well up within. But the day is coming when God will wipe all tears, every last one of them, from our eyes. Wonderful thought, indeed! More than eight hundred years earlier, the prophet Isaiah held out the same promise to the people of God. "The Sovereign LORD will wipe away the tears from all faces" (Isa. 25:8).

The "silent sound" of tears echoes throughout much of Scripture. Who of us, when confronted with the death of one's own child or the child of a relative or close friend, has not thought of David's anguished cry, "My son, my son Absalom! If only I had died instead of you" (2 Sam. 18:33). Remember Job, pleading for vindication as his eyes poured out tears to God (Job 16:20).

Most of us can vividly recall the poignant picture painted by Luke of the repentant woman who "brought an alabaster jar of perfume . . . and began to wet [Jesus'] feet with her tears. Then she wiped them with her hair . . . and poured perfume on them" (Luke 7:37–38). The apostle Paul tells many times of shedding tears. "I wrote you out of great distress and anguish of heart and with many tears, not to grieve you but to let you know the depth of my love for you," he told the Corinthians (2 Cor. 2:4).

Tears! How many are being shed at this very moment all over the world? Tears of pain and suffering. Tears of heartbreak and affliction. Tears of fright and terror. Tears of anger and frustration. Tears of failure and betrayal. Tears of loss and ruin. Tears of disappointment and disillusionment. Tears of bitterness and alienation. Tears of shame and self-reproach. Tears of remorse and repentance.

For us who belong to Christ, however, the day is coming when our heavenly Father himself will wipe away every last one of these tears from our eyes with his own hand. And all heaven will ring with the thunder of our hallelujahs!

Richard Allen Bodey

259

21:4a

The Death of Death

There will be no more death.

Revelation 21:4b

If you could make one change in the world—just one—what would that change be? If you could avoid one experience in life—any one—what experience would you choose? I have not a flickering doubt that, from the fall of Adam and Eve right up to the latest ticking of the clock, you and every normal human being on this planet would answer immediately and intuitively, "The elimination of death."

What thoughts leap into your mind when you think of death—your own death and the death of your dearest loved ones and friends? Separation? Loneliness? Loss of all that matters most to you? The unknown? An eternal void? Endless night? A permanent and unalterable state of unconsciousness? Annihilation? Judgment? Retribution? Untold pain and suffering?

The Bible takes a no-nonsense, straightforward, unhesitatingly realistic attitude towards death. Unlike morticians, it nowhere attempts to hide the ugliness of death or conceal its terror beneath attractive trappings. It never paints its pale and repulsive face with pleasing cosmetics. It nowhere conceals its dismal and forbidding shroud beneath soft and silken coverings. "The last enemy"—that is how Saint Paul labeled it in his first letter to the church at Corinth, but he didn't stop there. "The last enemy to be destroyed is death," he continued (1 Cor. 15:26).

A little later in this same letter, harking back to Isaiah, he added, "Death has been swallowed up in victory. 'Where, O death, is your victory? Where, O death, is your sting?' But thanks be to God! He gives us the victory through our Lord Jesus Christ" (1 Cor. 15:54–55, 57). In the words of John Donne, "Death, thou shalt die."

Richard Allen Bodey

260

Everything New!

He who was seated on the throne said, "I am making everything new!"

Revelation 21:5a

We bought the house we live in when it was twenty years old, and we have been living in it now for twenty-four years. Because it is nearly forty-five years old, there are some stains I will never be able to remove, some cracks in the tile that can never be repaired, some wear and tear that can give a house a frayed, worn-out look. When I visit some of my friends in their brand-new homes, I look longingly at the fresh, unmarked woodwork and painted walls; the fresh, unstained carpet; the fresh, glistening tile and appliances; the fresh, unscratched windowpanes—it's all fresh! New! Unsoiled and unworn by age!

Planet earth is thousands of years old. Some think it may be millions of years old. And it is showing signs of age. It is getting frayed and worn out. The air is polluted, and natural resources like oil, coal, trees, and fresh water are all running out. Some of it is damage we have willfully and selfishly inflicted on it, but some of it is simply due to age. It was not created to last forever!

In contrast, our heavenly home is going to be brand-new. Not just restored but created fresh. It will not only *look* fresh and new, it will *feel* fresh and new!

Wherever God comes, there is freshness and unspoiled newness; not made-overness but total renewal. "Therefore, if anyone is in Christ, he is a new creation; the old has gone, the new has come!" (2 Cor. 5:17). Life always takes on new freshness when God comes in Christ. Today, bring those situations in your life that need Christ's new touch to him in prayer.

Anne Graham Lotz

261

Whose Child Are You?

I will be their God and they will be my children.
Revelation 21:7 NRSV

Tom Nelson, a history teacher from Tennessee, told me about one of the great stories in that state's history. Newport, Tennessee, in 1870, was a small community where everybody knew everything about everybody else. Ben Hooper's father never married his mother. He never learned who his father was. Other kids called him, "Bennie No-name!" Ben grew up with a deep sense of shame that made him increasingly withdrawn. When Ben was twelve, a new pastor came to the little community church, and Ben slipped into church to hear him. He sat alone on a back pew.

He was so caught up in the service, that Ben didn't notice the preacher walk towards the back door as the people sang the final hymn. Suddenly, he felt the preacher's strong hand leaning on his shoulder. "Who are you, son?" the pastor asked, "Whose boy are you?" Ben's heart skipped a beat at that troubling question. Suddenly the preacher said, "Wait a minute! I know who you are and whose you are. The family resemblance is unmistakable. You are a child of God." He slapped Ben on the back and added, "Son, what an inheritance! Get out and claim it."

That brief encounter changed the direction of Ben Hooper's life. He came alive. His spirit soared. His school grades got better. Other kids' taunts didn't bother him anymore. He was somebody. Ben became an attorney. He served in the state legislature and was twice elected governor of Tennessee.

Today, we have a number of ways of establishing paternity (blood types, DNA, etc.), but none to compare with this: We can call God "Daddy."

Get out today and claim your inheritance. Put a spring in your step. Dream big dreams. Set great goals. Yours is an unbeatable heritage. Live up to it!

Robert Leslie Holmes

The Dark Side
of the Good News

Their place will be in the fiery lake of burning sulphur. This is the second death.

Revelation 21:8

In Revelation 21:4, we read, "There will be no more death." In our text today, however, we read of a lake of fire, which is "the second death."

A glaring contradiction? Hosts of professing Christians—theologians, pastors, and laity alike—think so. Many proclaim dogmatically that it is so. The naked truth is that no one in all of human history warned people of the awful reality of eternal damnation more clearly and more emphatically than the loving Savior himself. Did he not say, "I tell you, my friends, do not be afraid of those who kill the body and after that can do no more. But I will show you whom you should fear: Fear him who, after the killing of the body, has power to throw you into hell. Yes, I tell you, fear him" (Luke 12:4–5)? Did he not hurl this chilling challenge to the teachers of the law and the Pharisees: "You snakes! You brood of vipers! How will you escape being condemned to hell?" (Matt. 23:33)? Indeed, on the cross, he himself endured nothing less than the agonies of hell so that all who put their trust in him, but only they, would be liberated forever from this terrifying destiny.

These are not the ravings of an uncontrolled maniac. Still less are they the reckless outbursts of a sadistic fiend. They are the solemn words of the loving Savior, who on the cross endured the worst horrors of hell so that all who commit their eternal destiny to him will never get within sight of hell, but will share with him the glories of heaven forever. If you belong to him, you may die once, but you will never fall prey to the second death. Hallelujah! Amen.

Richard Allen Bodey

Immeasurable Beauty!

He carried me away in the Spirit to a mountain great and high, and showed me the Holy City, Jerusalem, coming down out of heaven from God. It shone with the glory of God, and its brilliance was like that of a very precious jewel, like a jasper, clear as crystal. It had a great, high wall with twelve gates, and with twelve angels at the gates. On the gates were written the names of the twelve tribes of Israel. There were three gates on the east, three on the north, three on the south and three on the west. The wall of the city had twelve foundations, and on them were the names of the twelve apostles of the Lamb. The angel who talked with me had a measuring rod of gold to measure the city, its gates and its walls.

Revelation 21:10–15

If you could build a memorial to remember the one you love most of all, what would it be? In the middle of the seventeenth century, Shah Jahan, the Mughal emperor of India, faced that problem when his wife, with whom he had had an inseparable relationship, died in childbirth. Shah Jahan's grief resulted in the construction of the Taj Mahal, one of the world's most beautiful buildings. Taj Mahal was, in fact, his wife's name.

264

The Taj Mahal is a mausoleum, a burial place, set within a complex of gardens and other buildings. It took twenty-two years and more than twenty thousand workers to complete. A council of architects from India, Persia, Turkey, and Italy were recruited to design it. Shah Jahan insisted that it must be the most exquisite building the world would ever see. Upon his own death, Shah Jahan was laid there with his beloved wife.

There is a place more beautiful by far than even the Taj Mahal. It is not designed for the dead but for the living who will never die. It is the City of God, a place beyond description. John stretches the limits of his imagination to describe this place he saw, where we shall go to live forever with our Savior, Jesus.

Rejoice in the Lord today that you have a place such as this to look forward to as your eternal abode. More than that, the One who loves you more than any other will be there, alive forever with you.

Robert Leslie Holmes

The Light
of the New World

*The city does not need the sun or the moon to shine on it, for the glory of
God gives it light, and the Lamb is its lamp.*

Revelation 21:23

I have been in some of the great cities of the world at night. I have
looked out at Hong Kong from Victoria Peak during the Chinese
New Year, and I have seen the lights transform the hills surrounding the harbor into a virtual fairyland. I have seen Capetown,
South Africa, looking like a jewel-studded skirt wrapped around
Table Mountain! I have seen Paris from Montmartre after dinner,
stretched out for miles in an endless sea of light, with the lighted
outline of the Eiffel Tower beckoning like a finger to those who
love beauty.

But even in those great cities with their millions of lights, there
are still pockets of darkness. In our heavenly home, there will be
no darkness at all! No one will ever stumble or be lost or unable
to find his or her way. Jesus said, "I am the light of the world"
(John 8:12), and he also said that we "are the light of the world"
(Matt. 5:14). The sole light of heaven will be the light that comes
directly from God through Jesus Christ, which will be reflected in
the life of each believer. The entire city will be saturated with the
glory and light of Christ!

What a wonderful prospect. What a wonderful present. Today,
determine to let Christ's light shine through you wherever you
go.

Anne Graham Lotz

He Knows Your Name!

Nothing impure will ever enter it, nor will anyone who does what is shameful or deceitful, but only those whose names are written in the Lamb's book of life.

Revelation 21:27

A mother, quizzed by a census taker, was asked, "How many children do you have?" She replied, "Well, there's Michelle and Elizabeth and . . ." "I don't need their names," interrupted the official, "just give me the number!" The mother smiled back, "They don't have numbers, mister, they've all got names." For her, each one was special.

"He calls his own sheep by name" (John 10:3). Today's verse explains why. It is that our "names are written in the Lamb's book of life." Our names are important to Christ because he desires a personal relationship with each of us. Paul, writing to Timothy, gave the assuring word that "the Lord knows those who are his" (2 Tim. 2:19).

To others, we may all look alike, and our names may be easily forgotten. Christ, however, has no anonymous disciples. We are not lost in a crowd. "My sheep listen to my voice; I know them" (John 10:27). "The very hairs of your head are all numbered" (Matt. 10:30).

Not everyone will enter the New Jerusalem, only those "whose names are written in the Lamb's book of life." This book contains the names of all who have put their trust in Jesus. It symbolizes God's intimate knowledge of all who believe in his Son, Jesus.

We will not enter heaven because of our heritage, background, personality, or good behavior but only because, on Calvary, Christ remembered our name. How can we know he remembers our name? Because in our hearts we have heard his call and responded by following.

If you have not responded to his call before, do it today. Rejoice that you have a personal Savior.

Robert Leslie Holmes

Come to the Water!

Then the angel showed me the river of the water of life, as clear as crystal, flowing from the throne of God and of the Lamb.

Revelation 22:1

A stone marker in Bath, England, honors that city's medicinal waters for bringing healing to generations of people. These words are inscribed upon it, "These healing waters have flowed from time immemorial. Their virtue is unimpaired, their heart undiminished, their volume unabated." Wonderful words!

Yet here are even better ones: God's angel showed John an endless stream, flowing freely and giving health for all eternity. Those who drink it never die. Jesus pointed this water out to the woman at the well. "Whoever drinks the water I give him will never thirst. Indeed, the water I give him will become in him a spring of water welling up to eternal life" (John 4:14). This water flows from "the river of the water of life."

When I was traveling through the Sinai Desert, our guide related an age-old desert custom that is reenacted every time a caravan needs new water. The leader commissions a rider to ride his camel off into the distance. Soon after the first rider departs, the leader sends another, then a third, and so forth, each following a short distance behind the one before. Upon finding water, the first rider dismounts and shouts to the rider following him, "Water! Come!" The second takes up the cry and passes it to the third until, all the way through the camel train, the desert seems to reverberate with the good news.

Jesus, the Lord of glory, calls to us, "Water! Come!" Come to this water, rich, pure, and unmatched anywhere on earth. Come and drink the water that brings life forever for free!

Robert Leslie Holmes

267

Three Trees

On each side of the river stood the tree of life, bearing twelve crops of fruit, yielding its fruit every month. And the leaves of the tree are for the healing of the nations.

Revelation 22:2

"The LORD God made all kinds of trees grow out of the ground" (Gen. 2:9). Three biblical trees are of special interest to Christians. The tree of life in this verse is one of them.

The first two trees, in Genesis 2:9, are "The tree of life and the tree of the knowledge of good and evil." These trees were God's gift to Adam and Eve. One promised life. One brought heartbreak. Tragically, love for the second tree cost us the benefits of the first one. Eating the forbidden tree's fruit, Adam and Eve lost the joy of life lived in perfect fellowship with God. At that moment, history took a wrong turn for us all.

Now God's tree of life reappears as the tree of healing for the nations. Why would the nations need healing in this perfect environment? John quotes from Ezekiel's vision, "Fruit trees of all kinds will grow on both banks of the river. . . . Their fruit will serve for food and their leaves for healing" (Ezek. 47:12). John does not imply that sickness and sin will invade God's new world, for nothing accursed can live there (see Zech. 14:11). John's point is that this true-life tree will achieve what God first intended, health and strength for his people.

How? Only through the grace revealed on a third tree, the tree of Jesus. This tree was in the form of the cross that held God's Son in our place.

Today, thank God for the forgiveness he makes available through the redeeming tree of Jesus and for the promise of full restoration for all who believe on his Son.

Robert Leslie Holmes

268

Face to Face!

They will see his face, and his name will be on their foreheads. There will be no more night. They will not need the light of a lamp or the light of the sun, for the Lord God will give them light. And they will reign for ever and ever.

Revelation 22:4–5

An Irish legend tells of a wealthy nobleman's son who was born nearly blind. Through childhood, adolescence, and into manhood, he lived in semidarkness. Eventually, he fell in love. Around that time, surgeons developed a new surgery they said would clear his sight. The wedding was delayed while his eyes recovered.

"How wonderful," he marveled. "The day I marry my beloved will also be the day I will see her clearly for the first time!" An intriguing idea came to him: "Suppose I have my bandages removed at our wedding ceremony so that my bride will be the first one I shall ever see clearly." The more he thought about it, the better he liked it. His fiancée liked it too.

The big day arrived. The bridegroom, blinded by bandages, anxiously took his place in front of the congregation. The bridal march, played on the organ, signaled the arrival of his beloved. As she took her place beside him, the dramatic moment they each anticipated arrived. His surgeon gently removed his eye bandages, and the bridegroom blinked to adjust to light brighter than he had seen before. He turned towards the young woman beside him and exclaimed in sheer joy, "At last! And more beautiful than I ever dreamed!"

One day, we are going to see Jesus just like that. One day, we will see him in his full splendor. That day we will exclaim, "At last! And more beautiful than I ever dreamed!" Until that day, "we see but a poor reflection as in a mirror" (1 Cor. 13:12).

Today we see by faith. One day, we shall see his face! Hallelujah! Glorious day!

Robert Leslie Holmes

269

Ready? Aye, Ready!

"I am coming soon!"
Revelation 22:7, 12, 20

Three times this chapter says Jesus is coming soon. "Soon" is not about time measurement but the unexpected manner of his return. It means "suddenly and unannounced."

As a youngster, I heard a story about a wealthy man who visited a one-room schoolhouse in a poverty stricken village. As he left, he pledged to the students, "I will return and award a college scholarship to the student who makes the most improvement and keeps the tidiest desk." For those students, that offer was a ticket out of poverty. The next day, Betsy, notorious for her untidy desk and casual study habits, announced that she would win the prize. Her classmates taunted her. "Betsy, your desk is always untidy and your grades are always poor," they chided. "I know," Betsy replied, "but from now on, I'm going to study hard and clean my desk out every Friday afternoon." "What if he comes on Thursday?" they asked. "You're right," exclaimed Betsy, "I'll clean it out every afternoon." "Well," they quizzed, "what if he comes just before lunchtime?" Betsy smiled. "You're right again! I'd better keep my desk clean all the time." Sure enough, from that day forward, Betsy's whole approach to life and learning was remarkably different.

The motto of the famous Scottish Highlanders reads, "Ready? Aye, Ready!" That should be every Christian's motto. The Bible says Jesus will return when we least expect him.

There is an Irish saying, "Live each day as though it will be your last, and one day you will be right!" It's humorous but true! If you knew Jesus was coming today, would there be a significant adjustment to your attitude and actions? What would you do differently? Do it now. It could be today!

Robert Leslie Holmes

Even the Angels

I, John, am the one who heard and saw these things. And when I had heard and seen them, I fell down to worship at the feet of the angel who had been showing them to me. But he said to me, "Do not do it! I am a fellow servant with you and with your brothers the prophets and of all who keep the words of this book. Worship God!"

Revelation 22:8–9

An elderly lady in our neighborhood told of an experience when she helped make ready for a momentous occasion. It was 1953. The place was Westminster Abbey. The coronation dress rehearsal for Queen Elizabeth II was underway. The orchestra ended its prelude. The Archbishop of Canterbury, robed in clerical splendor, stood near the altar. Nearby, top military brass stood proud in full dress regalia. Beside them, other dignitaries talked together, bedecked in official finery. Suddenly through the air came the spine-tingling fanfare of ceremonial trumpets to signal the new queen's arrival. At that very moment, the huge abbey doors, through which she would process to assume her throne, swung open.

271

This day, however, there was no queen. There were only some cleaning ladies pushing vacuum cleaners in the vestibule on the other side of the doors. They were there to do their final cleaning before the great ceremony and were totally unaware that they were encroaching on this almost royal moment. Stunned by the brilliant finery before them, the cleaning ladies curtsied. The archbishop assured them that all these dignitaries and nobles had gathered for the same reason. All were there to prepare for the next day's royal moment. "Her Majesty is not here," he assured them; "you need not curtsy until she comes."

John fell to worship the angel, but the angel quickly corrected him, "Worship God!" The angel reminds John that God alone, who comes to us in Jesus, the risen Lord of Calvary's cross, is worthy of worship and adoration.

The angel's charge to John also challenges us to let nothing temporarily beautiful steal our devotion from the King of kings and Lord of lords, whom even the angels worship.

Robert Leslie Holmes

Open the Book!
Live the Message!

Then he told me, "Do not seal up the words of the prophecy of this book, because the time is near. Let him who does wrong continue to do wrong; let him who is vile continue to be vile; let him who does right continue to do right; and let him who is holy continue to be holy."

Revelation 22:10–11

A leading pollster once declared, "Most Americans think a lot of the Bible, but very few think much on it." He meant that we hold the Bible in high regard but neither read it nor live its message.

John was told to open the book that the world might see. His vision was not ethereal but relevant for every generation. As the Lord's return comes ever nearer, we must read the book, heed its teaching, and apply its message to our lives.

William Wilberforce, born into wealth, demonstrated even in childhood that he was a clever debater. At age twenty-one, he used his skills to get elected to parliament. Once there, he proved he was also a shrewd politician. At the time, England hovered on the brink of spiritual bankruptcy. Morality was at an all-time low, the poor were oppressed, and the slave trade flourished. At first, Wilberforce adopted a "go along and get along" attitude toward these things.

At age twenty-five, however, Wilberforce joined a friend and favored teacher, Isaac Milner, on a trip to France. While there, Milner opened the Bible to Wilberforce. The two studied it together. As a result, William Wilberforce committed his life to Christ. The Bible became his life guide and, gradually, his attitude changed. The plight of the poor, which he once ignored, burdened his heart. He became their champion in the British parliament. Slavery was abolished in England in 1833, principally due to the influence of the Bible on this man who read the book and told God's story.

Make it your resolve to open God's book and tell his story by lip and life.

Robert Leslie Holmes

272

The Undated Man

"I am the Alpha and the Omega, the First and the Last, the Beginning and the End."

Revelation 22:13

The Bible begins with the record of the world's beginning and ends with the close of history. In between, its central character is Jesus. His name is revealed in many ways. Here it is "Alpha and Omega." Using the first and last letters of the Greek alphabet, Christ reveals himself as history's transcendent Lord.

In almost every field of endeavor, some people have provided critical leadership or made outstanding contributions. For this, their names are preserved in history. Almost always, history books make a parenthetical note of their date of birth and death. Not so, Jesus!

Think of any great historical character. Their name, when recorded, is often followed by their dates of birth and death in parentheses. Yet, this never happens with Jesus. This is because who he is and his contribution to human betterment transcends time. He is undated and undatable.

273

Think of any great discovery. It was not new to him. It came into being by his power. Not only that, his power also sustains it.

Think of life. Think of death. As Alpha and Omega, Jesus was not born. Neither did he merely die; he became dead in order that we might have a better grasp of life as he created it. After death, he rose again.

Alpha and Omega! No one but Jesus could take such a name for himself. He alone can save us from our sins and give us a life that transcends the earth. Without him we have nothing that really lasts.

Is he Alpha and Omega of your life? Today, honor him for who he is, transcendent Lord of all existence, power, and wisdom.

Robert Leslie Holmes

Does the Blood Work?

"Blessed are those who wash their robes, that they may have the right to the tree of life and may go through the gates into the city. Outside are the dogs, those who practice magic arts, the sexually immoral, the murderers, the idolaters and everyone who loves and practices falsehood."

Revelation 22:14–15

An elderly preacher, now deceased, told me a story that gives life to this passage. One day in a church service, a young woman surrendered her life to Christ. Her sordid past included drugs, prostitution, and a host of public sins. But she clearly demonstrated the sincerity of her newfound faith. With a willing heart, she gave herself enthusiastically wherever she could to help God's work.

Her joyful spirit caught the attention of a young pastor. The two fell in love and began to make wedding plans, but some church members objected. They did not think a person with her past should be a pastor's wife. Someone even objected at a congregational meeting and publicly cataloged her sins in greatly exaggerated form.

274

In response, a gentle old saint rose to speak. "Does the blood work?" he asked. "If it does, she is forgiven. If it does not, none of us is. Your problem is not her past but your present. If you believe Christ's blood forgives, her past does not count." Her critics were shamed into silence.

"Though your sins are like scarlet, they shall be as white as snow," Isaiah prophesied over seven hundred years before Jesus was born (Isa. 1:18). Now, here is John seeing the prophecy fulfilled in Revelation by way of Calvary. The difference between "those who wash their robes that they may have the right to the tree of life" and those "outside" is their belief in the efficacy of Christ's blood, shed on Calvary.

Does the blood work? Our answer to this question determines how forgiven we feel and how forgiving we are.

Does the blood work? Make it work for you and through you.

Robert Leslie Holmes

Ultimate Stardom

"I, Jesus, have sent my angel to give you this testimony for the churches. I am the Root and the Offspring of David, and the bright Morning Star."

Revelation 22:16

Many years ago, someone told me this story: A fierce afternoon storm gave birth to a tornado that forced two amateur forest explorers to find refuge in a cave. After it passed, they surfaced to observe only devastation. Huge trees lay like kindling. Familiar pointers were extinct. The pathway home was obliterated. One sat down, despaired, but the other said, "We are not lost. When darkness comes the stars will guide us home."

In his last amazing self-declaration, Jesus first claims God's holiest name for himself: "I am," a name that calls for surrender and obedience. When he calls himself David's root and offspring, he claims to be Israel's Messiah. But, when he says, "I am . . . the bright Morning Star," he makes his clearest claim to eternal Lordship.

Today we apply the term *superstar* to figures in entertainment, sports, business, academics, and almost all professions. Our superstars come and go. Yesterday's "superstars" are often today's unknowns.

At least three times the Bible reverences Christ as the ultimate morning superstar (see also 2 Peter 1:19 and Rev. 2:28). The morning star outshines all others. It appears just before the dawn, when night is darkest, coldest, and bleakest. When all other stars have burned out and our world seems drab, dreary, and hopeless, the one eternal superstar, Jesus, still guides. One day he will burst forth in his final, unfading brightness. Until that day, we have his Spirit and his Word to guide us home.

Long ago in Bethlehem, wise men followed his star. If you are wise, you will too.

Robert Leslie Holmes

275

Invitation to a Wedding

The Spirit and the bride say, "Come!" And let him who hears say, "Come!" Whoever is thirsty, let him come; and whoever wishes, let him take the free gift of the water of life.

Revelation 22:17

In a story I heard years ago, a train clickety-clacked along the tracks. A little man in a wrinkled suit curled beneath a seat, where he was attempting to hide from the conductor. "Ticket, sir?" the conductor demanded when he spotted him. "Please, sir," the old man pleaded, "I can't afford a ticket and my only son is getting married. Please don't keep me from his wedding." The conductor was visibly touched. "Okay," he smiled. "I'll buy your ticket myself." In the next car, the conductor spied another old man hiding under a seat. "Ticket?" he asked once more. The old-timer replied, "What ticket? I don't have a ticket. My friend invited me to a wedding and said he'd pay my way."

The bride is the church. It is you if you belong to Christ. The Holy Spirit partners with us as we invite the whole world to come to this wedding, where the drink of choice is living water that only Christ can give.

Of that water, Jesus told the woman at the well, "Whoever drinks the water I give him will never thirst. Indeed, the water I give him will become in him a spring of water welling up to eternal life" (John 4:14).

Come to the wedding! There is no need to hide. Come openly and with great joy, for your way was paid long ago on a hill called Calvary. Invite others to join you. Their way was paid too. "The Spirit and the bride say, 'Come!' And let him who hears say, 'Come!'"

Robert Leslie Holmes

276

This Book of Books

I warn everyone who hears the words of the prophecy of this book: If anyone adds anything to them, God will add to him the plagues described in this book. And if anyone takes words away from this book of prophecy, God will take away from him his share in the tree of life and in the holy city, which are described in this book.

Revelation 22:18–19

Christian historian J. Edwin Orr told me about a student of his who asked, "What makes the Bible different from other books?"

The teacher replied, "Forty different writers, who spoke a variety of dialects and came from unrelated backgrounds, including a king, stutterer, physician, herdsman, tax-collector, an adulterer, a theologian, scribe, former Pharisee, widow, fiery-tempered fisherman, two murderers, and a runaway preacher. Personality studies of them make us realize that God chooses some strange characters to do his work. They lived before e-mail, telephones, and fax machines. They held no organizational or editorial meetings. Their lives spanned sixty-four generations, more than one thousand, six hundred years. Most had no idea the others existed. Yet, they produced sixty-six flawless books that possess the complete unity and harmony of a well-made jigsaw. This book has been challenged by more people than all other books combined. Yet, it passes the tests of its critics every time. Of all the books ever written, in all the languages of the world, this one exists in a class of its own."

Having stated this record, Edwin Orr asked his student, "What would you say about a book like that?" The student exclaimed, "I'd say it's a miracle!"

No wonder Christ puts a warning on his book.

The Bible is the book of books. Read it and heed it!

Robert Leslie Holmes

277

Grace for the Gap!

*He who testifies to these things says, "Yes, I am coming soon." Amen. Come,
Lord Jesus. The grace of the Lord Jesus be with God's people. Amen.*

Revelation 22:20–21

We do not know for sure when Jesus will return. We know only that he promised.

Two tiny sisters, Hannah and Cameron, overheard their grandparents saying that they would come back soon to visit. For the little girls, "soon" meant the very next day. Early the next morning they awoke and made ready. Throughout the day, they watched by the front window, certain their grandparents would drive up at any minute. It did not happen as Hannah and Cameron expected, but the grandparents did return soon. The difference was simply a matter of scheduling. Similarly, we are to be always expecting Christ's return. He will come on his Father's schedule (see Mark 13:32).

What about the meantime? In the meantime, "the grace of the Lord Jesus be with God's people." Revelation, like every book of the Bible, is a book about grace.

278

What is grace? It is unmerited favor. It is undeserved reward. It means, finally, that we get what Christ deserves because on Calvary he took what we deserve. Grace is **G**od's **R**iches **A**t **C**hrist's **E**xpense.

"In this world you will have trouble. But take heart! I have overcome the world" (John 16:33). Revelation shows us that no matter what happens on the nightly news, Jesus Christ, the King of kings and Lord of lords, is in control. From his throne he still forgives us. He loves us even though we sent him to the cross. Every day he treats us better than we deserve. That is grace, grace for the gap.

So, with saints from all the ages, we pray expectantly, "Come, Lord Jesus!"

Robert Leslie Holmes

Notes

1. M. Eugene Boring, *Revelation: Interpretation, A Bible Commentary* (Atlanta: John Knox Press, 1989), 61.
2. Quoted in Donald Jay Grout, *A History of Western Music*, 3d ed. (New York: W. W. Norton, 1980), 524.
3. Richard Chenevix Trench, *Commentary on the Epistles to the Seven Churches in Asia* (London: Macmillan, 1867), 137.
4. Leon Morris, *The Revelation of St. John* (Grand Rapids: Eerdmans, 1969), 118.
5. A favorite illustration of Herbert Lockyer Sr., appearing in *Moody Monthly* (November 1954): 40.
6. Flannery O'Connor, *Collected Works* (New York: Library of America, 1988), 479.
7. T. F. Glasson, *The Revelation of John* (Cambridge: Cambridge University Press, 1965), 58.
8. G. B. F. Hallock, *Five Thousand Best Modern Illustrations* (New York: Richard R. Smith, 1931), 317.
9. Jim Cymbala, *Fresh Wind, Fresh Fire* (Grand Rapids: Zondervan, 1997), 57.
10. Eugene Peterson, *Reversed Thunder: The Revelation of John and the Praying Imagination* (San Francisco: Harper & Co., 1988), 143–44.
11. Ibid., 143.
12. Claire Martin and Janet Bingham, "Columbine—The Victims," *The Denver Post* (online), 23 April 1999.
13. George Eldon Ladd, *A Commentary on the Revelation of John* (Grand Rapids: Eerdmans, 1972), 252–53.